Premeditated *Mercy*

Premeditated *Mercy*

A SPIRITUALITY
OF RECONCILIATION

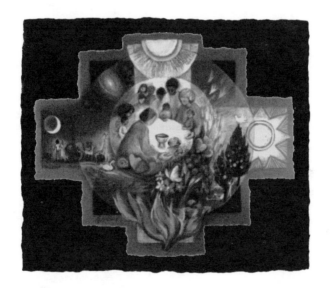

Joseph Nassal, CPPS

FOREST OF PEACE
Publishing

Suppliers for the Spiritual Pilgrim
Leavenworth, KS

Marywood
UNIVERSITY
Campus Ministry

Other Books by the Author:
(available from the publisher)

The Conspiracy of Compassion
Rest Stops for the Soul

Premeditated Mercy

copyright © 2000, by Joseph Nassal

Library of Congress Cataloging-in-Publication Data

Nassal, Joe, 1955-
    Premeditated mercy : a spirituality of reconciliation / Joseph Nassal.
      p. cm.
    ISBN 0-939516-49-7
    1. Mercy. 2. Reconciliation—Religious aspects—Christianity. I. Title.

    BV4647.M4 N37 2000
    234'.5—dc21

                  99-053862

published by
Forest of Peace Publishing, Inc.
PO Box 269
Leavenworth, KS 66048-0269 USA
1-800-659-3227
www.forestofpeace.com

printed by
Hall Commercial Printing
Topeka, KS 66608-0007

1st printing: January 2000

Cover Art: "One Sacred Community" by Mary Southard, CSJ, LaGrange
                Image available in prints, cards and prayer cards through their Ministry
                of the Arts: www.ministryofthearts.org

DEDICATION

To Tren Meyers,
to honor and celebrate
thirty years of friendship
marked by mercy and compassion,
laughter and tears.

Acknowledgments

I write about what I most need to learn. In seeking to learn more about the practice of premeditated mercy, I am grateful to all who have shown me the favor of forgiveness through the years, all those whose pardon gave me a sign of peace. To those with whom I am still broken, I believe the Sufi poet and prophet had it right: "Beyond the field of right-doing and wrong-doing, there is another field. I'll meet you there." Someday, I hope to meet you in this field.

As a member of a religious congregation committed to reconciliation through the Blood of Christ, I am grateful to those whose eloquence in spoken and written word, and in the language of their lives, have taught me much about mercy, especially Robert Schreiter, Barry Fischer, Dave Kelly and Mark Miller. I am grateful to all the members and companions of the congregation who have reflected to me in various ways the challenge of premeditated mercy.

I am most grateful to the Adorers of the Blood of Christ of Ruma, Illinois, who have given me a place at their table, a place to live and to pray, to work, write and worship.

I am indebted to all those friends, family and folks I've met along the way who have taken the time to tell me their stories, to articulate their experiences and struggles of reconciliation. Thank you for taking off your shoes on the holy ground of our common identity as children of God. This is the ground of our being: We are made in the image of God. I pray this may be a millennium of mercy. May we become a new creation.

Finally, to Tom Turkle, my publisher, and Tom Skorupa, my editor, at Forest of Peace Publishing, thank you for your encouragement and friendship, and for being so merciful with this manuscript.

CONTENTS

Introduction Premeditated Mercy.....*9*

Chapter One Raising Cain:
The Roots of Evil.....*12*

Chapter Two Making Peace:
A Recipe for Reconciliation.....*29*

Chapter Three Preparing a Meal of Mercy:
Following the Recipe.....*44*

Chapter Four Setting the Table:
Spiritual Exercises Before Bringing Our Gifts to the Altar.....*61*

Chapter Five A Table for All:
Finding Room for the Beloved and the Betrayer.....*83*

Chapter Six Reconciliation at the Round Table:
Seeking Common Ground.....*102*

Chapter Seven Prayer from the Crawl Space:
Celebrating God's Extravagant Mercy.....*119*

Chapter Eight Drinking the Cup of Mercy:
Sipping Sour Wine and Swallowing Hope.....*139*

Chapter Nine Seeing Our Shadows on Mercy Street:
Finding Our Way in the Dark.....*157*

Chapter Ten The Ministry of Mercy:
Finding Our Footing in the Shadow of the Cross.....*175*

Chapter Eleven Waiting Tables and Washing Feet:
Seeing Inside and Seeking Out the Lost.....*194*

Chapter Twelve Becoming a New Creation:
Feeding the Multitude with Mercy.....*213*

Epilogue Go in Peace: Finding Room for Reconciliation.....*236*

If you bring your gifts to the altar and there recall that your brother or sister has anything against you, leave your gift at the altar, go first to be reconciled with your brother or sister, and then come and offer your gift.

— Matthew 5: 23-24

INTRODUCTION

Premeditated Mercy

We cannot love God unless we love each other,
and to love we must know each other.
We know God in the breaking of bread,
and we know each other in the breaking of bread
and we are not alone any more.

— Dorothy Day

There is an anecdote about Leonardo da Vinci when he was working on his famous painting of The Last Supper. He had become very angry with one of his assistants. With a flurry of furious epithets, he berated the man without mercy. After banishing his assistant from his studio, he went back to work on the painting. But as he tried to paint the face of Jesus, he couldn't do it. No matter how hard he tried, he was unable to paint the face of Christ. So he stopped painting, went to the man who had received the full force of his anger and asked his forgiveness. Only when the man forgave him and they reconciled was da Vinci able to return to the table of the Last Supper and paint the face of Jesus.

This story reflects what Jesus suggests in the verses from the Sermon on the Mount:

> You have heard it said, "You shall not kill; and whoever kills shall be liable to judgment." But I say to you that if you are angry with your companion you shall be liable to judgment; if you insult your companion you shall be answerable to the high council…. So if you are offering your gift at the altar, and there remember that your companion has something against you, leave your gift there before the altar and go; first be reconciled to your companion, and then come and offer your gift (Matthew 5: 21-24).

The challenge is clear enough: We are to reconcile with one another before bringing our gifts to the altar. Like da Vinci, we cannot come to the table of the Eucharist if we hold anger or resentment in our heart toward another. Or if we know another is nursing a grudge against us or harboring a hatred toward us, we dare not approach the table of Eucharist, for that table reflects God's desire that we live in a holy communion with all people. In this brief passage from Matthew's Gospel, Jesus offers a radical approach to the relationship between reconciliation and worship. We might call this approach *premeditated mercy* because it invites us to prayerfully consider in the depths of our hearts where we need forgiveness, where we need to be reconciled, where we need to experience God's mercy before we come to the table of communion.

We normally hear the word *premeditated* in conjunction with murder. It implies a willful intent. A person charged with the crime of premeditated murder has taken considerable time to plot and to plan the taking of another human life. It is not a crime of passion or the consequence of a sudden burst of insanity. Premeditated murder implies a thoughtful, calculated act of violence that results in the killing of another human being. The accused has deliberated for a long time, covered every option, thought about every detail. Premeditated murder is a deliberate act of violence committed by an individual who has undertaken careful consideration of the action beforehand. This is not self-defense. This is not a crime committed in the heat of the moment. Rather, the perpetrator of violence has gone to extreme lengths to eliminate the one who is the focus of the murderous intent.

Premeditated mercy is the parallel opposite of premeditated murder. Premeditated mercy implies a deliberate, thoughtful and willful act to forgive, to be reconciled, to live at peace with others, even those who have betrayed us, forsaken us, abandoned us, threatened us. Sitting in prayer before the altar, we may recall an argument with someone we know or a disagreement that settled into an unholy kind of silence. Jesus advises that before continuing the ritual of offering our gifts at the altar, we should leave the table and address the attitude that has caused the separation. Ultimately we are called to make peace with the one from whom we are estranged. Premeditated mercy suggests that in our silent prayer before the altar we ponder the breach in relationship and plot a strategy that will lead to reconciliation.

This book will explore how we make these sacred connections within ourselves and in our relationships. As we begin, then, may this be our prayer:

Prayer for Premeditated Mercy

Compassionate Creator,
as we approach the tables of our lives,
tables where we gather to dream and to dialogue,
tables where we gather to break open your word and break bread,
tables where we pass around a cup of wine,
which holds both our hopes and our hurts,
give us the grace to face
whatever anger, resentment or disgrace
we hold in the fragile chalices of our hearts.
In our prayerful meditation before we come to the table,
may we sip holy silence and taste the flavor of your forgiving love.
Before bringing the many gifts of our lives to the table,
enable us to see how your mercy will free us from our fears.

O Gracious God,
help us to meditate on your mercy,
to remember your mercy
and to radiate your mercy and your love.
+ Amen.

Raising Cain:
The Roots of Evil

Human beings suffer,
They torture one another,
They get hurt and get hard.
No poem or play or song
Can fully right a wrong
Inflicted and endured.

— Seamus Heaney, *The Cure of Troy*

It was a particularly vicious crime. The older brother, a farmer, a tiller of the soil, invites his younger brother, a shepherd, to go for a walk in the fields, presumably to check on the crops. Because the younger brother is often away tending his flock, he doesn't see his older brother very often. So the invitation to go for a walk offers a chance to catch up on their lives.

The only thing the younger brother catches, however, is a jolt to the back of the head. When he bends low to pick up a handful of dirt, his brother strikes a blow that kills him.

Is this a case of premeditated murder or a crime of passion? If we were to investigate this crime, in order to charge the older brother with premeditated murder, we must first look for a motive. His motive seems clear enough: jaundiced jealousy toward his brother. Cain became angry because Abel found favor with someone from whom Cain had wanted more than anything to win approval. Angry because Abel received the approval he so desperately wanted, Cain invited his brother out into the field and killed him.

Cain, the firstborn, the oldest, the farmer, offered the best fruit he could find, the best produce his land produced, but it wasn't good enough. Abel, on the other hand, brought a fat lamb from his flock and found favor with God. Evidently, in God's early days, the Divine One was not a vegetarian. God liked lamb.

God's disposition toward Abel's offering and the divine disregard for Cain's own gift infuriated the farmer. When he saw God smile at the lamb Abel presented at the altar, Cain became jealous of his brother. "Why are you angry, and why has your countenance fallen?" God asks. "If you do well, will you not be accepted?" (Genesis 4: 6-7). Cain thought he did well — the best he could do — but it didn't measure up.

Isn't there a part of us that can identify with Cain's plight over this slight from God? When we've done the best we can but others tell us it just isn't good enough, we're disappointed and probably a little bit angry. When we're in competition for a job or a promotion at work, but the job or the promotion goes to someone else, aren't we jealous of the other's good fortune? Few of us would go to the extremes that Cain did, but in the process of premeditated mercy proposed by this book, it is important to acknowledge these feelings. It doesn't help to bury them under halfhearted congratulations to the one who won the position that we coveted.

Cain's rejection slip was even more dramatic and dangerous because this wasn't a promotion or a job that obsessed him but an offering, a gift. And this offering wasn't to the chairperson of the board or the president of the company, but to God. Cain desperately wanted God's approval, and when that approval went instead to his younger brother Abel, the seeds of two garden variety sins that now are so familiar to us — anger and envy — started growing quickly in the field of Cain's heartland.

God noticed this sudden growth of sin in the heart of the farmer. So God proceeded to tell Cain that he must master this anger, for if the anger should get the best of him, violence and death would follow. Before the weeds of anger and jealousy had a chance to take over the ground of Cain's being, God said, the farmer needed to uproot the sin.

But it was too late. Cain could not master the sin inside. It got the best of him, and he invited his brother Abel "out to the field." And soon enough the story takes a deadly turn.

SIN: GETTING THE BEST OF US

Cain was jealous at his brother's favored status in the eyes of God.

He was angry with God's rejection of his gift at the altar. But rather than seeking to reconcile with his brother, he allowed his anger to get the best of him. This is what sin does: It gets the best of us, the best in us, and brings out the worst instead. When anger gets the best of us, it grows into violence. Perhaps we don't kill other human beings, plotting acts of premeditated murder, but we may unleash violent words that wound spirits and threaten souls with great harm. When jealousy and resentment rise within us, they get the best of us.

When we see that our best is not good enough, we tend to turn on the one who is deemed better than us. It may be a family member or a friend, a coworker or a companion, in some cases even a spouse. Sometimes silence is the weapon we use to try to get the best of the one who sparks our envy. It's a time-honored weapon, the silent treatment. This sullen kind of silence creates distance and damages souls. Extreme cases of violent silence may even kill a commitment toward another. Vices like jealousy and anger are so insidious because they get the best of us. They seek to destroy the best in us.

The best in us is God's image.

In planning Cain's defense for the premeditated murder of his brother, a skilled attorney might draw upon an "image of God" defense. The lawyer might take the jury on a journey back to the Garden of Eden to trace the genealogy of these two siblings. The attorney would remind the jury that Cain and Abel are only the second generation. Their parents, Adam and Eve, ran into a problem similar to Cain's, though perhaps even more elemental. The sin of the first parents was pride. They wanted to be God. They forgot to look in the mirror and see they were already made in God's image and likeness. They grasped for something they thought was within their reach — the fruit of the tree of good and evil. But in their reaching, their grasping, they fell off the ladder. They fell from grace. Their apple-picking time in the garden of good and evil led to their fall.

Maybe this is why God was not pleased with Cain's offering. It brought back too many painful memories for God. Cain's parents, Adam and Eve, were God's pride and joy. But it was Adam and Eve's pride that killed God's joy. At least in the beginning. So when Cain brought the fruit of his land and offered it to God, the memories of the fruit of the tree of good and evil was fresh in God's mind.

Not again, God thought. Not more fruit. This is what got Cain's parents in trouble: plucking the fruit from the tree of knowledge. Now here was Cain bringing more "brain food." Maybe God saw Cain's offering as something from the head instead of from the heart. Whatever the case may be, Cain's defense attorney might plead, "It wasn't Cain's fault! God was not disposed to accept Cain's offering. Blame Abel's death on God's rejection. Or blame it on Adam and Eve, since Cain was predisposed to fall because of his parents' fall from grace." The lawyer might also suggest that because of his parents' sin Cain and his brother Abel had to work for a living. Cain had to till the land east of Eden; Abel took care of the flock in the pasture beyond the gates of the old home place. Was not the hard labor of tilling the soil too hard on the soul? After all, until recently his parents had known only leisure in the garden. Was not having to work hard too stressful an adjustment?

In defense of Cain, a lawyer might next invite the jury to look closely at the face of Cain. Since he and his brother were only the second generation of creation, the lawyer might point out how these two brothers bore more than a slight resemblance to their creator. "Look closely," the lawyer might say, "or even casually, and you can see the resemblance." Then the lawyer might suggest that when sin entered the human psyche because of Cain and Abel's parents grasping for something which was already within their reach, namely, being made in God's image, this family resemblance began to be buried deep within the human spirit. They forgot who they were. They forgot the best in themselves.

In pleading for mercy, the lawyer might try to persuade the jury that this was not a crime of premeditated murder but just an act of blind passion. Then, logically, the lawyer might raise the issue of temporary insanity: "For a brief, blinding moment, Cain forgot who he was. In a rage fueled by anger and jealousy, sins sown in the hearts of the second generation because of the sins of the father and mother, Cain struck a blow that killed his brother." In this scenario, Cain could, at most, be charged with second-degree murder or even manslaughter, since Cain's crime was one of passion, of jealous rage, rather than premeditation.

Ultimately, though, Cain's crime — whether premeditated murder or manslaughter — is indefensible. It was a violent crime that even now is visited upon so many families. Reclaiming our identity as people made in the image and likeness of God is basic to the process of reconciliation. When we fail to reclaim this image within ourselves, we forget who we are. When we fail to recognize this image in the other, we risk violence. For most of us, our weapon of choice is the tongue. Our words become the weapons that wound the spirit of another because we fail to recognize this image of God, the very best in us and in the other.

ACCEPTING RESPONSIBILITY

The story of the "Cain mutiny" early in the book of Genesis reflects how far we have fallen from grace. Cain could not claim self-defense in the murder of his brother, but neither did he accept responsibility, at least initially. When God asked Cain where Abel was, Cain replied, "How should I know? Am I my brother's keeper?" (Genesis 4: 9). Cain refused to acknowledge he had anything to do with his brother's disappearance. In response he gave us the above quoted line that has been echoed throughout history to distance ourselves from responsibility for one another.

We begin to sense how deeply this attitude of refusing to accept blame runs in Cain's family. In the story of his parents' fall from grace to disgrace, Adam said, "The woman made me do it." When God then confronted the woman, Eve said, "The devil made me do it." This condition of not accepting responsibility for our actions seems to be etched in the human psyche soon after our creation.

Very early in life I learned a lesson from my older siblings, Ed and Sharon, about accepting responsibility. It was a Saturday morning before dawn. I was eleven years old. I remember I was eleven because it was 1966. It had to be 1966 since my parents had just purchased their first brand new car: a 1966 Olds 88.

We awoke that Saturday morning to a house filled with smoke. Somewhere a fire was smoldering. My mom woke up my little three-year-old sister, my younger brother, my older sister and me and rushed us outside. My older brother went with my dad in search of the cause of the smoke. As we stood outside in the warm early-morning summer sun, suddenly the garage opened and my dad backed the brand new car, now filled with smoke, out into the driveway. Dad and my brother Ed had found the source of the smoke: a smoldering cigarette in the back seat of the Olds 88.

Mom and Dad had let Ed and Sharon use the car the night before to attend a Catholic Youth meeting at church. They had taken some of their friends for a ride in the new car after the meeting. And evidently, someone smoking in the back seat had forgotten to put out a cigarette.

In revisiting this incident more than thirty years later, I asked Dad if he had punished Ed. Both Mom and Dad said, "No," because "it was nobody's fault." Someone was at fault, of course. The cigarette had not landed in the back seat on its own. Mom and Dad could have punished Ed and Sharon but chose not to since it wasn't their fault. Yes, they had used the car. Maybe they were smoking. But both Mom and Dad realized a disaster had been narrowly averted. The car was parked next to the furnace and if that smoldering cigarette in the back seat of the car had ignited before Dad and Ed had found the source of the smoke, the whole house could have gone up in flames.

As I recall, Ed and Sharon were willing to take responsibility for the damage that was done. They did not point fingers at one another, saying, "It was your friends who were riding in the back seat." Instead, they accepted full responsibility for what had happened.

I have often interpreted the story of Cain's parents, Adam and Eve, as "Pride Comes Before the Fall." But maybe the story of the fall is more about not accepting responsibility for our actions. Maybe the story says something to us about how often we point fingers at others rather than accepting responsibility for what we've done or failed to do. I learned a little something about taking responsibility that day in 1966 when smoke filled our house. I learned something from my parents, who chose to look at the whole picture — that a more serious disaster had been avoided and their family was safe. I also learned a lesson from my older brother and sister, who didn't point fingers, who didn't go looking for scapegoats, who didn't say, "The devil made me do it."

As we seek to educate the Adam and Eve who still surface from time to time in our fragile and fearful hearts, we might remember what someone once wrote about accepting responsibility and placing blame: "The one who blames others for one's problems hasn't begun one's education. The one who blames oneself has begun one's education. And the one who blames no one has finished one's education."

Like his parents, Cain had not yet begun his education when he asked God, "Am I my brother's keeper?" But the syllabus for our soul's schooling in premeditated mercy requires that we move from blaming others (including God) for our problems, through blaming ourselves, to blaming no one. Only when we truly believe that for some of life's problems there is no one to blame can we celebrate our soul's graduation to mercy.

THE MARK OF CAIN

The Cain saga doesn't end with the murder of Abel. Now the tiller of the ground, the farmer, has blood on his calloused hands and blood soaking the land. He could wash his hands, but the land would not remain silent. "Listen," God says to Cain, "your brother's blood is crying out to me from the ground! And now your land is cursed: It will no longer yield to give you its strength" (Genesis 4: 10-11).

The blood of Cain's brother that has seeped into the soil is weeping so loudly that God hears the wailing and responds: "Where is your brother Abel?" And the tiller of the soil, descendant of Adam and Eve, firstborn after the fall, shows his progeny by saying, "I don't know; am I my brother's keeper?" (4: 9). Abel was the keeper of the flock; now the ground tilled by Cain will be the keeper of his brother's bloody body. The ground "has opened its mouth to receive your brother's blood from your hand" (4: 11), God says to Cain. Cain's land is now cursed. Nothing will grow in this land again. And Cain is banished. His punishment is not imprisonment. Rather, it is solitary confinement as a fugitive "and a wanderer on the earth" (4: 12). Cain recognizes that this punishment is far worse than a prison cell. Now he will be alone as he wanders the earth. Always on the run. Always looking over his shoulder. Always sleeping with one eye open for the bounty hunter who is following the trail of his brother's blood.

Cain was sentenced to the netherworld of neither here nor there. Maybe this is what hell is: neither this place nor that, an aimless wandering for eternity, the netherworld where one is not tethered to anyone or anything. There is no sense of belonging, just an endless longing. Yes, this sounds like hell.

"Am I there yet?" Cain spent his life asking.

His brother Abel would have been more suited to be a wandering missionary. A shepherd would be on the move to feed his flock or to find the lost or to find water. Farmers like Cain are homebodies; they prefer to stay at home, till the ground, stay close to the earth.

Now Cain will have to keep his ear close to the ground for fear that someone might come from behind and kill him. As he keeps his ear close to the ground, he hears the cry of his brother's blood. Cain begs for mercy. He pleads with God that sending him out into the world would make him an easy target. "Lock me up!" Cain suggests to God. "At least I would be safe." This punishment "is more than I can bear" (4: 13), he says to God. He is driven away from his land. Any farmer who loses his land through foreclosure or sale can tell you the depth of this loss. It is equivalent to a death. The farm is not just a livelihood; it is a life. And to have it taken away is comparable to the loss of life.

Cain loses his land not because the crops fail and God forecloses on his property. Cain loses his land because he could not master his anger and his jealousy. His brother's blood will cause the crops to fail. Cain will go in debt — a deep debt, far deeper than the shallow grave where he buried his brother, the very grave from which Abel's blood screams for justice.

Not only will Cain lose his land, but he will also become a nomad. He will be a fugitive, always on the run from the long arm of God, the long arm of the law. God, the just judge, does not give Cain a death sentence for taking his brother's life. On the contrary, God tells Cain he will not die because of his crime. God will not avenge Abel's death with an "eye for an eye." Nor will anyone harm the fugitive farmer, because God "put a mark on Cain, so that no one coming upon him would kill him" (4: 15).

This mark, like a tattoo, identifies Cain as a marked man. But he is not marked with a "bull's eye" to serve as target practice for a revenge seeker. Rather, it is a mark of mercy. It is a mark that will keep Cain safe. But it will also remind him of his crime, his past, his brother. The echoes of his brother's blood crying out from the ground will ring in his ears and his heart for as long as he lives.

This is severe punishment. This is God's justice and mercy. This is what happens when sin gets the best of us: We bear the mark of Cain. Our sin is tattooed upon our heart, our soul. From the Christian perspective, the only way to erase this tattoo etched much deeper than skin deep, the only way to reverse the vengeance of this vicious crime, is for God to shed God's own blood. To stand in Cain's place. To replace the mark of Cain with the mark of Christ. That mark, the sign of the cross, etched upon the souls of all Christians at baptism, will be the means by which Cain's name will be redeemed.

CAIN: A NAME REDEEMED

Let's explore the process of redemption that leads to reconciliation by looking at another story. Imagine with me that many centuries after Cain murdered his brother Abel there was a *shepherd* whose name was Cain. He roamed the hill country surrounding Judea. Like his ancestors before him, he was a keeper of the flock. Cain cared for his sheep with a tenacious tenderness. He called each one by name and knew the ones who were prone to wander away or get caught in briers or were too slow to find their way back home.

Tracing his life would leave a few scars on one's fingertips from the jagged edges of his story. He had tried his hand as a soldier, and his body bore the wounds of war. His boots bloodied once too often, he now preferred the open fields of a herdsman to the battlefields of a warrior. In his quiet moments late at night when the sheep were sleeping and the stars were shining, Cain could sense the guilt that gathered like gloom in his conscience and the sin that stained his wandering soul.

Cain never considered himself religious or righteous, so he had little to hide — except his name. That was the only thing that haunted Cain. He resented his parents for naming him after the legendary brother who killed Abel. Why couldn't they have named him after the one who was the original shepherd rather than the farmer with bloodstained hands? He felt his name had become a self-fulfilling prophecy. His life had reflected the life of his namesake, the one who murdered innocence out of envy and for his punishment became a fugitive farmer, a nomad in the land of Nod. He knew the story by heart. It was not a name to live up to. He had spent his life living it down.

One night Cain was thinking about his past as he rubbed the tattoo on his arm, another family heirloom that bore witness to the legacy he claimed. Legend had it that when Cain was punished for killing his brother he was banished and became a wanderer. But God made him the original marked man: A tattoo served notice to any would-be attackers that this one, guilty though he was, still was protected by an unseen hand and divine plan. Cain, the shepherd, carried this tattoo like he carried his name, keeping it covered by his sleeves. He didn't want anyone to see it or know that he felt strangely secure, even as the sins of his past stalked his days and serenaded him at night. This sense of serenity allowed him to spend these dark hours without the slightest fear that he would be threatened by thieves, murderers or marauders.

This night, however, as he gazed at the sky while keeping watch over his sheep, he would be threatened by something else. He noticed a brilliant star, one he had seen before. But this night the star seemed particularly revealing. He stared at it for a time, mesmerized by a memory of what it might mean. The memory was from a prophet's words spoken to Cain by his mother long ago: "The people who walked in darkness have seen a great light; upon those who dwelt in the land of gloom, a light has shone" (Isaiah 9: 2).

"Could this be that light?" Cain wondered aloud shortly before falling into a gentle sleep. He rarely slept very soundly, not only because of the sheep but because he knew that when one sleeps too soundly one's dreams become too distant and deep to retrieve.

Suddenly, Cain was startled by the sound of his rustling sheep. He heard someone call his name. He recognized the voice of another nomad who had settled in for the night on a hill nearby. When the voice came closer, he could see four or five other shepherds who looked as if they had seen a ghost. With a mixture of fear and fascination in their words, they described what they had just witnessed: a holy ghost hovering over the field where their flock was sleeping. They all had seen this ghost, so they knew they were not dreaming. And what made it even more real was that the ghost spoke.

"What did she tell you?" Cain asked, brushing a cobweb from his eye.

"She told us we have nothing to fear," one of the shepherds said. "She told us that tonight in David's city a savior has been born."

"And when she said this," another shepherd picked up the story, "there was a great chorus of others singing like we've never heard before."

Cain did not know what to make of their story but agreed to go with them to the town of Bethlehem as the ghost had instructed them. He knew this town. It wasn't much, no more than a bump in the road, but he had visited there a time or two when he'd needed supplies. Before going with the other shepherds, though, he wanted to wake his sheep and take them along.

"There isn't time for that," one of the shepherds said to him, grabbing Cain's sleeve.

Cain pushed the shepherd's hand away. "Don't touch me," he said sternly. The other shepherd had touched the sleeve that covered his tattoo. Even in the strange happenings of this most unusual night Cain could not forget that he was a marked man.

"Come on, Cain," another said. "Pull yourself together."

"But I've never left my sheep alone," Cain protested.

"There's a first time for everything," the one who had grabbed his sleeve said. "And tonight is that night."

When Cain and the others arrived at a small shed on the edge of the town of Bethlehem, they found a young couple with a newborn child. Seeing this scene stirred something inside Cain as he remembered the rest of the prophet's story told to him by his mother:

> For every boot that trampled in battle,
> every cloak rolled in blood,
> will be burned as fuel for flames.
> For a child is born to us, a son is given to us;
> upon his shoulder dominion rests.
> They name him Wonder-Counselor, God-Hero,
> Father-Forever, Prince of Peace (Isaiah 9: 5-6).

In reading this story written upon his heart, he remembered his name. But for the first time in his life, he felt no shame. The young woman who held the child in her arms asked each of the shepherds to speak their names. When she looked at him and he met her eyes, he was not ashamed. "My name is Cain," he said.

The woman smiled, and the baby bowed his head at the sound of a name now redeemed. The legacy of the name had come full circle. Cain was among the very first Israelites to see the given Son, to witness the birth of New Innocence — and the fulfillment of humanity — in the world.

GOD'S CRIMINAL MERCY SYSTEM

The story suggests that we are redeemed not by justice but by mercy. God's mercy. God's premeditated mercy. God meditated on how this mercy might come to earth since the fall of the divine beloved ones, Adam and Eve. Reflecting on this mercy plan for centuries, playing and praying with the possibilities in the divine heart for ages unknown, God chose to save the world not by justice but by mercy. Our spiritual system, then, our belief system, is based on mercy, not justice.

But we live in a world where the legal system, the system of checks and balances, of law and order, is based on justice, not mercy. We call it the "criminal justice system," not the "criminal mercy system." Justice is blind, or so both the statue and the statutes suggest. Everyone is equal under the law, or so we are told, and so we hope.

God, though, is not blind. God is not so much interested in human justice as in divine mercy. Ever since Cain took his brother out on the land and killed him with the force of his hand, God planned to reclaim creation, to reclaim the land. God's premeditation exercise began with marking Cain to protect him from those who would seek to avenge Abel's death by bringing Cain to justice. Though we recall certain biblical stories where it seems God's premeditation exercises had certain ups and downs — raising the divine hand in Noah's time, for example — God's plan of premeditated mercy would reach its epoch, its eternal effect, in sending the Son to walk the land God created.

The sacred story of the birth of Jesus in a manger in Bethlehem begins the final stage of God's plan of premeditated mercy that would bring about not a return to the first creation but an entirely new creation. In the person of Jesus, mercy becomes more than a theory. Now mercy is embodied in a human person. This is important to remember as we explore the roots of premeditated mercy: We are not interested in returning to the Garden of Eden but in becoming a new creation.

NO EXIT: THE GARDEN OF EDEN

We sense God's plan of premeditated mercy at the beginning of Jesus' public ministry. We also see the purpose of this plan and how it will be carried out. It will not be to reclaim but to redeem. Jesus, as the embodiment of God's mercy, doesn't seem interested in reestablishing the first creation but rather in showing the world how the practice of mercy makes a new creation. To symbolize this, Jesus begins his public ministry not in a garden but in a desert.

To put this in perspective, for several years now when considering some retreat and vacation time, I have heeded the call of Horace Greeley, the nineteenth century American journalist famous for the line "Go west, young man." (Of course, now that I'm in my forties I hear that call as, "Go west, middle-aged man!") Recently, when driving west on I-70 between Kansas City and Denver, I noticed a sign on the interstate that's always intrigued me. At Exit 206 in Kansas, there's a sign that says, "Garden of Eden." I'm not kidding! The sign says that the Garden of Eden is located sixteen miles north of Interstate 70. I confess that even though I have traveled this stretch of highway for many years, I have yet to take that exit. It's not that I wouldn't want to return to innocence — the Garden of Eden is, of course, the place where our innocence was lost. But I fear a return trip to the land of innocence would be more of a tourist attraction than a pilgrim's destination.

Our destination on this road of reconciliation is not the Garden of Eden, where our innocence was lost, but the wilderness where we begin to find our redemption. The process of reconciliation is not simply about recovering our lost innocence. It is more about discovering how we become a new creation, how we are redeemed by the suffering, death and resurrection of Jesus. A savior was sent by God not simply to reclaim our innocence but to grow our souls and engage them in claiming our redemption.

The symbols of garden and wilderness are important mile markers on mercy's map. The Garden of Eden is the place associated with paradise. It symbolizes all that is good and holy. All is in order in the garden where God is the divine gardener who keeps everything growing in harmony. The desert, or wilderness, on the other hand, symbolizes death. The first syllable of the word *wilderness* suggests the meaning of this symbol: wild. This is a walk on the "wild" side, where chaos, confusion and catastrophe linger at every corner. Danger lurks in the desert. During the day, the sun is so hot one can barely breathe. During the night, it can be so cold as to chill one to the bone. Whereas the garden is east of Eden — the east symbolizing sunrise and new life — the wilderness is in the west, where the sun sets and where death waits to take our breath away.

In the book of Genesis where the story of lost innocence is recalled, God places at the center of the garden the very best creation of the divine imagination — the human beings. They are the apples of God's eye because they are made in God's image and likeness. When God looks into the eyes of the man and woman, God sees a reflection of the divine self. So precious in God's eyes are these human beings that God has breathed into them the divine breath. The creation story from the book of Genesis says that the first man and woman, Adam and Eve, live because God has fashioned them from the ground and breathed into them the breath of life.

But these first humans, whom God created to be partners, became partners in crime. They could not resist the temptation to eat the forbidden fruit. Because of their crime of disobedience to God's divine plan, the breath of life is taken away from them. So we see that it wasn't so much the beauty of the garden that was breathtaking; it was Adam and Eve's disobedience that took their breath away. Adam and Eve didn't lose their life right away, of course. But when they gave in to the temptation to be like God, they relinquished God's dream that they live forever.

The Jesus story is about how this gift of everlasting life is restored through his obedience to God's will. Of course, the wilderness can also be breathtaking. But the story of Jesus beginning his public ministry by spending forty days and forty nights in the desert shows us how to resist the temptations that seek to take our breath away. It is by remaining faithful to God's word in the desert that Jesus initiated the redemption that will lead us through the wasteland of deferred dreams and distant or discarded relationships.

JESUS: GO WEST, YOUNG MAN

Instead of heading "east of Eden," back to the garden to reclaim innocence lost, Jesus heeds the advice to "Go west, young man." After his baptism and before beginning his public ministry, the young rabbi wanders west, into the wilderness, into the desert.

As Jesus discovered, when one heads west, one enters the nation of temptation. But it is here in the furnace of the desert that the new creation begins to be fashioned and forged by passing through this nation of temptation. We've all been this way before, haven't we? We may pray, "Lead us not into temptation," but to paraphrase the words on a T-shirt I recently saw in a mall, what we are really saying is, "God, you don't have to lead us to this nation of temptation because we know the way." Maybe that's why, when Jesus later teaches his disciples how to pray, this attitude of "lead us not into temptation" is so present in his mind. He's been there. He's done that. He knows how difficult it can be to live for forty days and forty nights in the nation of temptation. Jesus sees the *No Trespassing* signs in this nation of temptation, posted there because of the dangers that lurk in the desert. But he knows in his call to travel west that he will have to pass through the wilderness, for it is here that we begin to learn how to "forgive us our trespasses as we forgive those who trespass against us." As Jesus tells his disciples, to make it safely to the land of forgiveness we need to pray, "Deliver us from evil," for that is precisely what Jesus encounters in the wilderness: the presence of the evil one.

The three temptations Jesus encounters in the desert are very seductive. But then, by definition, temptation draws us in as cleverly as the serpent seduced Adam and Eve. The first temptation of Jesus is for *instant gratification*. He is hungry. He has fasted for forty days and forty nights and is famished. He is greeted by the president of this nation of temptation who suggests that if he is truly the Chosen One, he can calm his growling stomach, ease his hunger pangs, by turning a stone into bread. But Jesus resists this temptation for instant gratification by relying on the only weapon he has at his disposal: God's word. This is his defense to resist temptation: "One does not live on bread alone." Turning a stone into bread would have been an easy miracle for Jesus. But throughout his life — and the wilderness was his training ground for the kind of Messiah he would be — his miraculous interventions were not for self-gratification but for the fulfillment of God's plan through the fulfillment of others. Jesus was not a self-serving savior but one who sought to serve the needs of others.

On our sojourn to that sacred space of the soul where the practice of premeditated mercy finds its source, Jesus' resistance to this first temptation of self-gratification encourages us to look to the needs of others first before we seek to satisfy our own wants and desires.

The second temptation is for *popular acclamation*. The evil one takes Jesus up to the top of the temple and tempts him to throw himself down since God would send a SWAT team of angels to catch him "lest he dash his foot against a stone." This daredevil stunt would win Jesus popularity and wide acclaim. But Jesus resists the desire for fifteen minutes of fleeting fame. He is in the business of reclaiming the world for God, not making a name for himself.

Jesus' response to this temptation suggests that in our wandering in the wilderness on the way to reconciliation, we might focus less on our own desire to be popular and more on our pursuit to be holy. Our walk on the wild side is not about "leaping tall buildings in a single bound," but stretching out a hand to someone feeling too small to matter. Like Jesus, we are not interested in taking a flying leap from the pinnacle of a temple, but rather in seeing how each of us is a temple where the real presence of God resides. In the new creation fashioned out of the ground of this wilderness retreat, Jesus will not win any popularity contests. He will not meet with wide acclaim. Rather, he will take some unpopular positions that will lead him outside the gates of the holy city where he will be crucified. He begins to identify himself as the new temple here in the wilderness, the Temple of the Holy Spirit that will rise from the dust of the desert and the ashes of Calvary to form a new creation.

The final temptation is *worldly recognition and power*. From the top of a mountain, the evil one shows Jesus all the kingdoms of the world. If only he would sell his soul, Jesus would be the most visible ruler on the face of the earth. All the kingdoms of the world would be at his service. He would be king of the world. But Jesus resisted the temptation for recognition in the eyes of the world. He already knew who he was: the chosen one of God. He wasn't interested in being ruler of the world; rather, he was called to be savior of the world.

On our journey through this nation of temptation, recognition in the eyes of the world is certainly a seduction. We can sell out for more prestige, more privilege, more power. This was the leverage the evil one used in the garden to seduce Adam and Eve to sell out: They could be like God. But the New Adam, Jesus, resists this temptation by remembering his identity as the chosen one of God. We resist this temptation when we recognize that we are already somebody in the eyes of God. We are children of God, made in God's image and likeness. We carry within us the very breath, the very spirit, of God. When we recognize who we are, we can resist the temptation to be somebody we are not.

In his poem, "Murder in the Cathedral," T.S. Eliot wrote that "The last temptation is the greatest treason: to do the right deed for the wrong reason." As we journey west in the wilderness toward the land of redemption, our challenge is do right deeds for the right reasons. We are not to practice premeditated mercy for our own purification but, rather, for the reconciliation of the human race. Our desire to be reconciled in our relationships with others is not self-serving. We may, for example, seek an uneasy truce with someone we trusted who abused or betrayed this trust. We may want to be cordial and civil in the presence of one who has hurt us simply to avoid confrontation. We may shake hands as a sign of peace. But in our hearts, the pain that precludes the possibility of peace is still there. We hear the echo of the prophet Jeremiah screaming through the cracks of our broken heart, "Peace, peace, when there is no peace!" (Jeremiah 6: 14).

This is the greatest treason: to make peace for the wrong reason. Like Jesus wandering in the wilderness, the challenge of premeditated mercy is to resist the treason of doing right deeds for the wrong reasons. The road of reconciliation is so often paved with our good intentions. But, as the old saying goes, we know where this road leads. Instead, the challenge is to deflect our desire to be reconciled away from saving or serving ourselves. It is rather about believing that God saves us, and because we are saved we can serve one another.

When the jagged edges of life open cuts on hands and feet and fingers, after putting pressure on the wound to stop the bleeding, we may want to put the pedal to the metal and head west. Along the way, we may see the sign that says, "Garden of Eden," and we will be tempted to exit the highway of holiness to reclaim our innocence. As inviting and enticing as it may be to reclaim our innocence by returning to the Garden of Eden, it is really only a tourist trap. The Garden of Eden may offer us a nostalgic rendezvous with a memory, but it will not provide a remedy to ease the pain of our wounds.

In following the road of reconciliation, we realize there is no return to innocence, no way to reclaim the first creation. Rather, we are to become a new creation by claiming our redemption. We find our way to becoming a new creation by passing through this wilderness — resisting the temptations of instant gratification, popular acclamation and worldly recognition — and by remaining faithful to the image and breath of God that beats and breathes within us.

Making Peace:
A Recipe for Reconciliation

When grapes turn to wine,
they long for our ability to change.

— Rumi

One of the most dramatic examples of premeditated mercy that I have ever encountered is the story of Father Michael Lapsley. An Anglican priest, Father Lapsley was expelled from South Africa in the late 1980s for speaking out against apartheid and standing in solidarity with the victims of the racist regime. On April 28, 1990, he was living in exile in Zimbabwe. When he went to get his mail that day, hidden inside the pages of a religious magazine was a letter bomb. The bomb exploded and he lost both hands and an eye.

Speaking in Chicago at a conference on the theme of reconciliation in April, 1995, Father Lapsley said, "Personally, I am grateful that I can remember, and it is not a memory that haunts me. It is a memory that I can live with. I felt the presence of God with me in that bombing, sharing in my crucifixion. I was in darkness. All my senses were affected. Sight in one eye had gone; there was permanent damage to the other eye. Having lost my hands, feel and touch had gone forever. In my view," Father Lapsley continued, "to receive a letter bomb is to become a specific focus of evil in the world. People from all over the world responded with a flood of messages assuring me of their prayers and love and support. I became a focus of all that is beautiful in the human community — the ability to be kind, generous, loving and compassionate. I realized that if I became filled with hatred, bitterness, self-pity and a desire for revenge, I would remain a victim forever. It would consume me. God and the people of faith and hope enabled me to make my bombing redemptive — to bring life out of death, good out of evil. I was enabled to grow in faith, in commitment to justice, in compassion. I am no longer a victim, or even simply a survivor. I am a victor over evil, hatred and death."

A bomb exploded in this priest's hands. Those who sent the bomb plotted an act of premeditated murder. But Father Lapsley responded to this vicious and violent attack by plotting acts of premeditated mercy. He would not allow evil to have a permanent victory. The forces of evil had failed to kill his body. If Father Lapsley had developed a taste for revenge, the forces of evil would have surely damaged his soul. So, instead, this extraordinary witness quenched his thirst for reconciliation during his long and arduous recovery by meditating on mercy. "Being so physically wounded," he said, "I discovered how important healing is."

Today, Father Lapsley operates a trauma center for victims of violence in South Africa. In a country which is still seeking healing from the deep scars left by apartheid, Father Lapsley seeks to bring together those wounded by institutionalized racism. His community has endeavored to create a safe place, a trusting environment, where the persecutors and the persecuted, the violent and the victimized, might come together for reconciliation.

Father Lapsley's story offers a recipe that reflects the ingredients necessary for making peace:

- a magnum of memory
- a cup of blessing
- an ounce of yeast
- a cup of compassion
- several grains of salt

All of these ingredients are essential in order for others to "taste and see" the real, reconciling presence of Christ. By reading the labels of each ingredient, we can see why they are so important.

A MAGNUM OF MEMORY: CONFRONTING THE PAST

At the reconciliation conference in Chicago, Father Lapsley said the terrible trauma of being the target of a letter bomb is "a memory I can live with." Though one might think such a horrible experience would be something one would try to forget, Father Lapsley chooses to remember this pivotal and excruciatingly painful event from his past. He cannot forget what happened to him. Each time he looks in the mirror and sees his body indelibly scarred by violence, he is reminded. Each time he picks up a newspaper with the prostheses that now serve as his hands, he remembers.

Memory is an important ingredient in the recipe of reconciliation. A *magnum* is the measurement for mercy because a magnum, according to Webster, is "a large wine bottle holding about two-thirds of a gallon." A magnum of memory is just the right amount since a gallon of memory may be too much, causing us to drown our sorrows. But a magnum of memory may reflect what Jesus did on the night he was betrayed when he held up the wine and said, "Do this in memory of me." Each Eucharist is a celebration of this memory. We must not forget. We must never forget.

Memory, however, tends to play tricks on us. When I hear confessions, a familiar formula often surfaces that reflects what many Catholics were taught from their first experiences with the Sacrament of Penance. When a penitent finishes his/her list of sins, he/she often adds: "and for all the sins of my past life." My first inclination is to ask, "What were you in your past life?" Upon reflection, however, this token phrase uttered by many Catholic Christians who were taught a certain way of going to confession may reflect how many of us have never fully confronted — and, therefore, never fully reconciled with — the sins of our past.

It's because making peace with our past is such an essential element in the practice of premeditated mercy that the first ingredient in the recipe for reconciliation is memory. Indeed, it's by remembering the pain and tracing the wounds that have caused separation that we begin the process of healing and reconciliation. Of course, when we premeditate mercy, we take the risk of remembering all the bombs that have blown up in our faces. We might also become aware of all the little bombs that we have manufactured in the remote places of our hearts. Every now and then those little bombs are released and explode in words that wound others or deeds that damage others. However, by making peace with our past, we express our belief in our ability to face without fear the wounds we cause as well as the wounds inflicted upon us. We confront our capacity for violence as we enter the sanctuary of our heart shrines where the stories of wounds inflicted and incurred are remembered with great reverence.

On a global scale, we know what happens when we fail to remember the sins of our past. Global amnesia has led us to the killing fields of Cambodia, to the ethnic cleansing in Bosnia and Kosovo, to the massacre in Rwanda. When we fail to confront the sins of the past, we keep repeating the violence. Death spins a vicious cycle, a tornado of terror, a cyclone of catastrophe. But when we face into the violence of the past, we gather the resolve to make the fervent prayer "never again" a forever principle.

Confronting the sins of the past can lead to a change of heart and a break in the cycle of violence. Recently I met a woman named Sally Peck. She was introduced to me with these words, "Sally's mother was murdered several years ago." The person who introduced us went on to say that Sally is now very active in an organization of murder victims' families who are opposed to the death penalty. I visited with Sally one afternoon because I wanted to know how a person who has experienced the loss of a loved one through violence could reach such a profound place of reconciliation. It seemed especially rare when so many in our country, and even in our communities of faith, are in favor of capital punishment.

Sally told me that it was the memory of her mother's love and forgiveness that helped her to forgive her mother's murderer. You see, her mother's brother was killed in a labor dispute when Sally was nine years old. She remembers that her mother showed no desire for revenge against the one who murdered her brother. When Sally received the call that her mother, who was eighty-two at the time, had been murdered, she recalls driving over to her mother's house and thinking, "Whoever it was who did this, my mother would forgive the person and would have us forgive the person too."

The memory of her mother's love has allowed Sally to let go of the desire for revenge. She told me that her mother has spent her life bringing people together. Because of the witness of her mother, because her mother's teaching about love and forgiveness was so fresh in her mind and her soul, Sally's heart had become a home for peace.

If we want to make our hearts into homes for peace, we might place on the altar of our heart shrines the pictures of those women and men who have taught us to forgive. Think of people who have taken the risks of reconciliation by letting go of grievances — no matter how great —

that might clutter their hearts. With a magnum of memory, we toast those who have favored us with their forgiveness. With a magnum of memory, we begin to make peace with our past.

ONE CUP OF BLESSING: A GRATEFUL HEART

The second ingredient in this recipe for reconciliation is one cup of blessing. This cup of blessing creates a grateful heart. In reflecting on his experience of being physically mutilated, Father Lapsley never suggested he was grateful for the experience. But when he said, "I felt the presence of God with me...," he revealed a heart that was filled with blessing. It's only such a blessed heart that can reflect a hopeful and resilient attitude: Even though one's enemies may destroy one's body, they can never kill one's spirit. As Father Lapsley said, "I realized that if I became filled with hatred, bitterness, self-pity and a desire for revenge, I would remain a victim forever. It would consume me." So instead of filling his heart with hatred, Father Lapsley filled his heart with gratitude for "God and the people of faith and hope who enabled me to make my bombing redemptive — to bring life out of death."

Have you noticed that we sometimes *think* "off the top of our heads," but we always *thank* "from the bottom of our hearts"? To make peace, we take the lid off the "top of our hearts" to see what is stored at the bottom. A grateful heart has the capacity to see all as gift. With a grateful heart, we can look at the mistakes we have made and find new meaning even in our messy lives. A spirit of gratitude encourages us to see these failures as necessary teachers in the quest to know more about ourselves, our gifts, our relationships and, especially, the mercy of God.

One day when I lived at a house of prayer in Kansas, I was walking down the hall to my office when I came upon a member of the staff working on a project. It was obvious she was in the early stages of creativity. "What are you making?" I asked.

"A mess," she said.

The cup of blessing that symbolizes a grateful heart invites us to see that making peace always involves making a mess. At least at first. As we wrestle with our fears of loving and our failures in forgiving, we sometimes look around and look inside and whisper, "What a mess I've made." But this is where the creative process sparked by prayer begins. In the messiness of our lives, peace is found in the bits and pieces of broken dreams. With a grateful heart, we acknowledge the mess and allow God's creative hand to help us put together the peace.

With this grateful heart, this cup of blessing, we discover that wounds inflicted by life — illness, loss of loved ones, dashed dreams, death — can draw us closer to each other. At first, giving thanks for the pain and sorrow in life seems incomprehensible. When we're in the middle of it — when we're in the midst of the mess — it usually seems unfathomable to find even a sliver of a silver lining or a shred of evidence for which to be grateful. But a grateful heart will, over time, bring to the surface a sacred presence that brings more than a measure of healing.

Gratitude is an attitude of the heart. The grateful heart is a great heart indeed. A grateful heart enables us to view the world from a perspective of promise instead of penance, hope instead of hostility. The hearts of those who look at the world — at life — from the bottom of their hearts rather than the top of their heads are free to acknowledge that all is gift. With grateful hearts, we will not give in to discouragement or fear.

There is a story told about a woman who found the barn where Satan kept his seeds ready to be sown in the human heart. She noticed that seeds of discouragement were in large supply, far more numerous than others. Upon inquiry, she learned that such seeds could be sown almost anywhere. But upon further questioning, Satan admitted reluctantly that there is one place in which Satan could never get these seeds of discouragement to grow. "And where is that?" the woman asked.

Satan replied, "In the heart of a grateful person."

In the heart of a grateful person there is no room for fear or discouragement. Indeed, its opposite, encouragement, literally means, "with courage." Thus, when we add one cup of blessing to our recipe of reconciliation, we gather the courage to forgive. We may even find the answer to the prayer, "deliver us from all evil," because as the story suggests, the evil one cannot sow seeds of discouragement in the heart of a grateful person.

So, when we try to make peace but find we are only making a mess, we can take a sip from the cup of blessing and remember this prayer that comes from a grateful heart:

O Divine Dreamer of Eternal Designs,
grant me the vision to see your image within me.
I've tried so hard to make peace,
but often, it seems, I've only made a mess.

Help me to see your plan for peace taking shape
within this grateful but broken heart of mine.
Open for me that inner eye to see amidst the mess
the meaning and message you have for my life.

In the quiet of this hour
help me to focus on the power of your divine presence —
to see with new eyes the love you have for me
and for all peoples on this planet.
Help me see your truth
that unravels the mess made by headstrong lies:
peace through strength; might equals power.
Grant me the vision to see your dream for me
and the courage to live the truth of your peace.

YEAST: AN OUNCE OF FORGIVENESS, NOT A POUND OF FLESH

The third ingredient in this recipe of reconciliation is the yeast of forgiveness. Unless we knead into the dough of our daily bread an ounce of forgiveness, we will continue to look for the proverbial "pound of flesh" from those who have hurt us. The desire for revenge will fill us with rage, and the heat of this rage will kill the yeast of forgiveness so that reconciliation can never be realized.

Yeast is very temperamental. When yeast is used in baking, it must be placed in warm water before being kneaded into the dough. The water has to be just the right temperature or the yeast will not be effective. If the water is too hot, the yeast will die. When our temperature rises and our blood boils, the yeast of forgiveness will die in the raging inferno of the desire for revenge. There is a famous story about two survivors of a Nazi death camp who meet many years after the Holocaust. One of the men says, "Have you forgiven the Nazis?"

"Yes," the other replies.

"Well, I haven't! I'm still filled with rage for what they did to us. I hate them. I have never exacted my revenge, my pound of flesh."

Gently, the other man touched his friend's shoulder. "In that case," he said, "they still have you in prison."

Imprisoned by his own rage, the man remained a victim of the atrocities committed against him. Father Lapsley understood how one can remain incarcerated in the cell of victimhood. But reflecting on his experience of being the target of a terrorist attack, Father Lapsley said, "I am no longer a victim, or even simply a survivor. I am a victor over evil, hatred and death." Unless we forgive those who have hurt us or who hate us, we cannot escape past abuse or present persecution.

St. Paul, in his first letter to the church at Corinth, tells us how necessary the yeast of forgiveness is in seeking to live as a reconciling presence in the world: "Do you not know that a little yeast has its effect all through the dough?" (1 Corinthians 5: 6). Just as a little yeast goes a long way to make the dough rise, so does an ounce of forgiveness in the mix of mercy.

Moreover, this yeast of forgiveness is a double acting yeast. It affects and is affected by the one who forgives as well as the one who needs forgiveness. When we are willing to admit we've made a mistake; when we are willing to go to another who has been hurt by a word we have said or by our lack of attention; when we dare to forgive and be forgiven, this yeast of reconciliation goes a long way toward making peace.

But remember how this yeast works. In baking, after mixing the yeast with the dough, the baker covers the dough with a warm moist cloth and then does something else while the yeast works on the dough. As Jesus reminds us in the passage about premeditated mercy, "Before bringing your gift to the altar, if you hold something against your brother or sister, go and reconcile" before coming to the table. We must allow this yeast of forgiveness to work on us from the inside before we bake the bread of friendship. We must create space for the yeast to be active before we dare to approach the altar of worship where the bread is broken in a sacramental sign of God's infinite mercy.

Paul used the image of yeast to remind us to "get rid of the old yeast and to make of ourselves fresh dough, unleavened loaves." Because of Christ's sacrifice on the cross, Paul tells us to "celebrate the feast not with the old yeast, that of corruption and wickedness, but with the unleavened bread of sincerity and truth" (1 Corinthians 5: 8). These are the ingredients of yeast that will make this recipe of reconciliation rise or fall: sincerity and truth. These are the gifts that will either enhance our desire for intimacy or destroy our initiative to be reconciled with the other.

But just as yeast needs warm water to work, so the ability to forgive works best in an environment of warmth — of trust, acceptance and hospitality. As we have seen, if the water is too hot, the yeast will not be effective. If the one with whom we desire to be reconciled is still filled with rage, we must try to turn down the heat. Likewise, if the water is too cold, the yeast will also die. If a cold shoulder is all we receive from the one with whom we seek to be reconciled, an ounce of yeast will have little effect. Finding the right temperature for the yeast of forgiveness takes time. Moreover, maintaining the right temperature is often not easy. Yet, it's essential to the whole process of reconciliation and defines our commitment to the practice of premeditated mercy. The more we create an environment where this yeast can do its work, the more likely this leaven will have its effect "throughout the dough."

"The reign of God," Jesus says, "is like yeast which a woman took and kneaded into three measures of flour. Eventually the whole mass of dough began to rise" (Matthew 13: 33). In the practice of premeditated mercy, we work from within ourselves first so we can serve as a catalyst for reconciliation. Then we work within the group to which we belong. By adding an ounce of forgiveness rather than a pound of flesh to the mix of our relationships, we create the great-tasting bread of companionship that rises in the ovens of our own experiences. But to do this, we must know how to knead the dough, drawing upon experiences of being needy and being needed, of forgiving others and being forgiven by others. By working from within, we seek to create an atmosphere that is sincere and sacred, truthful and trusting. Eventually, we will see our community of remembrance rise to heights never anticipated or expected on this side of the reign of God.

ONE CUP OF COMPASSION: HANDLE WITH CARE

The fourth ingredient in this recipe, compassion, is vital to reconciliation. One cup is an arbitrary amount; the recipe calls for as much as is needed at any given time. Compassion is concerned with the way we handle loss — our own and others. On this package of compassion the warning label reads: "Handle with Care." Being compassionate means paying careful attention to any grieving we or others may be grappling with as a result of an experience of loss.

We see this compassion in action in Father Lapsley's efforts to establish trauma centers for victims of violence in South Africa. His suffering at the hands of terrorists left indelible wounds upon his body and scars upon his soul. But rather than covering these wounds, hiding these scars, he left them open, using them as his motivation to bring healing to both the victims of violence and the perpetrators of violence. By creating a safe and compassionate environment, stories of the violence can be shared, truth can be told and healing can happen.

A Gospel story that holds the key to understanding the need for compassionate presence in the recipe for reconciliation is the appearance of Jesus to his disciples after the resurrection (John 20: 19-31). The wounds of the crucifixion are still visible on the resurrected body of Christ. To sense the importance and the power of this image of a resurrected but scarred Jesus, consider an episode of the television series *Nothing Sacred*, in which Father Leo is a retired priest in residence at a parish where he is the former pastor. Father Leo was forced to resign as pastor because of rather serious doubts about the resurrection. In fact, Father Leo no longer preaches because of his doubts. He hasn't preached in five years. The issue for Leo is why, after the resurrection, Jesus still had the wounds of crucifixion visible on his body. Leo can't understand why God, whom he images as a loving father, would raise his son from the dead but keep the scars of his death visible on his body.

The story Leo ultimately uses to help him through this question, this doubt, is the story of his adopted patron saint, Thomas, the doubting one. Jesus tells Thomas to touch his wounds and believe. In reflecting on this invitation, Leo finally begins to understand what this means. As he reflects on these wounds — touches the wounds in his own life and the wounds of those who come to him for counseling — he begins to see these wounds as points of entry into another's life, another's experience. Then the wounds still visible on the body of Christ become his reason to believe again.

God kept the wounds of crucifixion visible on the body of Christ so that we can touch them. These are the openings, if you will, that allow us to enter the body of Christ. We keep the wounds open so we can get inside each other's lives. These wounds are our doorway into each other's experiences, the way we can crawl under each other's skin rather than allowing those we find most difficult to love to make our skin crawl. The way we can get at the truth of our relationships is to keep the wounds open!

In a world as wounded as ours, it is difficult to see and believe this truth. I was reminded of how hard it is while watching a story on the evening news during the Kosovo crisis. In a refugee camp in Albania two women who had been separated from their husbands and families in the forced exodus from Kosovo gave birth to babies within minutes of each other. In the midst of war, death, ethnic cleansing and utter hopelessness, the image of new life being born into the world was striking. Yet the doctor who delivered the babies seemed unmoved. He said something to the effect, "One has to ask why? It is beautiful — the birth of a baby is beautiful — but to be born into such misery? Why? What's the point?"

Each day the doctor saw the wounds caused by this war. But unlike Father Leo, he was unable to see the wounds as an entry point into another's suffering. Whereas the doctor asked, "What's the point?" Father Leo was able to ask, "Where's the point of entry?"

This is the point: When we believe, we begin to see. Our faith in the resurrection of Christ is not just about seeing and believing; it is often the other way around. When we believe, we see new life, new hope emerging in the most dangerous and deadly places imaginable. Thomas wouldn't believe until he touched the wounds of Christ — he needed to see first. But in that Gospel story, Jesus praises those who have not seen and yet believe. For when we believe, we begin to see clearly, we begin to see with the eyes of compassion.

The wounds on the resurrected body of Jesus are our reasons to believe that reconciliation is not only possible but a promise that can be realized through the grace of God. When we believe in the availability of this grace, what wonders we shall see!

We cannot escape the wounds of our world or of our own lives. We can dress these wounds, cover them up with bandages and gauze, hiding them from the eyes of others. Or we can, by our faith in the promise of the resurrection, invite Christ to probe the prints of our wounds and transform them. In this faith we can then, like Father Lapsley, address these wounds: speak to them, breathe on them and see through them to the very heart of God's compassion.

For Christians there is no other way to see. We believe that out of suffering and death come new life. Thomas finally saw this and believed as he proclaimed his faith, "My Lord and my God" (John 20: 28). When Jesus appeared to Thomas and the other disciples in that upper room after his resurrection, he was reminding us that we cannot experience resurrection without the cross. But suffering will either take us deeper into the mystery of faith that we enter through the wounds of Christ and our own wounds, or it will freeze us in our pain, causing us to lose hope or to make our worlds smaller in order to cope with life. Like the doctor in the refugee camp who delivered babies as the bombs were bursting and wondered about the point of giving birth in the middle of so much misery, we too may lose our faith altogether.

We must not be naive about these wounds. Whether they are caused by injury, by war, by violence, by death, by loss, by rejection or by fear, wounds can cause us to doubt God's presence and God's mercy. Father Leo doubted because he could see the wounds on the body of Christ. It made no sense. Why not heal these wounds? Why not make the resurrected body of Christ perfect? Why a nail-scarred, risen Lord?

We've seen so many wounds on the body of Christ this century — genocide, world wars, racism, apartheid, ethnic cleansing, hate crimes of every kind — do we still believe? Do we still believe in God's great mercy shown to us in the resurrection of Jesus? This is where the rubber of life meets the road of faith: Do we still believe after all that we have seen?

The cup of compassion we add to the recipe of reconciliation flows out of the cup of the Eucharist, the cup of sorrows that has been transformed into the nectar of healing and renewing life. As such, it challenges us to believe because of, not in spite of, the wounds we see on the body of Christ.

When we mix compassion into the recipe of reconciliation, we sense the truth that only when we believe in something, in someone, can we see our way through this dark and dreary, wounded and weary world. And, with our cup of compassion, we see these wounds as the openings through which we can enter each other's pain, suffering, doubt and fear. As the poet Henry Wadsworth Longfellow once wrote, "If we could read the secret history of our enemies, we should find in each person's life sorrow and suffering enough to disarm all hostility." When we read the wounds of even those we call our enemies — the wounds of those we find most difficult to love, whose presence in our lives we find most difficult to digest — then we are able to enter a place of understanding within that person's soul. And from this place within the other's soul, we *stand under* that one's suffering which was unknown to us before, and we begin to *understand* that a prerequisite for premeditated mercy, an essential ingredient in this recipe for reconciliation, is compassion: to handle each other, even our enemies, with care. When we are willing to look honestly at the losses of our own lives, to take inventory of our own wounds, we will find the courage to respond to the losses others experience. And we will handle them with care.

PASS THE SALT: THE FLAVOR OF GOD

The final ingredient in this recipe of reconciliation is a familiar condiment found on most kitchen tables: salt. In his Sermon on the Mount, immediately after offering his companions the Beatitudes, the attitudes of being that would shape their discipleship, Jesus uses the everyday image of salt to identify those who follow his teaching: "You are the salt of the earth" (Matthew 5: 13). It's a rich image that suggests many different perspectives from which to understand who we are called to be as disciples. For Jesus' audience, the spiritual significance of this identity was clear. Whereas we might see salt as something that enhances the flavor of food — without enough salt, food tastes bland — in Jesus' time, salt was primarily used as a natural preserver of food. It was a very valuable commodity — to give another salt was a priceless gift of hospitality and friendship. Sharing salt and bread with a friend was a symbolic gesture reflecting the everlasting nature of the relationship.

We've adopted this meaning in our own culture. When we say that someone is a "salt of the earth" kind of person, we mean he or she is down to earth, admirable, trustworthy, reliable, a friend. This reflects back to the ancient "covenant of salt" recorded in the Hebrew Scriptures in the books of Leviticus, Numbers and Second Chronicles.

At the time of Jesus, salt was also used in rituals of purification. Soon after a child was born, for instance, the infant was washed and then "rubbed with salt" as a protection against germs and as a skin conditioner. The Israelites also adapted the popular pagan belief that salt was a safeguard against demons.

This belief about salt and its protective qualities has found its way into our times. For example, have you ever thrown salt over your left shoulder for good luck? Or have you accidentally spilled salt and been struck by a strong sense that it was bad luck? If you look closely at Leonardo da Vinci's famous painting of the Last Supper, you will notice that Judas Iscariot is depicted as having just spilled salt on the table — a bad omen if ever there was one. We might view the throwing of a pinch of salt over our left shoulder as a silly superstition. Yet I wonder if we might reclaim it as a sacred gesture — not for good luck but for good grace. It could be a prayer for the grace that keeps evil at bay — the grace that protects us from the evil one while helping us reclaim our true identity as children of God, followers of Christ, salt of the earth.

From another perspective, we know that our bodies need salt to survive. Yes, too much salt in the diet can be harmful, and some people have to take salt substitutes. But from a spiritual perspective, a salt-free diet is disastrous. When Jesus calls us "salt for the earth," he implies that there is no substitute for salty Christian witness.

Furthermore, when someone tells us something and we take it with a "grain of salt," we mean we don't take it seriously. But in the context of Jesus' identifying his followers as "salt of the earth," our recipe of reconciliation calls for several grains of salt to help us take very seriously the challenge to flavor our relationships with forgiveness. Only reconcilers who take the challenge seriously are "worth their salt." Only when we season our friendships with forgiveness are we worth our salary as followers of Christ — understanding that the word "salary" comes from the Latin word *sal*, which means salt.

Or, we spread salt on a sidewalk or a street after an ice storm for safety's sake. But if we sprinkle salt on a wound after a fight with a friend, we don't do it for safety's sake but for a measure of revenge — because salt burns!

Well, you get the idea. The point is, when Jesus says, "If salt has lost its taste...it is no longer good for anything, but is thrown out and trampled under foot" (Matthew 5: 13), he is challenging his disciples to put their faith into action. When we are engaged in the works of premeditated mercy listed by the prophet Isaiah (58: 6-8) and adopted by Matthew (25: 31-46) in the teaching of Jesus just before his Last Supper — sharing our bread with the hungry, sheltering the oppressed and homeless, clothing the naked — we will season the world with the flavor of God. It is a taste the world longs to savor.

But not only that. When we've met the poor in their need and filled them; when we've met the wounded in their pain and healed them; when we've met the lost in their fear and found them; when we've met the blind in their darkness and opened their eyes to the wonders of God's abiding presence, then, in the words of the prophet Isaiah, our own wound "will quickly be healed" (Isaiah 58: 8). When we pass the salt of the earth to someone in need, we don't have to worry about the proverbial salt being poured into our wounds, because when we shake the salt of love around, we flavor the world with the taste of God.

We do this as Father Lapsley did when he established centers for victims of trauma in South Africa following his terrible ordeal. Rather than sprinkling salt on the wounds inflicted by violence, we sprinkle salt on the icy relationships between victim and oppressor — creating an environment where stories of truth can be shared. In these salty stories, the ice begins to melt so that no one will slip and fall from the experience of grace.

We add these grains of salt to the recipe of reconciliation with simple acts of kindness and friendship, gentle words of affirmation and hope. When we pass the salt of the covenant, we awaken in another his or her own goodness. When we stop and help another through a difficult day, we sprinkle a little salt along the way. When we throw a little salt on an icy situation, the ice begins to melt. When we take the time to comfort another who is grieving, we taste the mourners' salty tears.

In the practice of premeditated mercy, the recipe for reconciliation requires that we keep a salt shaker near our place of prayer. The salty container becomes the symbol of our covenant with one another and our commitment as followers of Christ. Then, when we are at the table in the company of friends or foes and someone asks, "Will you pass the salt, please?" we hear it as an invitation to sprinkle the other's life with hope and hospitality.

In the practice of premeditated mercy, we throw these grains of salt over our shoulders to protect us from evil and reclaim our identity as salt of the earth. We spread a little salt on an icy relationship so that the one we don't like will not slip and fall. We are the salt of the earth. More than ever, our world needs you and me to pass the salt around the table, around the world.

Pass the salt, please.

Preparing a Meal of Mercy: Following the Recipe

So hope for a great sea-change
On the far side of revenge.
Believe that a further shore
Is reachable from here.
Believe in miracles
And cures and healing wells.

— Seamus Heaney, *The Cure of Troy*

There are numerous examples in the Gospel story of how Jesus followed the recipe for reconciliation. We begin, though, at the end of the story when, after his resurrection, he appeared to the disciples on the beach and prepared breakfast for them (John 21: 1-25), for every good recipe inevitably finds its way into a meal. John writes that "Jesus came over, took the bread and gave it to his friends" (21: 13). To break bread with another is at its most profound level a sacrament because such shared bread is not only made from grains of wheat but also from grains of dreams baked in the ovens of our own experiences. This sacred gesture of giving another a piece of bread is an act of hospitality and hope. In its roots are coded Christ's template for reconciliation. It reflects the real presence of reconciliation that would shape the attitudes of those first disciples of Jesus after his resurrection. This simple ritual of preparing and sharing a meal with friends provided a formative memory for those first disciples, a memory that would nurture courage in their hungry hearts for living out their identity as companions of the Risen One.

The word *companion* literally means "to break bread with." As we reflect on the story in John's Gospel, we see how what Jesus did for the disciples on the beach that morning after his resurrection followed the recipe of reconciliation. For in the course of the meal he invited his disciples to live as companions and reconcilers in the world. When we likewise follow this recipe in our relationships, we prepare a meal of memory and practice premeditated mercy.

"Come and eat your meal" (John 21: 12), Jesus told his friends as he prepared brunch on the beach for them after his resurrection. This Gospel story, sometimes referred to as the "breakfast on the beach," shows us how a people of faith can become a community of memory and hope. We take a closer look now at this story that concludes John's Gospel as we seek to follow the recipe of reconciliation.

BREAKFAST ON THE BEACH

The first thing we might notice in the breakfast on the beach story is how many questions and incongruities are inherent in the narration. For example, the story is very specific in telling how many fish the disciples caught: 153. Why 153 fish? Why such a precise number? Who counted them? Why bother to count them anyway? Some scholars suggest that the precise number of fish refers to the inclusive nature of the early church — an inclusiveness that implies reconciliation. This theory is supported by the next line, which reflects the nature of real inclusivity: "In spite of the great number, the net was not torn!" (21: 11).

But there are other strange features in this story. Like the catch itself. Fishing through the night, the disciples had no luck at all. Seasoned fishermen, they must have been frustrated. After all, this was not a hobby to do on one's day off; this was their bread and butter, the livelihood that put food on the family's table. Adding to the frustration of not catching even close to their limit, it must have been a night of brutal heat. The Gospel says Peter was stripped. So, here they are, professional fisherman — one of whom is naked, others whose clothes are sticking to their bodies because of the heat of the night — being told by a stranger on the beach to "try the starboard side." Had they not thought of this during the night? Were they all fishing off the same side of the boat? But sure enough, once they follow the stranger's suggestion, they catch so many fish they "could not haul the net in."

This brings us to other inconsistencies in this scene. After the miraculous catch of fish has opened John's eyes and he screams, "It is the Lord!" (21: 7), Peter does a very odd thing. Like Adam and Eve in the Garden when they ate the forbidden fruit and realized they were naked, "upon hearing it was the Lord, Simon Peter threw on some clothes" (21: 8) and jumped in the lake. First of all, why put on clothing in order to jump into the water? Like Adam and Eve, was it a modesty issue? The primal parents hid in the garden; Peter seemed to go into hiding underwater. Yet, unlike the fruit of the garden, these fish were not forbidden. Jesus was not the park ranger ready to count how many fish they had caught and if they had exceeded their limit.

Then, after Peter swam, evidently fully clothed, by the side of the boat, "the other disciples came in the boat, towing the net full of fish" (21: 8). They caught so many fish — 153 — that all the disciples together couldn't bring in the net. But notice that when Jesus tells them to go get some of the fish they caught to throw on the fire, Peter, sopping wet, soaked to the bone, "went aboard and hauled ashore the net loaded with sizeable fish" (21: 11). Where did Peter get the strength to haul in the net by himself when earlier in the passage all the other disciples together couldn't bring the fish out of the sea?

Then there is this interesting little twist: When the disciples land on the shore — remember the fish were still being towed behind the boat — they see "a charcoal fire…with a fish laid on it." Okay, where did Jesus get the fish? The 153 were still flopping around in the net, weren't they? Maybe Jesus did have a fishing pole after all. But wherever Jesus got that fish to fry, it is no wonder that the early Christian community adopted the fish as a primary Eucharistic symbol.

Jesus then invited the weary fishermen to breakfast: "Come and eat your meal" (21: 12). In that simple invitation, Jesus initiated the final act of the drama of reconciliation with his disciples, each of whom had abandoned him in some way. In this breakfast, the real presence of the Risen Lord is reflected. Another meal — like the *last* one. This time, though, he didn't wash feet; he cooked breakfast. But in this simple act of service, "no one presumed to inquire 'Who are you?' for they knew it was the Lord" (21: 12). Finally, even though the disciples did certainly recognize Jesus, the fact that they might even consider inquiring about his identity suggests that it wasn't readily apparent who the fisherman was.

Perhaps we can explain all the incongruities and inconsistencies in this story by remembering that even though Jesus had already appeared to the disciples on two previous occasions, they were having difficulty integrating this remarkable event of the resurrection into their lives. So they did what many of us do when something happens that startles us or shakes us so much that we have trouble comprehending the event: We return to something familiar; we go back to the routine of our lives.

Peter said, "I'm going out to fish" (21: 3). Again, this was not a leisure activity for Peter and the others but what they knew best, what they had done for a living before Jesus came along and called them to follow him. After what they had just gone through — the arrest, crucifixion and death of their leader, the empty tomb and now his appearance to them on a couple of occasions — the disciples wanted to find their bearings again. They wanted to do something that was ordinary since all the events they had just experienced were so extraordinary.

In the practice of premeditated mercy, when the joy of living has been drained out of us because of events that are beyond our control, it is important to go back to what we know best. The disciples who had gathered on the beach that night were caught in a crossfire of crisis. Their leader, mentor, teacher and savior had been crucified. The fire in their bellies that engulfed their lives in the passionate pursuit of Jesus' prophetic message was now consumed. The cross had put out the fire of their fidelity in following Jesus. Though they had escaped into the night when Jesus was arrested, now they were lost in the darkness of suspicion that surrounded them and the deep darkness of shame and guilt within them at having run away.

The life they had anticipated as fearless proclaimers of a new reign of justice and peace seemed over. Their leader had been crucified. But in addition to this crisis of identity in the aftermath of their scattered and shattered dreams, they were also confused by the commotion caused by the empty tomb. What did this mean? Had someone stolen the body? Though two of them had visited the tomb early that morning to confirm what their friend Mary had reported breathlessly about the rabbi's body being missing, they did not yet fully understand. In this state of crisis and confusion, these disciples, who had been fishermen when they were called by Jesus to follow him, return to what they knew best: They went fishing.

After a time of loss or great confusion, we need to be reconciled to our lost dreams. When we are able to return to the routine of our lives — to simple pleasures we find in the sheer experience of daily living and doing what we know how to do best — we might find our joy rekindled in a way that will surprise us. For the disciples it was a surprise as real as a stranger kindling a fire on a beach to cook breakfast.

A second lesson we might draw from this story of Jesus teaching his followers the recipe for reconciliation is the need to keep an open mind. Sometimes a stranger might give us a suggestion that changes our fortunes. The disciples were professional fishermen. Since at first they didn't recognize it was Jesus on the beach, they could have easily closed their minds to this passerby who was pestering them about trying the starboard side. They could have sarcastically said, "Well, why didn't we think of that? How stupid we are! We've only been fishing this lake for years and it would never have occurred to us to try another spot!" A response like this would have stifled the possibility of catching some fish. Or, they could have said, "Look, friend, don't you think we've already tried that? We've been fishing from all sides of the boat all night long. We tried the starboard side, and it didn't work!" Being open to the one who calls us to a new possibility — even if we've already tried it — will keep our practice of premeditated mercy from getting stale. From listening to the advice of a stranger to finding, as Peter did, a strength we didn't even know existed — by keeping an open mind — we will deepen our belief that this great net cast upon the waters of our lives will not break. It will not let some souls slip through, will not leave some behind. Our practice of premeditated mercy with the Risen One will reflect the belief that everyone is caught in the joy of our God.

As to why Peter, who was naked, put on his clothes and jumped in the lake, well, let's just chalk that up to the wondrous reality that seeing the real presence of Jesus can make us do things that on the surface seem rather foolish. But when we plunge beneath the surface, we find the waters of reconciliation just right.

AFTER BREAKFAST: A MEMORY AND A RUMOR

There are two other parts of this story that occur after breakfast and that highlight important ingredients in following this recipe of reconciliation. The first concerns memory and how important it is to confront the sins of our past. The second concerns a rumor that got started that morning on the beach, a rumor that offers hope for us who seek to practice premeditated mercy in all of our relationships.

Remember that the first ingredient in the recipe of reconciliation is memory. In the practice of premeditated mercy, we must confront the sins of our past. The story of Jesus preparing breakfast on the beach for his disciples has its beginning at the Last Supper when Jesus warned Peter and the other disciples that they would desert him. Peter was indignant, saying that even though the others might leave, he would stay with Jesus to the bitter end. But we know what happened. After Jesus was arrested, Peter denied that he even knew Jesus.

Peter's denial of Jesus is an example of a sin of omission: how we can betray another by what we fail to do. Before Jesus could commission Peter to "feed my lambs" and "tend my sheep" (John 21: 15, 16), Peter had to confront this sin of omission. In this story, Peter is the personification of an ancient Persian saying: "There is no saint without a past. There is no sinner without a future." After sharing breakfast on the beach after the resurrection, Jesus engages Peter in an act of premeditated mercy. He invites the saint to face the sin from his past and offers the sinner a future.

The story reflects Peter's rehabilitation and transformation as a compassionate companion of the Risen Christ. It is a story of how confronting the sins of *omission* can lead to *mission*. By coming to terms with what we have failed to do, we are commissioned to be a reconciling presence in the world. In Peter's case, the triple denial he uttered that fateful night, "I do not know the man" (Luke 22: 57), is unraveled by Jesus asking him three times, "Do you love me?" (John 21: 15, 16, 17). Just as he had three times denied knowing Jesus, now Peter asserts his love for him three times. After the third question, Peter simply asks Jesus to read his heart: "Lord, you know everything; you know well that I love you" (John 21: 17).

As he affirms his love for Christ, Peter is sent forth to "feed the flock." In Peter's call and commission, his rehabilitation is complete. Now the risen Jesus invites, inspires and challenges Peter and the other disciples to go forth and create communities of care and compassion, memory and hope.

In this second to last scene on the beach in John's Gospel, Peter's identity as a "late bloomer" is clear. One of the first chosen by Jesus years before, he finally comes to terms with his commission to be a companion of the Risen Christ. Peter's story reminds me of a student I knew in high school. Simon was a year ahead of me. He and I became pretty good friends during my sophomore year. Simon was very bright, although he never applied himself to schoolwork or studies. Instead, he used his creativity and imagination to discover new ways to bend or break the seminary rules. His fiery and free spirit was attractive to me since I was still trying to be the perfect little seminarian, which in those days meant following the rules to the letter of the law. Whereas I saw these rules as hurdles to jump over in order to reach the finish line of graduation, Simon was always looking for ways to sidestep the hurdles and run freely. While I was content to stay on the obstacle course constructed by the priests and brothers at the seminary, Simon's desire was to run cross-country and see if the priests and brothers could catch him.

Well, somewhere along the line, they did. I forget what breach of the rules finally led to Simon's sudden departure in the middle of the night, but most of us could see it coming for some time. In those days, the way the director of seminarians disposed of free spirits like Simon was to wake them up in the middle of the night, tell them to clean out their locker and drive them down to the bus or train station to catch the midnight ride home. That's what happened to Simon. One morning when we awoke, Simon's bed was empty, his locker was cleaned out, and we knew Simon had been told by the powers that be that he did not have a vocation.

I didn't see Simon again until fifteen years later when the seminary closed and the community invited all the students who ever attended the school to return for one final reunion. I was ordained by then, and Simon, who had been told he didn't have a vocation, had found one. He was a surgeon. Simon, who if he had stayed in the seminary would probably have been voted the least likely to succeed by the priests and brothers, had far exceeded most of his classmates. In talking with him, I could still detect his free spirit, but now that spirit had become focused on the art of healing. I also suspect that Simon could still bend or break a few rules if it meant providing for his patients.

When I asked the priest who had been the director of seminarians at the time of Simon's departure if he was surprised by what Simon had become, he replied, "Not really. Simon always had extraordinary talent. He just needed to focus his energies and grow up a little." Then the priest added, "I guess you could say Simon was a late bloomer."

Peter also needed to focus his energies. But instead of growing up, Peter had to learn to grow *down* a little. Peter is often seen in the Gospels as a kind of free spirit who speaks before thinking. Jesus must have noticed this spirit at work in Peter the first day he saw him on the beach and called Peter and his brother Andrew to follow him. Yes, we know what happened to Peter's free spirit: When Jesus was arrested, the other disciples fled. But Peter — perhaps because his bold statement about never abandoning Jesus was lingering in his mind — followed at a distance. When questioned about his allegiance to Jesus, Peter's free spirit was frozen by fear. Impetuous Peter denied he had been with Jesus, denied he was one of the disciples, denied even knowing Jesus. In his threefold denial his growing down had begun.

When Jesus later invited Peter to confront the sins of his past, we see how much Peter has grown down. Unlike earlier in the Gospel, he didn't boast that he loves Jesus more than the others; he simply asked Jesus to read his heart: "Lord, you know everything, you know well that I love you" (John 21: 17).

In asking Peter three times if he loved him, Jesus isn't rubbing salt in Peter's wound of denial or making him stretch for forgiveness. Rather, by unraveling the mistakes of the past, Jesus is calling Peter to move beyond the past, to focus his energies and take on the challenges of a new way of life. It's a life that includes feeding and tending the flock. It's a life that includes enormous risks, as Jesus tells Peter: "When you were young, you fastened your belt and set off wherever you wished. But when you grow old, you will stretch out your hands and another will fasten a belt around you and take you where you do not wish to go" (John 21: 18). In commissioning Peter and the other disciples, Jesus warns them that following this recipe of reconciliation will not be easy. The practice of premeditated mercy is difficult and dangerous. In reminding Peter of the ultimate risks of the love he proclaims, Jesus tells Peter that he will, like the Lord he loves, stretch out his hands on the cross and die a martyr's death.

Premeditated mercy challenges us to focus our energies of love. When we focus on the love that burns within our hearts, we will find, as Peter did and as Simon did, our hands stretching out to offer hope and healing to others. Whether we are late bloomers, like Peter and Simon, or early risers, the Spirit of God invites us into the realm of premeditated mercy by confronting not only the things we have done in the past, but also those things we have failed to do when another was in need. As we navigate this way of love, we need to remember the old saying: "There is no saint without a past. There is no sinner without a future."

THE RUMOR OF RECONCILIATION: HOPE IN THE FUTURE

Not all of those who gathered on the beach that morning were to die a martyr's death. At the conclusion of John's Gospel, Peter and Jesus are walking along the beach when Peter points to John and asks Jesus, "Lord, what about him?" (John 21: 21). In Jesus' answer to Peter are sown the seeds of how rumors get started. "If it is my will that he remains until I come, what is that to you? Your bisiness is to follow me!" (21: 22). The rumor that circulated after Jesus' Ascension intimating that John wouldn't die was not a rumor bent on damaging or destroying another's reputation. Rather, it is an example of "holy hearsay" or "godly gossip" that suggests how the practice of premeditated mercy, as risky as it is, does not always lead to martyrdom. Yet it does always lead to a deepening and widening of relationship.

The story goes that when John was an old man he gathered his friends around him shortly before he died. He told them that he would die a most unnatural death. "You see," he said, "my friends Peter and the others who followed the Master are the ones who died truly natural deaths since martyrdom, as the Master taught, is the natural consequence of following him. Because the cross is the normal consequence of discipleship, I am dying a most unnatural death.

"But before I go," old John continued, "I want to put to rest certain rumors about my death which have been greatly exaggerated."

So this beloved friend, the silent witness who leaned against Jesus, resting his head on the teacher's chest, who held the teacher's mother at the moment of Jesus' death, who raced to the tomb on that first day of the week to find it empty and was later to tell the Gospel story of this resurrection rumor, now told his own disciples how the rumor about him got started.

Indeed, Jesus' simple statement in response to Peter's pondering: "Lord, what about him?" sparked the rumor that John would not experience death. Rumors like this spread like wildfire. But as the Scripture points out, this is not exactly what Jesus said. As a matter of fact, Jesus never told Peter that John was not going to die. All he said was, "Suppose I want him to stay until I come?"

Rumors. Whispers in the shadows that are carried on the wind. These soft-spoken words, whether true or not, are passed from person to person, house to house, until the original remark and the current rumor bear no resemblance. There can be some truth in rumors. Don't we sometimes ask, "Is there any truth to the rumor...?" But more often than not rumors are taken out of context, born out of wisdom's wedlock with truth and given a life of their own.

Rumors are contagious. They are like a virus that begins with the moment of infection: "Did you hear about so and so?" We lean closer to catch the virus. Like a cold, it only gets worse. And like the common cold, there is no cure for rumors. We can control the rumor's symptoms — not with medication but with meditation. Silent prayer. By holding in our prayer both the one affected by the rumor and the one infected with the rumor virus, the hearsay is silenced. The rumor stops here.

What makes a rumor destructive is the lack of a reliable source. Rumors spread because they feed on the insatiable appetite called curiosity. Rumors are rarely given voice in public settings but are reserved for private places. "Don't tell anyone," the contagion begins, "but I heard that Jesus told Peter that this disciple would not die until Jesus comes again." The murmurs begin. "How can this be?" Curiosity satisfied, the one infected with this virus promises not to be a carrier: "You have my word, I won't tell anyone."

But the promise is broken because the rumor is so delicious and our appetite so large that we can't keep it to ourselves. "Did you hear about John — you know the one who spent the Last Supper leaning against Jesus' chest — well, I heard he is going to live forever."

If we believe that by definition rumors can never be true, that they only carry a piece of the truth spoken out of context, then it might be a stretch to consider rumors ever being holy. But if we believe that rumors can be tracked down to determine whether they are true or not, and if we find evidence, circumstantial or otherwise, from the source that there is truth in a holy rumor, then it seems we are obliged to pass it on.

By following the recipe for reconciliation, by following the Risen One who cooked breakfast and cooked up a compassionate presence in the world, we spread this holy hearsay, this godly gossip, this rumor of reconciliation. Remember, the resurrection of Jesus started as a rumor. There was only circumstantial evidence: an empty tomb, a linen cloth, a stone that had been rolled away. Mary and the other women ran back to the others and reported that the tomb was empty. John and Peter ran to the tomb. They saw and they believed. But they kept it a secret until the source of this resurrection rumor, the Truth, wounded and scarred but very real, appeared in their midst to dispel any false rumors about whether he was dead or alive.

Mary Magdalene, whose presence at the breakfast on the beach — or at the last supper for that matter — is not verifiable (but for the sake of godly gossip let's start a rumor that she was present at both events!), offers another example of holy rumor mongering. Recall that Mary is weeping in the garden after discovering the empty tomb when the Truth appears in the clothes of a gardener and calls her by name. Hearing the Truth say her name confirmed her faith: The rumor is true. And the Truth tells her: "Go and tell the others" (See John 20: 17). And so, Mary becomes the patron saint of resurrection rumor mongering, managing the truth of her experience with uncontrollable excitement: "I have seen the Lord" (John 20: 18).

When we practice premeditated mercy, we spread the rumor that the resurrection is real and so reconciliation is possible. We see that this rumor of life is true every spring when Mother Nature believes the rumor of resurrection and becomes green, not with envy but with hope. So we can look outside at spring's new birth and see the truth of the resurrection rumor. But the question becomes: Can we also look inside and see the truth of the resurrection? When we practice the premeditation exercises of prayer — of holding those who hold opposite views, those who seek to harm us or who have hurt us — in the silence of our hearts, new life begins to emerge. When we show mercy to those who have harmed us, we prove that the rumor of resurrection is true in our real, reconciling presence.

This is how we discern the difference between false rumors and rumors of faith — of truth. When Peter asks the question, "What about him?" Jesus replies, "How does that concern you? Your business is to follow me." When we make it our business to follow Jesus, then the false rumors will take care of themselves. They will lose their energy, run their course, and then be left for dead by the side of the road. Rumor roadkill. When we make it our business to follow Jesus, our focus will be on spreading the truth that will set the world free — free from falsehood, free from hatred, free from envy, free from death.

BEARING SALTY WITNESS TO THE RUMOR

After their encounter with Jesus on the beach that morning, Peter, John, Mary Magdalene and the other disciples went about bearing witness to this rumor of resurrection that leads to reconciliation. They were changed by their encounter with the risen, reconciling presence of Jesus. The truth of this rumor was confirmed not in private whispers but in public proclamation. The truth of the rumor was written on their faces: They could not live a lie. The truth of this rumor rumbled in their hearts and was released by their hands as they reached out to others in joyful service.

Bearing witness to this rumor is where the salt we talked about in the recipe for reconciliation is revealed. To taste this salty witness of the first disciples of the Risen One, consider the story of the child who was made entirely of salt.

The salt child very much wanted to know where he had come from. So he set out on a long journey and traveled to many lands in pursuit of this understanding. Finally he came to the shore of the great ocean. "How marvelous," he cried, and stuck one foot in the water. The ocean beckoned him in further, saying, "If you wish to know who you are, do not be afraid." The salt child walked further and further into the water, dissolving with each step, and at the end exclaimed, "Ah, now I know who I am."

Like the child made of salt, with every step the disciples took in the direction of the resurrected Jesus, a bit of their identity dissolved and they began to take on a new identity. They began to understand who they were as rumormongers of reconciliation. In the story of their breakfast on the beach with Jesus, we have already traced certain steps the disciples took in this process of disintegration that leads to a new integration. When Jesus first appeared to them on the beach, the Gospel says, "none of the disciples knew it was Jesus" (John 21: 4). Only after Jesus suggested they try another spot and they caught so many fish that their nets were at a breaking point did they recognize the identity of this one combing the beach. "It is the Lord!" (21: 7). And when they sat down for breakfast, "not one of the disciples presumed to inquire, 'Who are you?' for they knew it was the Lord" (21: 12).

Like the salt child, the disciples came to the shore and slowly dissolved into a new identity that involved being part of a larger reality. They were no longer what previously identified them — fearful, skeptical, doubtful and confused — but took on a new identity as members of the resurrected body of Christ. Fear of death dissolved as they ate a meal on a beach prepared by the one who was dead but is now alive. Regrets over running away when he was arrested and denying they even knew him disappeared as Jesus appeared to them and served them bread and fish.

As their own personal ambitions and inhibitions evaporated, the disciples took on the identity of the Risen One. Now they no longer would return to the routine of their former way of life; now the resurrection would become their routine. They would spend the rest of their lives giving to others what they had received: belief in the power of life over death.

As we mentioned in the first chapter, the goal of premeditated mercy is to become a new creation, to take on a new identity as a reconciling people of life. Like the disciples after the resurrection of Jesus, we are reminded again that this new identity takes time to take shape. The disciples didn't recognize the presence of the Risen One right away. Yet the longer they spent in his company after his resurrection, the more they dissolved and dared to take on their new identity.

In our premeditation exercises, then, we might consider what needs to dissolve within us so that a new identity, a new understanding, a new hope might evolve. What do we need to let go of in order to embrace fully the resurrection of Jesus and the reconciliation it reveals? What fears need to evaporate, what regrets need to dissipate, what self-centered attitudes need to disintegrate so that the fullness of the new life we are offered might absorb us?

As people whom the Risen One once called "salt of the earth," it is precisely in the practice of premeditated mercy that we come to know who we are, our true identity as people of reconciliation. In the silence of our prayer before bringing our gifts to the altar, the grace of God will dissolve whatever it is that is keeping us from becoming who we truly are. As our worries and fears dissolve in the silence of our prayer and the expression of our compassion, the voice of the Risen One says, "Do not be afraid to become who you are."

LISTENING TO ONE'S CRY

Premeditated mercy engages us in this process of becoming who we are by naming our own truth. We do this by coming into touch with our passion. How do we find our passion in life? As a way of answering that question, consider another episode from the television series that ignited a firestorm of controversy in some religious circles when it went on the air a few years ago, *Nothing Sacred*.

The pastor of the parish, a young priest named Father Ray, encounters a young man speaking in tongues and seeing visions of the Blessed Mother. Father Ray is skeptical of this young man's close encounters of the divine kind and works with an even more skeptical doctor to try to snap the young man out of his delusions. At one point in the show, Father Ray is sitting in church trying to pray and trying to figure out how to reach this young man. He looks at the statues of saints that crowd the church and concludes that most of them, if they were alive today, would probably be diagnosed as schizophrenics because of their bizarre behavior.

As Ray sits in church and tries to figure out whether the young man's visions are a figment of his imagination that reflect his insanity or signs of the infrastructure of his sanctity, the business manager of the parish, the resident atheist on staff, comes in and sits behind Father Ray. The priest reflects with him on the sanity-challenged status of so many saints. He tells him the story of the famous pole-sitting saint, Simon Stylistes, who built a tower in the center of his city, climbed the tower and spent his life sitting there because he wanted to be closer to God. Ray jokingly tells the business manager that he could never follow Simon's example because of his fear of heights.

The business manager says, "I've never had a problem with people speaking in tongues because everyone has a cry buried deep inside." Ray asks him what he means. So the business manager proceeds to tell him about his grandfather, for whom, underneath everything he said, "there was a cry for justice." He tells Ray about his parents, whose motivation in life was a "cry for comfort." Ray asks him what his cry is. The business manager pauses and says, "It's a cry for reconciliation" with his wife from whom he's separated.

Then the business manager leans over the pew and whispers to the priest, "Ray, what's your cry?" His meaning is clear. Ray can only help the young man when he allows his cry from deep within to find its voice.

When we find our cry, we find our passion. What is the cry that shapes your life, that underscores your every word, your ever deed? Is it a cry for justice, for peace, for prayer, for reconciliation, for inclusivity, for hospitality, for hope, for joy? One way to identify your cry is to reflect on what others will say about you when you die. The cry that shapes and sustains our life is what others see in us and will remember about us when we are no longer physically present to them. When I taught a course on "Death and Dying" to high school seniors, one of the assignments was to write your own obituary. It was an exercise to touch one's passion by listening to one's cry.

Near the end of the episode from *Nothing Sacred*, the young man who has been hearing voices and seeing visions goes to the roof of the hospital and sits on the edge, several stories above the street. Father Ray, though afraid of heights, goes to the young man and sits on the edge with him. His cry to embody compassion has found its voice.

When we gather at the table of Eucharist — in the midst of the real presence of Christ on the table and the real presence of Christ reflected in the people sitting in the pews — we sit on the edge of several stories that reflect the fundamental truth, the primary cry, of our lives. We hear it proclaimed in Scripture; we see it as we sit in silence before the presence of Christ embodied in bread, in wine and in each person gathered at the table. Each Eucharist offers us the opportunity to listen to that cry buried deep within our soul. When we hear that cry and allow it to find its voice in our lives, our truest passion begins to emerge and take shape.

When we come to the table of Eucharist in the company of our friends, we realize that the table of Word and Sacrament cannot be separate or distinct from all the other tables around which we gather in the course of our day to tell stories, break bread and share the cup of kindness and care.

As we gather around the table, we notice just the hint of a scent of fresh-baked bread. It's the bread of life that nourishes this body we call the church. As we gather around the table, we take the cup of blessing and taste the vintage wine, the blood of Christ, which will pulse through this body and bring us all life. We allow that sweet wine to linger upon our lips, if only for a moment. And when we drink it, we swallow the hope that will give us courage to go forth from the table to meet others in their need, be it a need for food or friendship. It is at this table that we find all the ingredients that make for a meal of mercy, the meal that nourishes us to become ministers of reconciliation and premeditated mercy.

FINDING OUR VOICE

The experiences of the first disciples of Jesus recorded in the Acts of the Apostles reflect this challenge of finding our voice. After their encounters with the Risen One in the upper room, on the road to Emmaus and on the beach, the stone rolls away from the tomb of their hearts where their cry has been buried. Peter, John and the others begin to bear witness to the reconciliation won through the blood of the cross and the resurrection of Jesus. This is the effect their encounter with the Risen One has on these first disciples: The cry of life, of resurrection, of hope buried deep within them finds its voice.

We hear this cry finding its voice when Peter and John, imprisoned for healing a beggar at the Beautiful Gate and proclaiming the resurrection of Jesus, stand before the religious authorities. "Filled with the Holy Spirit," Peter finds his voice. "Leaders of the people! Elders! If we must answer today for a good deed done to a cripple and explain how he was restored to health, then you must realize that it was done in the name of Jesus Christ the Nazorean who was crucified and whom God raised from the dead" (Acts 4: 8-10). The resurrection has removed the stone from Peter's heart that was covering the cry buried deep inside. Now, all his words, all his actions, will reflect this cry, this belief in Jesus' resurrection. "This Jesus, 'the stone rejected by the builders has become the cornerstone'" (4: 11). This is the cry that will shape the rest of Peter's life and will lead him to accept even death, death on a cross, because of his belief in the death and resurrection of Jesus.

As we practice the spiritual discipline of premeditated mercy, after we ask ourselves: What is my cry? We need to ask: How do I give it voice? How do I allow this cry that underscores my every word, my every deed, to shape my life? In the practice of premeditated mercy, all our cries find their voice as we stand before the world and shout with our lives that Jesus, who suffered, died and was buried, is now alive in the action of our becoming a new creation, a minister of reconciliation.

But becoming a new creation does not come without cost. Again, we turn to the first disciples of Jesus, who came together as a reconciling community. Remember that one of the ingredients in this mix of mercy is compassion — and that we find compassion by going through the wounds on the scarred but resurrected body of Christ. Those who were the first to profess their belief in the Risen One found a community that nurtured their faith. It was a community that "shared all things in common" (Acts 2: 44). When I hear about the generous nature of this early Christian community, it seems almost idyllic: selling their property and their goods so that no one among them would be needy, going to the temple each day to pray, eating their meals in common, breaking the bread in their homes, praising God all day long and "winning the approval of all people" (2: 47). And I wonder: Where are the wounds? It's such an ideal community that it seems to mock the appearance of Jesus to the disciples in the upper room when he showed them his wounds. Where are the scars on the early church, the body of Christ?

They do, of course, show up later in the Acts of the Apostles. But if we base our understanding of what it means to be a new creation community on the experiences of the disciples in the early chapters of

Acts and then look at the wounds on the body of Christ that is the church at the turn of a new millennium, we might be tempted to throw up our hands in hopelessness. But the key phrase here is: "Those who believed shared all things in common."

All things. Not just material possessions and goods, but all things: hopes, dreams, forgiveness, faith, doubt, fear, scars and even sin. The goal of a community of faith formed and fashioned by God's great mercy, shown to us through the death and resurrection of Jesus, is not to create communes of idyllic anticipation of the Second Coming. We've had numerous examples of fundamentalist interpretations of Biblical passages — especially in the approach and early aftermath of the new millennium — and we give them a name: cults.

No, the goal of a faith community fashioned by forgiveness, formed by God's premeditated mercy — which implies, of course, God meditated on this plan long before the world began — is to be a community of believers who "share all things in common." Such a community bears the scars of crucifixion. Members of this community touch these wounds each day. We touch these communal wounds as we see the flaws in our own bodies and souls, as we see the holes in our own commitment of faith. And, again, rather than believing in spite of these wounds, these holes, we believe because we have met the Risen Christ in them.

In this experience of reconciliation we are able to share all things in common — not only our wounds but also our faith in the resurrection — and thus find our voice.

Following this recipe and becoming a reconciler, a practitioner of premeditated mercy, means following the footprints left on the beach by the one we know as Jesus. This is how we will find our voice. When we do, we discover that our pace quickens and our feet race to that place of reconciliation. Once we are there, we smell the aroma of fresh-baked bread and see the fish frying over a charcoal fire. We hear Jesus say, "Come and eat your meal."

And like the disciples, we will not presume to inquire, "Who are you?" for we will know it is the Risen Lord.

Setting the Table:
Spiritual Exercises Before Bringing Our Gifts to the Altar

The practice of Eucharist is a practice of awareness. When Jesus broke the bread and shared it with his disciples, he said, "Eat this. This is my body." He knew that if his disciples would eat one piece of bread in mindfulness, they would have real life. In their daily lives, they may have eaten their bread in forgetfulness, so the bread was not bread at all; it was a ghost. In our daily lives, we may see the people around us, but if we lack mindfulness, they are just phantoms, not real people, and we ourselves are also ghosts. Practicing mindfulness enables us to become a real person. When we are a real person, we see real people around us, and life is present in all its richness....To me, the rite of Eucharist is a wonderful practice of mindfulness. In a drastic way, Jesus tried to wake up his disciples.

— Thich Nhat Hanh

Premeditated mercy embraces Jesus' teaching about what we are to do before coming to the altar to celebrate the extravagant forgiveness of God. If we are having a disagreement with someone, are holding a grudge, are harboring resentment or know someone who is angry with us for something we've done or failed to do, we are to go to that person and work it out, talk about it, discuss and dialogue about it. When we do, we begin to set the table where all might find a place. It is the grace of God that begins to move us to this place of premeditated mercy that will lead us to reconciliation.

Jesus advises his disciples to be reconciled before bringing their gifts to the altar. By following the recipe for reconciliation, we set the table for the feast of forgiveness. Forgiveness is the last step in the process of premeditated mercy. Reconciliation is the result of this forgiveness. But before true reconciliation can occur, the individual who has been hurt or betrayed must engage in a lengthy process of premeditated mercy.

That is what Jesus proposes when he says he has "come not to abolish the law and the prophets but to fulfill them" (Matthew 5: 17). Matthew records this verse in the Sermon on the Mount. It occurs immediately following Jesus identifying his followers as being "salt of the earth" and "light for the world" and just before his teaching about premeditated mercy: "first be reconciled to your brother or sister, and then come and offer your gift." In this passage (5: 17-26), Jesus offers himself as the fulfillment of the law of love. He advances a radical way of living out relationships. Jesus offers a way of holiness that "surpasses that of the scribes and Pharisees" (5: 20) and sets us upon a road that leads to the new creation, the reign of God.

It is important to remember that these words of Jesus in Matthew's Gospel were first addressed to Jewish converts to Christianity — converts who were especially concerned with how the teaching of Jesus reflected Moses' teaching and that of the prophets. While Moses taught that it was wrong to commit murder, Jesus goes even deeper by saying it's wrong to even entertain angry thoughts. Jesus dares to go beneath the surface, beyond the consequences of our actions, to the angry thoughts that are the seeds of sin, that bubble inside of us until they spill over into acts of violence. These thoughts, Jesus says, make us liable.

Premeditated mercy implies that we confront these thoughts before they boil over into words that harm another's reputation or into actions that do violence. When we premeditate mercy, we carefully, thoughtfully, prayerfully calculate a response of reconciliation rather than revenge. Just as we might otherwise premeditate how to get even, now we plot and plan how to forgive someone who has hurt us, or how we will seek forgiveness from someone we have hurt with our words or our deeds or our apathy.

Yes, we do this meditation on mercy before we come to the table. That is why we call it premeditated mercy. Moreover, the Eucharist is the supreme symbol of God's mercy, of God's forgiveness, of God's desire that human beings be reconciled with the Divine Being. The

Eucharist is the ritual action of reconciliation, during which we remember what Jesus did on the night he was betrayed. We celebrate the forgiveness of that betrayal, of the betrayal of all our sins, believing that the debt of our sinfulness is paid in full at the enormous price of Christ's blood. It is because of this great sacrifice of Jesus on the altar of the world that we are to make sure we are reconciled with one another before we come to the altar in our places of worship.

ANGER: ON THE BACK BURNER

As we consider how premeditated mercy surpasses the prescribed practices of religious rules and regulations, we see that Jesus uses specific examples from the Mosaic law to carve out a teaching that goes much deeper than words etched on stone. Now they become engraved upon the heart. Jesus declares that acts of premeditated murder begin to take shape when anger begins to boil on the back burner of one's heart.

Anger is an emotion that is often associated with heat. Tempers flare. Blood boils. Temperature rises. When experiencing anger, the advice often is, "Cool off" or "Calm down." Notice the direction of calmness: down. When anger boils, we are advised to turn down the heat. To "simmer down."

In times of anger, Jesus' advice also implies turning: Turn away from the altar and be reconciled with the one who turned up the heat; turn to that one before offering your gifts in worship. We are to step back from the altar and go to the one who caused our heart to burn and our stomach to turn. Calm down. Turn down the heat.

The connection between offering our gifts at the altar and offering our heart in reconciliation is so close that we cannot separate the two. "Lose no time" (Matthew 5: 25), Jesus says. I wonder why Jesus is so insistent about making reconciliation quickly such a priority? Why is making peace with the one who has made us angry so necessary *before* coming to the table? After all, the advice to "Calm down" implies letting our temper simmer for awhile before we approach the one who has hurt us.

Perhaps it's because of what happens to anger that has been boiling on the hot plate of our heart after it simmers and cools down. It becomes solidified, causing the heart to harden toward the one who has hurt us, the one who made us mad, the who has cooked up our anger in the first place. Arteries harden, stopping the flow of blood from the place where love originates, the heart. "Lose no time," Jesus admonishes or else you may lose a relationship forever.

In the silence of our premeditation exercise, before we offer our gifts, we check the person we are holding hostage outside of our heart because of the hurt inflicted or the anger kindled. We need to be honest about our feelings toward the person who caused our heart to burn. Then we take Jesus' advice to calm down, to cool down, but we can't let this cooling process go on until our heart becomes cold and hard toward the other.

The work of premeditation is to visualize this one who has harmed us or the person in our life we find so difficult to love or forgive. We don't just see that person in our mind's eye and calm down; we hold that person in our heart. The challenge is to pray for that person and ask God's blessing to be with that person this day. Yes, that person may have made us angry, but by following Jesus' recipe for reconciliation, we seek to make peace rather than anger. Following this recipe will make the meal of mercy and memory easier to digest.

BEING AWARE

In formulating this recipe, note that Jesus refers specifically to those who are holding a grudge or a grievance against us. This calls for a wide awareness on our part. A woman once asked me after hearing this admonition, "How do I know if another is holding something against me?" The answer is found in the kind of awareness that is deepened and widened through silent prayer. Sometimes, of course, we can tell others are holding something against us by their body language. We can tell by their distance or their silence when we greet them. Faces can be canvasses where the pain we caused is painted in shades of red. The daily practice of premeditated mercy encourages an increasing awareness and sensitivity toward those around us with whom reconciliation is needed.

Awareness is a key spiritual exercise in making the connection between our private lives and our public worship, between reconciliation and real presence. There is an Anthony deMello parable about a priest who was ecstatic because the most famous preacher in all the land was scheduled to come to the parish for a revival. Because this guest's preaching was so passionate and his reputation so remarkable, they had to book him five years in advance. The next Sunday this legendary evangelist and missionary was to arrive at their church and preach at all the Masses. "Yes," the pastor said, "Next Sunday, Jesus will be here to conduct our parish revival. Let us be prepared to have our lives changed forever."

The people too were excited, and when Sunday arrived all the Masses were packed. Even the 7:00 A.M. Mass, which normally had only a few early risers, was standing room only. The people waited anxiously through the Scripture readings. Then the pastor introduced the missionary who would preach their parish revival. "My dear friends," the pastor said, "I give you Jesus."

Jesus stood up and walked to the pulpit amid thundering applause. When the cheering subsided, Jesus smiled and said, "Did you hear the one about the agnostic fleas? They're standing in a forest of fur and one says, 'Sometimes I wonder if there really *is* a dog!'"

When the laughter subsided, Jesus left the pulpit and returned to his seat in the first pew. After a long period of silence, it became evident that Jesus had finished his sermon. So the pastor turned on his wireless mike, coughed and said, "Well, uh, thank you, Jesus. Uh, now, the revival begins tomorrow night. So please come to hear even more profound truths hidden in simple but inspiring stories. Please stand to profess our faith."

After the Masses, many people came to Jesus to meet him and invite him to their homes for dinner. But Jesus graciously refused their invitations. Of course, the people thought, he wants to fast and pray before the first night of the revival. The pastor offered him a room at the rectory, but Jesus said he preferred to sleep in church. What a holy man, the pastor thought to himself.

The next morning, before the pastor arrived to unlock the church for the 6:30 Mass, Jesus slipped away. While the pastor was still in the rectory, one of the faithful daily Mass-goers banged on the door. Breathless, she said, "Father, come quickly, the church has been vandalized!" The priest ran over to church where a few other people had gathered at the door. There, written with spray paint on the front door of the church was the word *BEWARE*. When they went inside, they couldn't believe their eyes. Written on all the walls, all the pews, the pulpit and the altar, the baptismal font and even the cross, was the same word, *BEWARE*. It was written in various colors of spray paint. Wherever they looked, in every nook and cranny of the church, *BEWARE* was looking back at them.

Their shock soon gave way to anger and confusion, fascination and even terror. Their first impulse was to call the police. The pastor said he would call the bishop to report the desecration. "Who could do such a thing?" they wondered both inwardly and aloud. "And where is Jesus?" they asked. He slept in church all night, but he was nowhere to be found.

Then a woman named Clare, who had attended daily Mass since she was a little girl, said, "What if Jesus did this?" The others looked at her with skepticism and shock at such an outrageous idea. But Clare continued, "What if Jesus spray-painted the church with this word *BEWARE*? Even though we don't know for sure and we certainly don't know what it means, perhaps this is part of the revival."

After much discussion and an emergency meeting of the parish council, it was decided that they would leave the church, stained and scarred with the word *BEWARE*, as it was for the duration of the revival.

That evening as people arrived for the revival, they were shocked and scandalized by what they saw. The word *BEWARE* was everywhere. However, the ushers calmed them down and said that Jesus would explain everything when the sermon started. Meanwhile, the pastor paced nervously in the vestibule. Jesus had not been seen all day. He expected that Jesus rose early and went by himself to an out-of-the-way place to pray. But now it was almost 7:00 and the revival was scheduled to begin.

Jesus never arrived. The people sat shoulder-to-shoulder in the pews, standing in the aisles, waiting to hear Jesus. But Jesus was a no-show.

For an hour, the pastor and the people sat in silence staring at the word *BEWARE*. That night, and each night of the revival, the people gathered and just stared. Slowly they let that mysterious word sink into their minds, their hearts, their souls.

The saw the word *BEWARE* on the pulpit and began to realize how they sometimes listened to the Word of God, but instead of being changed by the Scriptures they used God's Word to prove a point or win an argument. In their silence, they heard: "*BEWARE* of using my Word for false ends instead of as a means to the truth."

They saw the word *BEWARE* on the altar and began to see how the Eucharist was meant to sustain and sanctify them, nourish and change them, and how they sometimes fell into superstition and even scrupulosity about the sacraments. In their silence, they heard: "*BEWARE* of misusing the sacraments."

They saw the word *BEWARE* on the baptismal font and began to realize how their religious belief sometimes made them self-righteous and exclusive. In their silence, they heard: "*BEWARE* of seeing yourselves as the only ones who will be saved."

They saw the word *BEWARE* on the crucifix and began to sense how they sometimes used power and control in putting others in their place, how they failed to reverence the wounds of others, how they practiced competition instead of compassion. In their silence, they heard: "*BEWARE* of power that destroys rather than builds community."

Each night as they gathered for the revival, Jesus was a no-show, but the people saw that word *BEWARE*, and in their silence they became aware of how their prayer was often filled with too many words and not enough witness. They became aware of how their faith was lived routinely rather than passionately. They became aware of how narrow religious rules blinded them to the larger purpose of the law of love.

Because that word *BEWARE* was burned on their souls, at the end of the last night of the revival the parish council met with the pastor and decided that they would inscribe the word *BEWARE* over the entrance of their church so that all who walked or drove by at night would see it blazing above the door in multicolored neon lights: *BEWARE*.

On the Sunday following the revival, as the pastor stood at the pulpit still etched with the word *BEWARE*, he said, "I told you this mission would change our lives forever."

The practice of premeditated mercy suggests that the word *BEWARE* be emblazoned upon our hearts and minds and souls. It's not an easy word to hear, but if we make a space and add an "a," the word *BEWARE* becomes: *BE AWARE*. This is mercy's challenge: to be aware of any attitudes or actions, thoughts or ideas that crowd the temple of our heart and keep us from focusing all our attention, all our energy, on the Divine Presence in our midst. We are especially to be aware of the presence of God in the one who may be holding something against us.

The challenge is to be aware of any fear or fault lines, any self-centeredness or self-righteousness, any pride or prejudice, any shame or guilt that may shrink our spirit and clutter the temple of our heart so that we cannot move, or breathe or have our being.

TITANIC SYNDROME:
CLEANSING THE TEMPLE OF OUR HEART

This story of *BEWARE* suggests what Jesus did that day he went to the temple to pray and found the moneychangers and traders buying and selling in the house of prayer (John 2: 13-22). We see a side of Jesus we don't like to look at: He became angry. His anger was on the front burner but it was fueled by a passion, a zeal for God's house that consumed him. It is interesting to note that in John's Gospel Jesus' cleansing of the temple occurs early on — just after the wedding feast at Cana. In the Synoptics, this incident occurs late in Jesus' ministry, and some scholars point to it as a decisive moment leading to Jesus' arrest and crucifixion. But regardless of where it is placed in the life of Jesus, this much is clear: It is a prophetic action that brought to peoples' minds the fire and fury of the Old Testament prophets who called the people to reform and renewal.

In this prophetic moment, Jesus' challenge of premeditated mercy is meant to drive out from the temple of our heart those things that distract us from what is truly important in life. Those things that keep us from being what God calls us to be. Those things that distort or devalue our relationship with God or with one another.

A spring, or even seasonal, cleaning of the temple of our heart is not sufficient. The practice of premeditated mercy suggests that whenever we dare approach the altar to offer our gifts in worship, a ritual of cleansing the temple is necessary. It is like the story of Mark, a young man who lived alone in a small but tidy apartment. Since he learned early in life the prescription for holiness — "Cleanliness is next to Godliness" — Mark kept his living space spotless. He did this not because he was afraid someone might drop by unexpectedly and notice dust on the end table or dishes in the sink, but because Mark was by nature a perfectionist. Everything he did had to be perfect, and so his apartment simply reflected this attitude about himself.

A quick tour of Mark's apartment would render this view: Everything had its place and there was a place for everything. Even his closets were well organized — none of this "out of sight, out of mind" sleight of hand to give the appearance the apartment was clean. Go ahead, check the closets — Mark had nothing to hide.

There was no unsightly wax buildup on the kitchen floor. The counters sparkled like a Mr. Clean commercial. Dust was a demon to be exorcised early and often. Cobwebs never had a chance to gather in the corners. His apartment was so clean that he wouldn't mind if you performed the dreaded white-glove test on the tops of his windowsills. Be assured there was no sin lingering in those hard-to-reach and neglected spaces of his living space.

But Mark did suffer from what might be called the "Titanic Syndrome." For example, when he heard laughter coming from the apartment next door, he would vacuum the carpets to drown out the sound of joy. Or when he learned that a friend from college had received a promotion, Mark would move his desk and a couple of bookcases to give the room a new look. When he found out his former girlfriend was getting married, he cleaned his bedroom with a vengeance and moved around the furniture.

Mark rearranged the furniture in his outer space so that he would not have to enter his inner space. That's why it's called the Titanic Syndrome: It's like rearranging the deck chairs on a sinking ship. You know the ship is going down, but don't you think the sofa would look better against that wall?

Mark spent all his energy trying to be so perfect in his outer life that he never noticed the wax of envy building up on the floor of his heart. He didn't see the dust of resentment covering the mantel of his mind. He didn't bother the cobwebs of callousness clinging to the corners of his soul. Where he might welcome the white-glove test on the outside, he resisted such a dangerous enterprise on his inner space.

Jesus knew how much safer it is to stay on the surface, dealing with outer realities rather than inner attitudes. That's why he invited his followers to go deeper, beneath the surface of our actions to the attitudes that cause us to "act out" in the first place. The task of getting our inner house in order is difficult, maybe even dangerous, because, like Mark, most of us are much more comfortable rearranging the furniture than changing our heart. But if the old maxim "Cleanliness is next to Godliness" is true, then the practice of premeditated mercy is concerned with our inner space and not our outer space. When we daily cleanse the temple of our heart, we leave the mops and brushes and dust cloths behind. We focus our attention instead on that sacred space of our heart and mind and soul, where no cleaning tools are helpful.

When we approach this inner space, we don't need elbow grease but only some silence. As Jesus reminds us in his Sermon on the Mount, "When you pray, go to your room, close your door and pray to your God in secret" (Matthew 6: 6). In this sacred silence, we find no high-powered bleach to aid our efforts. The only *Pledge* we need is the lemon-fresh scent of the Spirit-Wind stirring in our souls. By spending even a few minutes each day in silence and prayer, we will begin to sense the movement of God's grace that takes us to a new place, a place of awareness. Then we trace the Spirit's movement within us to gather the courage to go to that person who is holding something against us and seek to be reconciled.

The more we explore this inner house of prayer, this temple of our heart, we tackle perhaps the greatest challenge of all: to empty the closets stuffed with resentment and anger and bitterness. To symbolize our desire to clean out the closets, we might place a garbage bag near our prayer place. The bags come in various sizes — from the small size that lines the trash container in the bathroom to the lawn and garden variety. The size we choose all depends on how much "stuff" is crammed into our closet. Each day we can symbolically place in the bag a piece of resentment we have stored for safekeeping because we thought it would protect us from ever being hurt in the same way again. Then, at least once a week, we can ritually take the trash to the curb.

CREATING SPACE FOR ATONEMENT

After taking out the trash, we return to the house of our heart and set the table. It's wise to leave an empty place or two around the altar in our heart. Our desire to set an extra place begins to heal the wounds caused by our indifference. Around the table of our common need, God offers us a second helping, a helping that will enable us to see and recognize the presence of God in those we welcome to our table.

Premeditated mercy demands creative space from us. How do we create a space where remembrance and reconciliation can be practiced? We find a clue in an ancient word *atonement*, which some have dissected into three words, at – one – ment. This word recognizes that all our relationships are grounded in the truth that God is holy. But the holiness of God, the wholeness and oneness to which we are called, is not some distant dream to be realized only when the reign of God comes upon us sometime in the future. The holiness of God is etched upon our souls because we are made in God's image and likeness. We create space for mercy by realizing that God's Spirit already dwells within us. In the temple of our heart, we make space for God's holiness to be active by practicing certain spiritual exercises that strengthen our resistance to evil, our resolve to forgive and our ability to make peace.

We create space for mercy when we hold within the fragile temple of our heart those who have hurt us. When a friend breaks our heart by betraying a confidence or telling a truth that tempts a vulnerable spot within us, we hold that friend as securely as we possibly can in our silence and our prayer. We sit as close as we possibly can to this friend who has hurt us, preferably sitting together in the front pew of our heart's temple. In this way, we practice the art of at-one-ment with this friend, this kin, this neighbor of ours, and we receive the grace to hold our friend instead of our grudge.

In the process of creating space in the temple of the heart for one who has hurt us, we soon recognize that this is the place where our hatred and distrust first visit us. By serving as ushers of a new reign of reconciliation, we will seat these enemies of the spirit, hatred and distrust, not in the front seats of our heart but in the back row of our mind. We will invite them to stand in the back, way back, maybe even in the "cheap seats" of the balcony, as we seek to focus all of our attention on the one who has hurt us. We place his or her picture on the altar table of our heart shrine. We meditate on the features of this friend who has hurt us, seeing this person in the best possible light. We then ask God to enlarge the space of our heart to welcome this friend and offer him a front row seat. We listen to this friend's words and to her silence. We allow both the words and the silence to instruct us and pray within us as we seek to develop a spirit of at-one-ment with this friend.

In his book *Compassion in Action*, Ram Dass writes of a time when he was aggravated with the policies of then Secretary of Defense, Casper Weinberger. So he found a picture of Casper in a newsmagazine and put it on his prayer table among all his spiritual heroes. Each morning, when he lit incense and honored all those with whom he felt a sacred connection, he would feel "waves of love and appreciation." He would say, "Good morning" to each of his spiritual heroes. Then, he would come to the picture of Casper Weinberger. Initially, he writes, "I'd feel my heart constrict, and I'd hear the coldness in my voice as I said, 'Good morning, Casper.' Each morning I'd see what a long way I still had to go."

But then, Ram Dass began to wonder, "Wasn't Casper just another face of God? Couldn't I oppose his actions and still keep my heart open to him? And wouldn't it be harder for him to become free from the role he was obviously trapped in if I, with my mind, just kept reinforcing the traps by identifying him with his acts?" He recalled what the Indian poet Kabir wrote: "Do what you do to another person, but never put them out of your heart." Granted, it's a tall order. But then, as Ram Dass says, "What else is there to do?"

Indeed, when you aspire to be a friend of Christ, what else *is* there to do? Conventional wisdom, the wisdom offered by the world, would suggest that there are many other things we could do. For example, following Ram Dass' reasoning, it was difficult for many in the Western world to see the face of Slobodan Milosevic as "just another face of God." During the crisis in Kosovo, his picture appeared on the cover of a newsmagazine with the headline: "The face of evil." As the bombs fell on the former Yugoslavia in what was called a humanitarian effort to stop the ethnic cleansing and return the thousands of refugees from Kosovo to their homeland, I suspect the prayers of most people focused on the victims of these terrible atrocities. How many of our prayers focused on Milosevic? How many of us took that picture from the cover of the newsmagazine and placed it on our prayer tables to send our prayerful energy toward this one who seemed to be evil incarnate, asking God, pleading with God, to change his heart and stop the killing?

In our personal lives, making room for the friend who has injured us — or, on a global scale, making room in our heart for someone like Slobodan Milosevic — may seem impossible on the surface. But remember, Jesus invites us to go beneath the surface, to that sacred space where we discover that reconciliation is a gift from a gracious God. In the temple of our heart where the Spirit of God dwells, we know we are not perfect, not yet. But the purpose of premeditated mercy is not perfection but to touch the image of God that beats within our own fragile heart. On this holy ground around the altar tables in the temple of our heart, we commit ourselves to compassion, not perfection, by making room for all.

If we remain open to the grace of God's compassion, we will learn a way of holiness that leads us to live with integrity. This growing sense of integrity helps us bridge the distance between our broken relationships and our worship. When we walk with integrity, our approach to our place of worship will rise from deep within hearts that have been jump-started by the grace of God. This integrity demands hearts that constantly seek a wholeness shaped by our own *and* the other's truth, hearts that are striving for a holiness that surpasses the "minimum daily requirements" of religious legislators or ecclesial codes of conduct.

Practicing premeditated mercy involves embracing the larger and deeper vision of who we are as God's beloved, as people made in God's image and likeness. With the Spirit of the divine presence stirring in our souls, we seek to unleash our unlimited potential to love and to forgive, to inspire and animate others. We seek to take risks and dare dreams and to do so for no other reason than because it is the grace of God welling up inside us. Premeditated mercy calls us to stretch out our hearts and our hands in acts of love by inviting us to take risks that are extraordinary because they are expansive. Such risks surpass the *conventional* wisdom of holiness by reflecting the *covenant* wisdom of a merciful and compassionate God.

In her autobiography, *The Story of a Soul*, St. Therese of Lisieux, "the Little Flower," tells a story of taking such a risk and the dividends it paid. It concerns a particularly cranky sister who had such a sour disposition that she became an outcast within her own community. The other sisters avoided her because they found it so difficult to be around her. Her bitterness about life was like a rash that the others were afraid of catching. Therese also found this woman dangerous to be around, but she decided to follow the recipe for reconciliation.

Each day St. Therese made it a point to smile at the old sister who was so sour and bitter about life. Each day she tried to do something nice for the sister. Sometimes she brought her flowers from the garden. She writes in her autobiography that what she was doing for this sister who was most difficult to love, or even like, was what she "would do for the person I love the most." Gradually, the unpleasant, disagreeable old woman began to change. She began to smile a little more and became less negative and critical of others. One day after St. Therese gave her a bouquet of flowers, the old nun asked, "Would you tell me, Sister Therese of the Child Jesus, what attracts you so much towards me? Every time you look at me, I see you smile!"

In the process of premeditated mercy, we have to reverse the way the world expects us to react in a given situation. Instead of treating those who are unkind and hurtful with contempt and disregard, we seek to treat them with kindness and compassion. This is reconciliation in reverse: We reverse what seems to be our natural reactions to those we find most difficult to love and instead put forward our very best selves as we seek to reverence the dignity and integrity of others. As St. Therese said, it means treating them as we might treat the person we love the most.

To do this we need to trust that the grace of the divine presence is already at work in the holy temple we call our heart. For without this trust in the grace of God's forgiving love, our own efforts at reconciliation will be impossible. They will become shallow, feeble attempts to mend fences rather than positive, prophetic actions to bridge the gaps that keep us apart.

Setting the Table: Paper, Scissors, Rock

In addition to the pictures of people we find most difficult to love and those in our world who inflict so much violence and cause so much suffering because of their evil deeds, there are three symbols found in most of our houses that also might be placed on our prayer table. These three symbols — paper, scissors and rock — are the elements used in a game many of us played when we were children. In this game, we didn't use actual paper or scissors or rocks; rather, we made hand gestures to symbolize these elements. The competitors in the game would count to three and then simultaneously show their hands. Two fingers spread apart symbolizes scissors, an open palm represents paper and a fist stands for a rock. As I recall, paper covers rock, scissors cut through paper and rock smashes scissors. If only the world could resolve conflicts with such simple precision.

In the middle of Matthew's account of Jesus' teaching about premeditated mercy, Jesus says, "Be perfect as your Divine Parent is perfect" (Matthew 5: 48). Someone once said that the closest to perfection a person ever comes is when he or she fills out a job application or sends in a resume. Yet, if the "paper perfection" of a resume is a reflection of our quest for excellence, remember this basic rule in the game of life: Scissors beat paper.

In the mid-1990s, a major long-distance telephone company used scissors as a symbol of its communications capability to cut through red tape. Jesus might have used scissors as a teaching tool to show his listeners how his new way of loving not only one's neighbors and friends but one's enemies and antagonists cuts through to the heart of discipleship. But if the perfect symbol of our quest for perfection is scissors, remember this basic rule in the game of life: Rock beats scissors.

For many years, I have placed on my prayer table rocks and small stones collected from various locations. One of these stones held a particular significance. It was no ordinary rock but a chip off the old block: the Berlin Wall, which separated East bloc countries from the West. A good friend gave me this piece of the rock when he returned from visiting Berlin shortly after the fall of the wall in November, 1989. The wall was a notorious symbol of how we learn to hate our enemies, of how difficult it is to pray for those who persecute us. It symbolized how turning the other cheek seems only to result in a sore face and how going the extra mile only leaves one with tired and aching feet. So, when the Berlin Wall came tumbling down, there seemed to be the possibility of a peace that would last.

But then came the Persian Gulf and the Middle East, Bosnia and

Northern Ireland, Rwanda and Liberia, Kosovo and East Timor. So I placed the rock on my prayer shrine as a memento if not a motivator. The bottom line of Jesus' teaching, "Be perfect as your Divine Parent is perfect" (Matthew 5: 48), seemed unreasonable and unattainable in a world of paper, scissors and rocks. For we live in a world where peace treaties written on paper are cut to shreds by car bombs, where scissors need to be kept out of the reach of children because of the violence they may do and where rocks become weapons to be thrown in the streets at those who look suspiciously like an enemy. We live in a world where lines are still clearly drawn, enemy territory is clearly designated and where the words of Jesus from this same section of the Sermon on the Mount, "You have heard it said, 'An eye for an eye and a tooth for a tooth,'" seem to satisfy an unquenchable thirst for revenge.

This is why we need mentors and models who put into practice what Jesus preached about premeditated mercy, about love for enemies and praying for persecutors. I found such mentors in a story from the Holocaust in the book *Grey: The Color of Hope*. A little more than a stone's throw from Berlin is a tiny village called Ravensbruck. In 1938, in the middle of a swamp just outside the village, the Nazis established a concentration camp exclusively for women. By the end of World War II, 50,000 women had died there. Some died from exhaustion in the slave labor camp. Others perished from the harsh, crowded living conditions. Still others died as a result of cruel medical and biological experiments too horrible to imagine.

When Ravensbruck was liberated at the end of the war, a piece of wrapping paper was found near the body of a dead child. Scrawled on the paper was this prayer:

O God,
> remember not only the women and men of good will,
> but also those of ill will.

But do not only remember the suffering they have inflicted on us,
> remember the fruits we bought thanks to this suffering:
> our comradeship, our loyalty, our humility;
> the courage, the generosity, the greatness of heart
> that has grown out of all this.

And when they come to judgment,
> let all the fruits that we have borne be their forgiveness.

Amen. Amen. Amen.

Whoever scribbled that prayer on the piece of paper at Ravensbruck had taken the message of premeditated mercy deep into her heart. That prayer for her persecutors proves that sometimes in the deadly serious game of life, paper beats rock — the rocks thrown from the palms of our persecutors that cause welts to rise on our bodies and wounds that scar our souls. Whoever wrote that prayer had a faith so deep that forgiveness was able to take root and flourish in the fruits of reconciliation reflected in her prayer.

We can scarcely imagine the torment and torture the author of that prayer endured. And yet she prayed for her persecutors. She asked God to accept her suffering and the suffering of her friends and family as atonement for the brutality of her enemies.

The spiritual exercises offered by Jesus in his teaching about premeditated mercy encourage us to make room in our heart shrines even for those we identify as our enemies. These exercises are even more challenging because they call us to love without limits. The heart-stretching spiritual exercises of Jesus invite us to expand the walls of our heart so far that the walls can no longer stand. When we take these lessons to heart, we cultivate a wholeness where no one is left out. In a heart without walls, we can carry the whole world.

With such a stretched heart, our first inclination is to forgive rather than strike back when we have been injured. When we experience persecution of any kind, our first impulse is to pray for those who treat us unjustly. When we identify another as an enemy, our first decision is to love that person. When someone asks us for a handout, we reach into our pocket without question. When someone asks us for clothes for the poor, we pick out our good coat. When others ask us to walk with them for longer than we expected, we keep going no matter how tired we might be.

In a world where an "eye for an eye" endangers the sight of every human being, we practice forgiveness and forego revenge.

In a world where it seems cowardly to turn the other cheek, we cultivate an inner strength that holds the seeds of transforming the other.

In a world where nonviolent resistance to injury seems a precursor for appeasement, our prayer for the persecutors seeks to touch the goodness in them, no matter how far beneath the surface that goodness is buried.

Worldly wisdom says: "Send a clear message; strike back with force." God's wisdom says: "Send a clear message of good news; strike back with the force of love and compassion, mercy and forgiveness." When we do this, the temple of our heart grows so large that everyone — the good and the bad, the just and the unjust, the innocent and the guilty — finds a place to sit and room to grow. In short, we cultivate the holiness of God.

That's why the prayer scrawled on a piece of paper in Ravensbruck's prison camp beats the rocks we throw at one another or use to build the walls that separate us. It is a prayer that reflects how the good in us can redeem the bad in the others, how the just can save the unjust, how love for friend or enemy is not only possible but is the only practical way the reign of God becomes visible in our world.

In the temple of our heart where the Spirit of God dwells, we know we are not perfect, not yet. That is why it helps to set the table with certain symbols that remind us to make some space for all, to leave some room even for those who are our enemies. When we make space for those who we find most difficult to love, we begin to make peace.

It is here in the silence at the table in our heart shrines where we are reminded of the call to be holy, as our God is holy. It is here where we touch again the holiness of God that beats within our own fragile heart. On this holy ground around this altar table, we commit ourselves to cultivate seeds not of perfection but of mercy and compassion. For that is how Luke translates Matthew's version of Jesus' teaching about perfection: "Be merciful as your God is merciful." Or, as some translations have it, "Be compassionate as your God is compassionate" (Luke 6: 36).

In summary, we might do this by setting the table in the temple of our heart with the symbols we've reflected on here: paper, scissors and rock. The paper could be our resume that reflects not so much what we have accomplished but what we desire to become — to be holy as our God is holy. The scissors might help us cut through any grudges that still grip our heart. A rock or two might remind us how God builds this temple of the heart, where the Spirit of God dwells, with mercy and compassion.

FOR GOOD MEASURE: THE RULE OF THUMB

As we sit before this table in the shrine of our heart, a mantra we might use for the practice of premeditated mercy is "for good measure." Jesus uses this mantra in Chapter 7 of Matthew's Gospel: "Judge not, that you be not judged…the measure you give will be the measure you get" (Matthew 7: 1-2). So we might add a ruler to the symbols on our prayer table. As we do, we might repeat the mantra, "for good measure."

We use this everyday phrase, "for good measure," in various ways. One more blow of the hammer, sending a nail into the wood, for good measure. One more swat of the hand upon the backside of a disobedient child, for good measure. One more pat on the back of a deserving employee, for good measure. One more prayer for one who is sick, for good measure. One more apology to someone we've hurt or neglected or missed along the way, for good measure.

The practice of premeditated mercy raises the crucial question: What measuring stick do we use? Do we measure our forgiveness in miles or inches? In teaspoons or tablespoons? In cups or pounds: a cup of blessing or a pound of flesh? If we measure our forgiveness by the pound, exacting a pound of flesh from the one who has hurt us, don't be surprised if our efforts make the other leaner, but also meaner. The way we measure our mercy has a lot to say about our pardoning practices. For good measure, try mercy.

For three years I was director of Shantivanam, a contemplative house of prayer for the Roman Catholic Archdiocese of Kansas City in Kansas. Praying at Shantivanam, we often read from the sacred scriptures of other faith traditions. This opened my eyes and my heart to how the basic teachings of the Divine One are reflected in very similar words in all the great religions of the world. Take, for example, the measurement we have come to know as the golden rule: "Do to others as you would have them do to you." We find remarkably similar interpretations of this rule in the sacred scriptures of all the major religions. In Judaism it is reflected in these words: "What is hurtful to yourself do not do to your fellow [human being]. That is the whole of the Torah and the remainder is but a commentary." Islam puts it this way: "Do unto all people as you wish to have done unto you; and reject for others what you would reject for yourselves." In Buddhism, "Hurt not the other with that which pains yourself."

In Confucianism, the golden rule is taught in the form of a dialogue as the student asks, "Is there one principle upon which one's whole life may proceed?" The Master replied, "Is not reciprocity such a principle? — what you do not yourself desire, do not put before others." And in Hinduism, the golden rule sounds like this: "This is the sum of all true righteousness: Treat others as you would be treated. Do nothing to your neighbor which hereafter you would not have your neighbor do to you."

In whatever form, the golden rule offers quite a challenging measurement for our heart. The full length of this measurement is captured in Jesus' teaching, "Love your enemies, pray for those who persecute you" (Matthew 5: 44). In the Buddhist Text *Compendium of Practices*, this teaching is translated in the form of a question: "Shantideva asks, 'If you do not practice compassion toward your enemy then toward whom can you practice it?'" In responding to that question, His Holiness, the Dalai Lama, the leader of an unjustly oppressed people, writes: "It is very important to develop the right attitude toward your enemy. If you can cultivate the right attitude, your enemies are your best spiritual teachers because their presence provides you with the opportunity to enhance and develop tolerance, patience and understanding."

Developing this "right attitude" is at the heart of Jesus' teaching about premeditated mercy. This right attitude takes on global, and perhaps eternal, consequences when we are very specific about whom our enemies are. In recent years, the world's public enemy number one was Saddam Hussein. Then Slobodan Milosevic surfaced in the former Yugoslavia to steal the crown from Saddam for awhile. If we take the teaching of Jesus and Buddha to our heart shrines and cultivate this right attitude, the command is to love Saddam Hussein and Slobodan Milosevic. If I understand the Dalai Lama's interpretation of this teaching correctly, if we have developed this right attitude, then Saddam Hussein and Slobodan Milosevic are at present our best spiritual teachers because their presence on the world's scene is providing us with a great opportunity to develop tolerance, patience and understanding. And, according to the Dalai Lama, "by developing greater tolerance and patience, it will be easier for you to develop your capacity for compassion."

Now there is a heart-stretching spiritual exercise: to think of Saddam Hussein and Slobodan Milosevic as spiritual teachers! But we might easily say: Be realistic! How can anyone love men who use children as human shields to protect their policies of oppression and death?

When we are in the midst of war with a Saddam or Slobodan, we are all prisoners of war, prisoners of fear. Because of our imprisonment, few politicians or pundits — or preachers, for that matter — mention the measurement of the golden rule found in all faith traditions as a basis for resolving a conflict. This suggests that the golden rule may sound wonderful, and may even be somewhat practical on a personal level — as in a relationship with a friend who has hurt us — but it simply is not practical or even relevant in a world order where policies of national self-interest take precedence.

The evidence indicates that the golden rule, at least in international affairs, has been replaced by another rule, also very ancient and familiar to us: the rule of thumb. Handed down through the ages, the rule of thumb reflects the measure of wisdom we have received from our ancestors in similar struggles and conflicts. For example, the wisdom of our experience in dealing with people like Adolph Hitler, Joseph Stalin, Saddam Hussein and Slobodan Milosevic is according to the rule of thumb — since a thumb equals one inch — if you give them an inch, they will take a mile. This rule of thumb has proven true so often in the past that it has effectively replaced the golden rule as a measuring stick.

When we find ourselves confronted with the presence of evil in the arena of the world, we are like the citizens of ancient Rome who gathered in the coliseum to watch the battle of gladiators. When the fight reached a point where one of the gladiators had the upper hand, he would look to the crowd for the rule of thumb. According to the rule of thumb practiced in ancient Rome — not unlike the gestures used by famous film critics — a "thumbs up" would mean the life of the enemy would be spared; a "thumbs down" would signal the enemy's death. We have a similar choice in determining how to deal with world conflicts: A "thumbs up" puts the golden rule above the rule of thumb. A "thumbs down" confirms Robert Frost's verse: "nothing gold can stay." Yet, when faced with evil threats in the world, whether our impulse is "thumbs up" or "thumbs down," the truth of premeditated mercy is clear: "the measure you give will be the measure you get back."

Before measuring by the rule of thumb, take a close look at the measuring instrument. Meditate upon your thumb and see its unique design, the only one of its kind in the world. Saddam Hussein and Slobodan Milosevic may have the people of their countries under their thumbs, but every man, woman and child in Iraq and Serbia have a thumbprint just as unique as yours and mine. But it's hard to make war so personal, isn't it?

I am reminded of a story I heard during the height of the Cold War. The Baptist Peace Fellowship sent a delegation to what was then the Soviet Union. A writer from Louisville, Kentucky, was part of this delegation. While in Russia, he met a young man named Andrew, an eighteen-year-old factory worker and part-time student. During the course of their conversation, the writer from the United States and the student from the Soviet Union discovered they had much in common. Though thousands of miles separated them, both in terms of geography and ideology, they became good friends. As he was leaving to return to the United States, the writer gave Andrew a sweatshirt with the logo of the University of Louisville imprinted on it. Andrew gave the writer a Russian-English dictionary. These simple gifts of friendship reflected the ideas they had shared and the common ground they had found. At their parting, Andrew said to the writer, "I will tell my country that I do not want them to drop bombs on your country because I have a friend in Louisville."

I don't have any friends in Baghdad or Belgrade. I don't know anyone in Iraq or Yugoslavia. But I wonder how different our views would be if each of us could add this measurement to the rule of thumb: "Do not drop the bombs on Iraq and Yugoslavia because I have friends who live there."

As a spiritual exercise for premeditated mercy, place some ashes or some dirt in a small bowl on your prayer shrine. With your thumb, take some of the dust and see how it collects in the whorls of your thumb. Perhaps you might make a print on the paper in your shrine and reflect on how this print reminds you of your uniqueness — how you bear upon your heart the image of God.

Then, with open hands, with dusty thumbs, imagine that halfway across the world in Belgrade or Baghdad, in Kosovo or North Korea, there is one who bears the same imprint upon his or her heart. And whisper the mantra: "for good measure." In these three simple and sacred words, you sum up this prayer for premeditated mercy:

For good measure I will love my enemies,
>   do good to those who hate me,
>   bless those who curse me,
>   pray for those who abuse me.
If anyone strikes me on the cheek,
>   for good measure I will offer the other cheek also.
From anyone who takes away my coat,
>   for good measure I will not withhold even my shirt;
>   for good measure, I will give to everyone who begs from me.
If anyone takes away my goods,
>   for good measure I will not ask for them back.
For good measure, I will do to others as I would have them to do me.

The practice of premeditated mercy invites us to set the table for a new creation as we seek to live no longer by the rule of thumb that returns hatred for hatred, vengeance for vengeance. For if, as Jesus says, we love only those who love us, only do good to those who do good to us, only lend to those from whom we hope to receive, then "what credit is that to you?" (Matthew 5: 46). Premeditated mercy involves replacing the rule of the thumb with the golden rule.

As we begin these spiritual exercises for premeditated mercy each day, we may not go as far as Jesus demands or as the "right attitude" the Dalai Lama proposes in making our enemies our greatest spiritual teachers. But we are invited to go as far as we can to measure our heart by the golden rule, trusting that God's grace will take us the rest of the way. For the golden rule of God's holiness measures not by the inch of our thumb but by the infinite miles of God's mercy.

A Table for All:
Finding Room for the Beloved and the Betrayer

*The most remarkable miracle is not
the transformation of water into wine;
it is the transformation of an enemy into a friend.*

— James Forest

When we have spent considerable time before the table in the temple of our heart — meditating on the spiritual exercises taught by Jesus and echoed in the teachings of Buddha, Confucius and other major faith figures and traditions — we begin to sense a desire to move from the solitude of our heart to find a place, a table, where we might practice our premeditation exercises of mercy.

We often use the image of the table as a euphemism for both dialogue and discussion. Though I often use those two words interchangeably, a friend of mine, Father Greg Comella, spoke recently on a retreat about the profound difference in the original Greek meanings of those two words. In Greek, *discussion* implies smashing things to pieces, whereas *dialogue* means "to have meaning flow through." This is a helpful distinction as we consider in this chapter what we bring to the table. When we gather for meetings, we put our ideas "on the table." Motions are made, and when no consensus is reached they are "tabled" to be reviewed further at a later time.

Tables are places where stories are told, discussions break open ideas, dialogue sifts through the meaning of what is spoken and what is left unspoken, and decisions are made.

As we seek to practice premeditated mercy, we observe that one of the first things we bring "to the table" is our diversity. At the table of the Last Supper, this diversity is reflected not so much in various cultures or creeds or gender (though the presence of women at that Passover Meal seems likely) or even ideologies (although there is evidence that one of the disciples Jesus chose to follow him was a Zealot who believed in the violent overthrow of the Roman occupation), but in the attitudes of those who gathered at the table. When Jesus came to the Passover meal on the night before he died, at the table were friends who would betray him and deny him, friends who would argue about ambition and about whom among them was making the greatest contribution to the cause. At the table for his Last Supper, we see how the practice of premeditated mercy becomes the real presence of reconciliation. This real presence is reflected in familiar words from Luke's Gospel:

> And he took bread, and when he had given thanks he broke it and gave it to them, saying, "This is my body, which is given for you. Do this in remembrance of me." And likewise the cup after supper, saying, "This cup which is poured out for you is the new covenant in my blood" (Luke 22: 19-20).

We understand these crucial words in terms of memory: "Do this in remembrance of me." The challenge of our companionship at the table of Eucharist is to keep alive in our minds and hearts the memory of what Jesus did on the night he was betrayed. But these words also are a mandate to be a living memory by becoming messengers of mercy at all the tables around which we gather in our lives.

The Eucharist is not only a meal of memory but also a celebration of mercy. In Matthew's account of the Last Supper, when Jesus offers the cup to his disciples and invites them all to drink "for this is my blood of the covenant," he adds, "which is poured out for many for the forgiveness of sins" (Matthew 26: 28). Here, the sacred connection between reconciliation and real presence is clear: Jesus offers his blood, which symbolizes his life, for the sole purpose of forgiveness. This mercy is not just for a few chosen people but "for many."

We explore this sacred connection by first examining the very common piece of furniture, a table, around which we share an uncommon meal. Before we can sit down to share this meal in the company of friends, we first have to set the table. But even before we can set the table, the table must be built.

THE TABLEMAKER

Once upon a time there lived a carpenter who specialized in making tables. Indeed, that is all this carpenter made: round tables, square tables, long tables, tables for two or four or forty. He made tables of all shapes and sizes from all sorts of wood — beech and birch, cherry and chestnut, elm and oak, maple and walnut. He made picnic tables and coffee tables, tables for the kitchen or the dining room or the conference room. His tables were used throughout the land because they were handcrafted, sturdy and beautiful. Everyone knew this carpenter as the Tablemaker.

Every now and then, a customer unfamiliar with the carpenter would come into his shop and ask for a cabinet or a chair or a bookshelf. But the tablemaker would smile and say, "I'm sorry, I only make tables." If the customer asked him why, he would motion the person to sit down at the sycamore table in the corner of his workshop, pour the customer some coffee and tell the story of how he came to make only tables.

I come from a long line of carpenters. Working with wood runs in my blood. My grandfather built many of the houses that still stand in this town. My father continued the tradition and my brothers after them. To this day, my family builds some of the finest houses in the land.

But when I was young and helping my dad in the construction of these houses, I felt something was missing. When the houses were finished, they were certainly beautiful to behold. But inside they were empty. These houses didn't become homes until people moved into them, bringing with them possessions that reflected in some way the story of their lives — where they had been, who they had known, what they believed. What the people put inside the house that my father had built meant more to me than the house itself. My father created a space for people to live in, and I wanted to create something to help the people fill those empty spaces.

So, one day, my father and I were out walking in the woods near our home. My father loved the woods. He felt a special kinship with the trees. As someone who worked every day of his life with wood, he never failed to thank the trees for their gift, which made his life, his vocation, possible. As we were walking that day, I told my father that rather than continue constructing houses I wanted to make furniture to put inside the houses he and my brothers built. I thought my father would be angry at my not wanting to carry on the family tradition. But he wasn't angry. He just stopped at the base of a large oak tree and put his hand gently on the trunk of the tree as one might rest a hand gently on the shoulder of a friend.

"What kind of furniture would you like to make, son?" my father asked.

"All kinds of furniture," I said. "Just like you make all kinds of houses."

"But is there one piece of furniture you'd like to make more than any other?"

I thought for a moment but admitted I didn't have a preference or a passion.

"Son," my father said, "I believe you should make tables."

"Tables?"

My father patted the belly of the oak tree and smiled. "You see, son, people gather around tables to eat and to talk, to tell stories and drink wine. When people gather around a table, there is a sense that people want to get along with one another. Whatever might be causing them to be hurt or sad or lonely or angry, when people gather around a table, when they sit to eat and to drink and maybe tell a few stories, they show they don't want to be alone. I don't know why, exactly. Maybe it has something to do with what God said after creating Adam: 'It's not good for the human to be alone.'

"Tables express God's desire for us to come together in some sort of community. Do you remember when your grandfather died and all our neighbors and friends brought over food for us? Remember how we sat at that table and nibbled at the food and told stories about Grandpa? Somehow that food and that table and those stories helped to ease the pain of Grandpa's death.

"And remember the time your brother got in trouble with the law and I had to bail him out of jail? Well, when I got him home, we sat for hours at the kitchen table just talking about what he had done and why he had done it. Somehow, just sitting at that table made forgiveness a little easier.

"I don't know what it is about a table, son," my father said finally. "But somehow it brings people together."

From that moment on, all I wanted to make were tables. Oh,

there were times when I thought about making other kinds of furniture, but then I would remember what my father said to me when we finished that walk in the woods. He said, "Son, you're going to make the finest tables the people of this land have ever seen. Your brothers and I will build the houses, and you make the tables that will go inside those houses. And if you ever doubt why you're making tables, or ever feel the need to make other things besides tables, you just come to me and we'll go for a walk in these woods. These trees and I will help you remember why making tables is so important."

So, you see, my friend, I only make tables. And though my father has been dead for many years now, whenever I am tempted to make other things, or whenever I doubt that the tables I make are making any difference, I just go for a walk in the woods where my father and I walked that day. I go to that old oak tree and put my hand on it like my father did. And I remember the story.

THE POWER OF MEMORY

At every Eucharist, we gather around a table to remember the story. This is the power of memory. We remember what Jesus did on the night he was betrayed. After giving his disciples the bread, he said, "Do this in remembrance of me." Immediately after giving the disciples the cup of wine, which he identified as "the new covenant in my blood," Jesus announced that "the hand of him who betrays me is with me on the table" (Luke 22: 21). This is how the power of memory influences our practice of premeditated mercy. This memory of what Jesus did on the night he was betrayed nourishes the courage we need to become a living memory of God's desire for reconciliation. It empowers us to practice mercy toward those who would betray us.

At the table of Eucharist, we listen to stories from Scripture that call us to live the reign of God. We bring simple gifts of bread and wine and call forth a blessing. We extend our hands — and our hearts — and invest these gifts with the resources we have at hand; we invest our very selves. We do what Jesus did on the night before he died: We raise our eyes to heaven, pronounce a blessing, break the bread and give these gifts on our table to one another to share. In this prayer we voice the power of our faith to ask God to change bread and wine into the body and blood of Jesus. Even more, we ask God to change us to be bread for those hungry for friendship, to be wine for those whose lives are thirsty for celebration. We ask God to make us the body of Christ for the life of the world, to be the blood of Christ for the salvation of the world.

Whenever and wherever we celebrate this ritual of remembrance, we become makers of the tables where the reign of God is being served. It's the space where we all can feast on forgiveness and faith, where friendships can be fashioned and commitments nurtured. Eucharist extends the table of holy communion where all might find a place, where all people might be fed.

In the living out of this ritual of remembrance in our daily lives, we will have some doubts and more than a few fears. But like the tablemaker, who goes to the woods to remember his father's story, we come to the table of the Eucharist to help us remember the stories that shape our commitment and nourish our courage. When we do this, we set the table for both stranger and friend and become the container of reconciliation and communion for all people, even those who would betray our love or deny our friendship. When we do this in memory of Jesus, we live the memory of the new covenant, and the reign of God, the new creation, is served.

REAL PRESENCE REQUIRES A ROUND TABLE

Reconciliation and the real presence the Eucharist reflects require that we gather at a round table. Few places of worship that I have seen use a round table for the breaking of the bread and sharing the cup. This was brought to mind in a vivid way a few years ago at the ordination of one of my brothers in community. I was sitting in the pew and noticed the altar and the view. The table seemed too large, and it was a square table in a round church. The bishop and the newly ordained and a few vested clergy were standing on one side of the table. The rest of us were standing more than a few feet away and a few steps lower, so we had to look up. I was distracted by the table. I kept thinking, "Shouldn't altars be round rather than rectangular? And shouldn't they be small enough so that every one can stand around?"

The way it is now in most churches I've seen, it seems more like a counter than a table. "May I take your order?" the presider might ask. (But because we've been here before and know the ropes, we say, "But I thought we're the ones who are supposed to take orders from you!")

I would like to see round tables in round churches where people can stand around the altar table and see each other's faces. Then, to paraphrase

King Arthur and his court, we may become lights of the round table.

How do you imagine the table at the Last Supper? The Scripture notes that they "reclined at table," giving us the impression that it was like a modern day coffee table and not like a countertop or our modern day altars. The scene many of us conjure up of the Last Supper is the one daVinci captured on canvas. Here were Jesus and the twelve apostles, the first concelebrants, on one side of a long table. If this was the first Eucharist, where was the congregation? Were there only men at the Last Supper? That is the view in the Roman Catholic tradition. This understanding is based on the accounts of the Last Supper by Matthew, Mark and Luke. Luke refers to those who crowded around the table that night as apostles: "And when the hour came, he sat at table, and the apostles with him" (Acts 22: 14). Roman Catholic tradition holds that the twelve apostles were all men.

But John, who instead of describing what was served at the meal (bread and wine) tells the story of the One who serves. He indicates that "Jesus...rose from supper, laid aside his garments and girded himself with a towel. Then he poured water into a basin, and began to wash the disciples' feet" (John 13: 5). Disciples included both men and women. Since one of the bases for reserving ordained ministry in the Roman Catholic Church only to men is that at the Last Supper only men were present, John's account of Jesus washing the feet of his disciples might cast a shadow of a doubt about who was present for his last meal in the company of friends. There is no argument that Jesus' friends included both men and women. Could it be that in washing the feet of his disciples, the symbolic act that indicates clearly the call to servant leadership in the community of faith, Jesus was opening the door for women also to serve as priests?

It is not within the scope of this book to debate the question of women's ordination in the Roman Catholic tradition. However, the question of who was on the guest list at the Last Supper is important in our understanding the inclusive nature of our companionship at the table of memory and mercy. For our consideration of this expansive vision, some practical questions surface. When hosting a dinner party for friends, do we care who sits where? Or do we say, "Sit anywhere you like." When eating with the family or our community, do we always sit at the same place at the table? When we invite acquaintances or new neighbors over for a meal to get to know each other better, do we write each invited guest's name on a card and strategically place them so that those who don't know each other might find by the end of the meal that they have made a new friend?

In one place where I lived with twelve other priests and brothers, we had large tables in the dining room. This was a source of some concern for members of the community. The table sat twelve and maybe even fourteen on a crowded day. It was difficult to have an intimate conversation with twelve people. But then, it would seem that's what Jesus did as he took bread and said, "This is my body." Have more intimate words ever been spoken?

In my family when I was growing up, we knew we had reached a certain level of maturity when at Thanksgiving Mom would say, "Let's move to the big table." The younger children would always sit at card tables set up in the living room while the adults ate at the dining room table. Could this be what Jesus said to some of his disciples right before dinner was served: "Come to the big table." Or might we assume, because of his love for children and his frequent references to becoming like little children before we can enter the reign of God, that Jesus gathered all the guests around the "little table" with very short legs designed especially for children?

Recall in Luke's account of the Last Supper, just after Jesus has given the cup as "the new covenant in my blood," he announced that his betrayer "is with me at this table." Then the disciples began to argue not only about who among them might be the betrayer, but who among them is the greatest. To this talk Jesus responds, "Who, in fact, is the greater — the one who reclines at table or the one who serves the meal? Is it not the one who reclines at table? Yet I am in your midst as the one who serves you" (Luke 22: 27).

It seems the disciples were still sitting at the "big" table and not ready to move to the "little" one.

THE ROOM WITH A VIEW

Now let's take a look around the room where this table is the focus of our attention. What kind of room is it? In Mark's Gospel, Jesus sends two of his disciples into Jerusalem with these instructions:

> Go into the city, and a man carrying a jar of water will meet you; follow him, and wherever he enters, say to the householder, "The Teacher says, 'Where is my guest room, where I am to eat

the Passover with my disciples?'" And he will show you a large upper room furnished and ready; make the preparations for us there (Mark 14: 13-15).

Mark describes this room as spacious. This indicates there was enough room for everyone. Perhaps this room had windows with a view toward that day when Jesus said he would drink the cup of wine anew in the reign of God. Yes, I imagine this place that the disciples prepared for the Passover meal was a room with a view to the reign of God.

If we unleash our imaginations a little, can we also see that maybe there was a skylight in the roof of this room so that people could see above them? Since this was an "upper room," maybe it had a glass floor too so that guests could see the folks celebrating in the room downstairs. And the walls of this upper room would be like windows so that the guests could see to the east, west, north and south. Yes, a room with a view of all six directions. It would be right to prepare the Passover in a room like this.

Now, imagine sitting in this room and savoring the sweet wine that lingers upon our lips. This wine stains our tongues with blood, precious and bold. Its bouquet arouses anticipation and stirs excitement. Swish and swallow. "Yes, this will do," the wine steward is told. The wine splashing in a glass of fine crystal is a sacred sound. "Careful, don't spill even a drop of this nectar that will warm wounds, ease pain, lighten head and heart, and restore remnant." We drink it slowly and savor each sip of salvation.

The wine steward pours this rare vintage but seems preoccupied. He is looking not at the guest or at the glasses as he pours, but at the windows. Imagine that these windows that look out toward the reign of God are stained with the faces of the poor. Yes, these are stained glass windows, over which are spread images of the saints from the street: holy images of the poor, the abandoned, the forgotten, the hungry, the homeless, the broken and the betrayed, believers and unbelievers, the reckless ones who abandoned all hope and the careful ones for whom hope has long been delayed. They stand at the glass door of this upper room; their images peer at us through the windows. As the wine steward pours, the poor ones watch and wait for a taste.

"You fool!" we shout at the steward. "Stop! The glass is full! Look what you've done!" Rose-colored stains cover the silk tablecloth. Look again: Blood stains the apron of the wine steward, who still looks at the window and wonders, "Who are these people whose images stain these glass windows?"

Still pouring, wine spilling, napkins sopping, guests yelling, the wine steward watches thirsty eyes gazing through the windows of this room.

"Sorry," he says at last — but not to the guests who are stunned and stammering insults at the one who pours the wine. "I'll bring you another bottle," he says. "This one is empty." But the glasses are full.

And the windows too.

Once I gave a retreat in a church that had no windows at all. In remodeling the church, the parishioners decided that because of the cost of replacing so many broken windows in the past, they would simply cover all the windows with bricks. Now the church is dark and tomb-like, though there is a large skylight over the altar where the sun can filter through a few healing rays. But for the people who gather there to pray there is no possibility to see outside. And there is no opportunity for those who walk by to look inside. I understand the economics of such a decision. This is, after all, a poor parish. But there is a cost to be paid by looking only at the skylight and not at the light in the eyes of those who live in the neighborhood, even if a few of them hold rocks in their hands. It would seem to me that finding ways to help those who carry the rocks to release them would be preferable. But then, I'm not a pastor, I don't live in the neighborhood, and I've never had a rock thrown through the window while I preached.

The question this image evokes is this: Whose eyes peer in through the windows of our souls when we gather to break the bread of friendship? Whose eyes pierce our hearts with their pain when we pass the cup of suffering around the table? It is important for us to look at those eyes that stare at us from outside the windows of our common life. But it is also necessary for us to see, really see, the eyes of those companions who surround us at the table.

STAYING AT THE TABLE

Once I had a vision about community life; I used as a metaphor the image of building a house with no closets. It was a place where there would be no secrets because those who lived together in community would be so open, so honest, so vulnerable, so fearless that we would be willing to be transparent and transformed in a spirit of unconditional love.

I was naive to think we could build such a house. Living in

community demands having ample closet space to keep our secrets, hide our shame, stuff our resentment, stow away our pain.

I realize now that my youthful vision about community life reflected my desire to return to the Garden of Eden. It was a dream drawn too much from the images of the creation story in the Book of Genesis, the original divine inspiration, where human beings live in harmony with all creatures and all of creation. The humans, Adam and Eve, are naked. They have nothing to hide. They bear no marks of shame or guilt. They are vulnerable and completely open. My mistake was in not drawing from the Last Supper scene, where secrets were kept not in closets but under the table.

One person whose writings I admire greatly is Parker Palmer. In an article a few years ago, he confirmed my learnings and raised some important points for people who seek to live and serve at the table of mercy and memory. He suggested that archetypes of community — those models or images that become etched in our minds — can be overly romantic and so leave us disillusioned. We have a deep yearning for community, for belonging to others. But in this process, the images we use to define our relationships within the larger community are often so ideal as to become dangerous.

But for those of us who live in community or who belong to a church, we know how unrealistic the image of the Garden of Eden is. After all, we live "after the fall." And so we tend to spend our lives picking up the pieces of our inability to love others and live in harmony with all creatures of the earth. In joining a community, we might hope that we will be able to live as Adam and Eve did. But soon we recognize that shame and guilt and the inability to be vulnerable in another's presence become the hallmarks of our common life. Our expectations dashed, we might then leave the community or place of worship disappointed and dejected.

Another Biblical image that has influenced me, and that many hold close to their hearts, is the image of the New Jerusalem, the Holy City, a place where unity is very real even amid the remarkable diversity of those who live within the city limits. This is a city that is safe and secure, a place where all are served and all are saved. This vision from the Book of Revelations reflects a wondrous gathering of peoples from every race and religion, culture and creed and way of life. It's an image that restores the original vision of God's heart: the Garden of Eden.

But as Parker Palmer suggests, a more realistic notion of community is the Last Supper. Here, around the table, in the company of his closest friends, we see Jesus give birth to a new creation community that can indeed be lived now. This is community in real terms. After all, Jesus was betrayed and denied by close friends. The table talk was about whom was the most important among them. Yet in the midst of these power struggles and conflicts, Palmer reminds us, "Jesus stayed at the table." He washed the feet of the ones who would betray and deny him; he broke the bread and passed the cup to each one at the table without questioning their motivations, their ambitions or their allegiance to him. Jesus realized he had not come to reclaim God's original vision of creation but to initiate a new creation. He stayed at the table long enough to pray for his disciples' unity and to show them how to love one another amid the ruins caused by ambition, fear, greed and deceit.

As he sat at the table that night he was betrayed, Jesus knew that soon enough he would return to a garden to pray. But the Garden of Gethsemane would not bear the slightest resemblance to the Garden of Eden. In the garden that night after supper with his disciples, Jesus' sweat and tears would become like drops of blood to water this garden with his anguish and his pain. No doubt Jesus knew that on our journey to the new creation most of us would spend considerably more time in Gethsemane than Eden.

So now if I were to build a new house or design a new room in this house we call community, I would keep ample closet space for those not ready to lay their hearts on the table. I would make the dining room the largest space in this new house. And, yes, closets instead of windows would line the room.

Then, once we all sat down and started telling stories, drinking wine, breaking bread, washing feet and entertaining doubt, someone might get up from the table and open closet doors. Secrets would come tumbling out, along with shame, resentment, fears and faith. Surrounded then by these closet concerns, rather than pushing them under the table — out of sight, out of mind — we'd make a toast and drink some more wine.

And behind these open closet doors there would be windows for all to see the coming of the reign of God. This reign is described in Scripture in terms of truth and love, justice and peace. It's a reign that bears the marks of crucifixion and the glory of resurrection. It's a reign that reflects the reality of redemption and reconciliation. It's a reign that falls from the skies and lands in our laps as we sit at the table of memory and mercy.

The Last Supper: Some Disenchanted Evening

We have looked at the room where the Passover table was set, but what was the mood of those who gathered that evening? Was the mood one of enchantment? Was this "some enchanted evening" Jesus was about to share with his closest friends?

According to the Scripture accounts, the atmosphere at the table that night was far from enchanting. Rather, this was some *disenchanted* evening. The mood was dark and foreboding. The air was thick with tension. Pass the knife. Mark's account reflects this mood: "As it grew dark he arrived with the Twelve. They reclined at table, and in the course of the meal Jesus said, 'I give you my word, one of you is about to betray me, yes, one who is eating with me'" (Mark 14: 17-18).

It is tense around the table. The others looked around with sadness etched in their eyes — and maybe a hint of surprise: "Surely not I," each one announced emphatically. But Jesus has given them his word and says it again: "It is one of the Twelve — one who dips into the dish with me" (14: 20).

Then, during this meal of memory and mercy, Jesus "took bread, blessed and broke it, and gave it to them. 'Take this,' he said, 'this is my body'" (14: 22).

Note that Jesus did not say, "Try this," as a gracious host who has prepared a new and unusual gourmet treat might say to her guests. "Try this and tell me if you like it." No, it was more than an invitation; it was an injunction. Here, Jesus was like an Italian grandmother I used to know in a parish where I once served. I'd often go to dinner at her house. I was never fat enough for her. I could never eat enough. There was always more than enough food. "Take, eat," she'd say, her words insistent and yet inviting enough for me to say, "Okay, but just one more."

"He likewise took a cup, gave thanks and passed it to them and they all drank from it" (14: 23). More wine to wash down the food. Always enough wine to celebrate in the company of friends. But this is no ordinary wine. No, this vintage was made from grapes of wrath and wonder and wisdom, grapes of tears and fears and failings, grapes washed with heavy rain, grapes clinging to the vines through violent winds, grapes harvested at just the right moment to be plump, ripe, juicy, sweet. This vintage is from grapes crushed in the winepress of our own experiences: "This is my blood, the blood of the covenant to be poured out on behalf of many" (14: 24).

Then he gives his friends the promise of a future: "I will never again drink of the fruit of the vine until the day I drink it anew in the reign of God" (14: 25).

So, it's in the stifling and suffocating air of betrayal that Jesus gives us this feast of abundance, the Eucharist.

I have an acute personal memory of feeling betrayed. Because of this betrayal, I once left the table. I could no longer sit at the same table as the one who had betrayed me.

Sometimes we have to leave the table for awhile just to fast and feel the hunger.

This betrayal drove me away from the table of community. It placed me outside the gates with souls who asked only for table scraps and found in those crumbs the hope to go on. I was fed at their table, by their manners, by their stories. Spending a few months' time in the company of these disenfranchised friends showed me the way back to the table. I have taken the memory of those I met outside the gates with me to the table ever since.

Standing at the table, which I often do now, I say those words of truth and invitation and am amazed that on the night Jesus was betrayed he didn't run away but stayed and spoke of love instead.

Though I am far from worthy to receive such an honored guest, I am reminded every now and then of my own betrayer and give thanks as I break bread and pour wine. The memory encourages me to place in the cup the sour wine of my betrayal and to taste the sweet nectar of God's grace. We say grace before a meal, but perhaps it's more suited to the meal itself.

God's grace takes us to places we'd rather not go, to people we'd rather not see. God's grace also keeps us in place around the table with both the beloved and the betrayer, with both the violent and the victim. And when this grace is felt inside, we see our reflection in the cup and savor the wine of gratitude.

This grace is reflected in a story from my first book, *Passionate Pilgrims: A Sojourn of Precious Blood Spirituality*. I recall it here because of how it reflects God's amazing grace.

ON THE NIGHT HE WAS BETRAYED

Maria was in her late seventies. She lived with her invalid husband, Joe. A devout Catholic, Maria went to Mass every day for many years, spending at least fifteen minutes before Mass kneeling in front of the statue of the Blessed Mother. But since falling and breaking her hip five years prior, she hadn't ventured outside very much. Maria still spent many hours praying the rosary beside the statue of Mary her children gave to her for Mother's Day many years before. A single silk rose ever stood guard beside the statue. Unlike Maria's memory, the silk rose never faded.

Every First Friday one of the parish priests brought Maria and Joe Communion. Maria lived from one First Friday to the next, preparing the candles, the white linen tablecloth and the small bottle of holy water on the Thursday before the priest was due to arrive. Though he only spent a few minutes with them, it was enough for Maria. Every now and then, when her mind wandered while she prayed the rosary, Maria thought about how often she took Holy Communion for granted when she was receiving the Eucharist daily. Now that she was receiving Eucharist only once a month, it meant so much more to her. Still, she wished there were a way for her to receive Communion more often.

One Friday, the priest asked Maria and Joe if they would like to receive Communion every Sunday. Maria's eyes beamed. "Of course, of course!" But Joe remained silent. He rarely spoke. When the car accident crushed his body ten years before, it also crushed his spirit.

"Maria, I must tell you that the parishioners will be bringing you Communion," the priest said. "We have many Eucharistic ministers in the parish who have volunteered to bring Communion to our shut-ins after the Masses on Sunday morning."

For a moment, the joy disappeared from Maria's eyes as she remembered how she used to switch lines during Communion to make sure she was in the one where the priest was distributing. She never understood many of the changes in the church, especially that one. But the thought of receiving Communion every Sunday was so strong that it loosened the grip her old ideas held on her mind. "Oh, Father, that's okay," she said. "It's still Jesus, no matter who brings him."

George and Juanita always received Communion side-by-side ever since they'd made a Marriage Encounter a few years back. They were excited when the pastor asked them to bring the Eucharist to the sick of the parish on Sunday mornings. Many years before, George had been in business with Joe. They were the best of friends and had built a very successful hardware store. But in the many years of their friendship,

George was never aware of Joe's penchant for gambling. It had become such an obsession that Joe no longer was wagering nickels and dimes but large amounts of money and merchandise. Maria had been aware of Joe's love for the poker table and had taken the problem to the Blessed Mother every morning in her prayer.

One morning, as George and Joe were in the store, George noticed how silent and depressed his friend seemed. When he tried to ask what was wrong, Joe turned away. But later in the day, George found out what had happened. In a big-stakes game the night before, Joe had put the store on the table — and lost. Even though George fought for his share of the business, the people Joe lost to were not the kind you take to court. When they won something and wanted it badly enough, they took it. No questions asked. No answers given.

The loss of the store was tragic enough, but George was able to find another job. What he never regained was his friendship with Joe. He could never let go of the feeling of being betrayed by his closest friend. He was never able to forgive Joe. Even when Joe was paralyzed in the car accident, George refused to show any sympathy. "He deserved it," Juanita heard George mutter under his breath.

On the first Sunday that the Eucharistic ministers were to bring Communion to the shut-ins, George looked at the schedule. His heart dropped. Maria and Joe were the first names on the list.

"I can't do it," George told his wife. "I won't do it. I'll just call Father and tell him to get someone else."

Juanita tried to calm him down and convinced him to go along with her. He could sit in the car while she visited Maria and Joe.

That morning at Mass, the priest spoke about the new ministry that was beginning in the parish and the commissioning of George and Juanita that would take place after Communion. George kept his head bowed during the entire homily.

Then, as he knelt during the Eucharistic Prayer, he heard words he had heard a thousand times before, but heard them really for the first time: "On the night he was betrayed, Jesus took bread and gave You thanks and praise. He broke the bread, gave it to his disciples and said, 'Take this all of you and eat it, this is my body which will be given up for you.'"

George started to cry. "On the night he was *betrayed*" rekindled the memory. Juanita looked at him and wondered what was wrong. She would ask him after Mass, for just then she heard the words, "Do this is memory of me."

Juanita stopped the car in front of Maria and Joe's house. They had been there so often in the past but this was the first time in ten years. For a moment, George stared through the walls and saw their children opening Christmas gifts with Joe and Maria's children on Christmas Eve. When Juanita touched his arm, it startled him. "I'll just be a minute," she said.

"No, wait," George reached out and held her hand. "I'm going with you."

Maria answered the door. Her look of surprise was buried in Juanita's shoulder as they embraced. George followed a couple of steps behind as Maria led them into the living room. The candles were glowing on the table next to the sofa where Joe was sitting, his eyes staring straight ahead.

"Please, sit down," Maria said.

"Oh, Maria," George's voice choked back the years of pain. "I'm sorry. I'm so very sorry." Then he went over to Joe and sat beside him on the sofa. He put his hand on Joe's shoulder and said in a whisper, "Hello, old friend, it's been a long time."

And they celebrated Eucharist.

After ten years of squeezing tightly the anger he felt toward Joe, after ten years of nursing the wound caused by Joe's betrayal, George was surprised by grace and finally was free to forgive. The grace had always been there, but until he heard those words, "on the night he was betrayed," he wasn't ready to go to the place where he never dreamed or never dared to go again. His memory was refreshed by the memory of what Jesus did on the night he was betrayed, George found the freedom to sit at the table with the one who had betrayed him. He could never have gone on his own. Only the grace of God had given George the courage to embrace his old friend.

This grace is present each time we gather at the table of Holy Communion. Just as Jesus, on the night before he died, broke bread and poured wine in the company of his closest followers — one of whom would betray him, another who would deny him, and the others who would flee in fear — the invitation of premeditated mercy is to be open to the grace that will enable us to find a place at the table with friend and foe, with beloved and betrayer. When we do this, we do it in memory of Jesus. It is, indeed, a memory that reflects God's amazing grace.

AMAZING GRACE: TRUST IN GOD

It is the real presence of God's grace at the tables around which we gather that inspires us to remain at or to return to those places where we know our betrayer will be. This grace is more powerful than whatever disgrace we may have embraced because of the betrayal. This grace is stronger than our desire to remain distant from the one who denied our friendship. This grace is more forceful than our longing to flee. It is the grace of God that will take us deeper into the mystery of our holy communion with one another. And in going deeper, we learn, in the words of Parker Palmer, "there is a God who is with us more fully than we are with each other, a God who will keep us together if we will only place our trust in God and not in the community."

Our search for community, for an experience of belonging, is not about fulfilling expectations we have about the people whose company we keep. Our search for community is about finding God. We may, of course, hold on to those high expectations and wonderful images that stir hope within us. But to stay at the table when our experiences in this community tempt us to lower our expectations or radically reshape the images and dreams we once had, we will need grace that will surprise us — indeed amaze us. This is radical grace. It is the grace that George received at Mass when he heard the words, "on the night he was betrayed," and remembered that Jesus gave his very self, his body and his blood, to his friends on the very evening of his betrayal.

It is the same grace I witnessed in a newspaper story some years ago about a married couple whose only son was murdered by a young man who was the same age as their son. This young man was convicted and sent to prison. The couple sat through the trial and saw that justice was done. Though devastated and heartbroken at the loss of their beloved son, they did not call for the young man's death in payment for their own son's life. They realized that the old law of an eye for an eye, a death for a death, would do nothing to solve the vicious cycle of violence. Instead, they began to premeditate mercy. They started to visit the young man in prison. Over the next several years, as they continued to resist the temptation for revenge and embraced the grace of God's mercy, they found themselves forgiving him for taking their son's life.

This couple's attitude of premeditated mercy disarmed the young man. They continued to see him, visit with him and pray with him. He became a model prisoner and became eligible for parole. And you know what this couple did when this young man was paroled from prison? They invited him to live with them in their home, as their son!

The quality of love that became flesh in that couple is a reflection of a radical grace that can come only from God. But to receive it, we must believe it is possible. We must believe that it really is possible to love in the manner of Jesus. When we lose our illusions and romantic notions about community and find instead the grace to stay at the table, we will begin to pay close attention to what Jesus told the disciples about his imminent suffering and death. We will begin to understand that maybe this kind of love can be a reality in us. In the process, we will become a living answer to the prayer of Jesus on that night he was betrayed: "May they all be one."

Reconciliation at the Round Table:

Seeking Common Ground

*Never does the human soul appear so strong
as when it forgoes revenge,
and dares to forgive.*

— E.H. Chapin

As we saw in the last chapter, in the practice of premeditated mercy it is the grace of God that allows us to find a place at the round table. God's grace holds us in this place even when we have been betrayed. Jesus, of course, knew more than most about the experience of betrayal. Since my presumption is that Jesus practiced what he preached, the scenario of the Last Supper takes on a sacred significance when we recall the basic premise of premeditated mercy: reconciling before offering our gifts at the altar. Following his own teaching, Jesus must have tried to reconcile with Judas, the one who would betray him, before offering his body and his blood as the gifts at the altar of the last supper.

We have also seen that in his portrait of this Passover meal, Leonardo daVinci depicted Judas as having spilled salt on the table. In the scene from the painting, Judas is also clutching a moneybag with his right hand while stretching his left hand across the table in the direction of Jesus. Between the outstretched left hand of Judas and the outstretched right hand of Jesus, there is a piece of bread on the table. DaVinci captures the essence of Jesus' teaching about premeditated mercy in this detail about hands stretched across a piece of bread. Jesus' left hand has its palm raised, motioning toward the piece of bread. From the look of surprise on the faces of the disciples, it must be the moment when Jesus says, "This is my body." With his right hand, Jesus has his wrist on the table, the palm slightly raised. Was he trying to reach Judas?

In this scene from the Last Supper, Jesus' left hand knew what his right hand was doing. Jesus is offering himself at the altar. Following his own teaching, then, Jesus has already forgiven Judas for what he is about to do. Indeed, it seems with his right hand open and stretched out in the direction of his betrayer, Jesus is seeking to reconcile with Judas even as he uses his left hand to say, "This is my body."

But Jesus' act of premeditated mercy does not change Judas' course of action. Judas is so coldhearted and intent on what he is about to do that when Jesus announces that the one who would betray him is at the table, Judas joins the chorus with the other disciples who ask, "Is it I, Lord?" He looks Jesus in the eye and states, "It is not I, Lord?" I can imagine Jesus looking with great love into the eyes of his soon-to-be former follower and friend, hoping that this gentle glance will give Judas another chance to change his mind. But the love in his eyes, the forgiveness in his heart, does not transform Judas.

What might this suggest to those of us who seek to practice premeditated mercy? When the one who harms us, or is about to harm us, is unwilling to accept pardon, forgiveness and love, reconciliation remains a distant dream. But at that Passover meal premeditated mercy is still present at the table. Jesus forgives Judas for what he is about to do. This forgiveness he is feeling in his heart at the Passover table would later be put into words as he hangs on the cross: "Father, forgive them, for they know not what they do" (Luke 23: 34). But this mercy is also evident at the table, particularly in the act of loving service Jesus renders to Judas and the other disciples as he washes their feet. But no matter how much love Jesus holds in his heart and is reflected in his eyes — no matter how long he holds Judas in this sacred gaze — if Judas is unwilling to change, the remedy of reconciliation is out of reach.

Judas is out of Jesus' reach. He has placed himself out of reach. Just as it takes two to tango and two to make ends meet, it takes two to practice reconciliation. One or the other can forgive, one or the other can practice premeditated mercy, but for reconciliation to reflect real presence both individuals must be open to the process. Unless the other is predisposed to change and to be reconciled, all we can do is continue to offer the bread of friendship, the bread of life — even as we know the other might not desire to be reconciled. Then, all we can do is drink the cup that contains the bitter wine of betrayal. If the other is interested only in revenge, and not in reconciliation, we swallow the sour grape wine and still try to love.

In meditating on daVinci's portrait of the Last Supper, one can imagine how sitting at the table with the beloved disciple, John, at his right hand, and Judas, the betrayer, sitting next to John, might make for some long silences and awkward glances. Peering into the beloved's eyes, what does one say that one's face does not convey? Yet Jesus' long, loving look is prayerful and serene, a sacred and eternal gaze.

Glancing at the betrayer, however, one would think Jesus would avoid direct eye contact. He had to be thinking, "How can this happen? How can we be seated at the same table?" If you have been betrayed, you know there is no love lost between you and the betrayer — that love was lost long ago at the moment of betrayal. Silence follows this table setting, too, but not a sacred silence — it is more a scared silence.

Jesus' real presence at the Last Supper with both his beloved and his betrayer suggests that premeditated mercy can switch a couple of letters, from *scared* to *sacred*. Maybe it can even transpose a couple of hearts by seeking to turn the betrayer into the beloved. Say but the word and it will be done: "This is my body, this is my blood."

Judas' presence at the table of the Last Supper suggests that sometimes we can take a wrong turn and still end up at the right place. He was at the right place at the right time. Jesus stretched out his hand to offer him mercy. But in the end, Judas was out of reach.

LOOSE ENDS: ACCOUNTABILITY AND RESPONSIBILITY

Before coming to the table of the Last Supper, Jesus reflects this basic thread of truth about premeditated mercy: that to mend the torn fabric of our relationships it takes at least two to make ends meet. In Matthew's Gospel (18: 15-20), Jesus outlines how, when we know the one who has injured us, there are four levels of accountability that lead to reconciliation: person to person, with a small group, with the larger community and, finally, to treat the person who has injured us as one would a Gentile or tax collector. To resolve the inevitable conflicts that arise in community, Jesus advises his disciples to bind the loose ends as best they can, not only by being personally accountable for our own actions, but also by having a sense of responsibility for other members of the community. We are all bound together, and we must be about strengthening the bonds of our common life. When someone has hurt us, we seek the person out and try to reconcile. We don't wait around brooding over our injury until the person comes to us. We practice premeditated mercy when we take a proactive stance, actively seeking reconciliation.

The purpose of Jesus' proactive stance of reconciliation is not to punish the person who has done the damage but to be persistent in our efforts to keep the person bound to the community. Every effort must be in the direction of inclusion — not exclusion — widening the circle rather than constricting it. Communication is the key in community; excommunication is the last resort. Communication conveys a sense that we are willing to dialogue about our differences; we are willing to talk through our opposing views in search of those common threads that bind us together; we are willing to listen to one another and discuss the options that are available to us. Excommunication implies the attitude that we can't communicate any more; we won't talk to one another any more. Whatever common threads might have tied us to one another are now severed; we are unwilling to listen or to discuss the issue. Case closed. Thread severed.

In the teaching from Matthew's Gospel, which is often seen as an outline of church discipline for the early Christian community, the emphasis is properly not on "loosing" but on "binding." Every effort is made to include, not exclude, the person. The due process is focused on forgiving the injury, not on promulgating a punishment. When we have individually and communally tried to bring back the person who has gone astray by following the steps of accountability and the individual has refused to listen or to cooperate or to show any inclination to be included, then that person freely chooses to be "on the loose." We have tried to put the person "in our bind," but he or she has chosen instead to be free of community. The individual severs the thread, not the community.

There are many loose ends in the fabric of our family, faith and cultural communities. The process of premeditated mercy raises this practical and fundamental question: Do we have a desire to make sure these loose ends are still connected rather than cut off forever? A loose end may make the community look ragged. But what is our passion: to look neat and orderly or to be a real community? Few living communities I know of can be characterized as "neat." Ragged edges and redemption are closely connected. If we keep pulling on that loose thread, who knows, the whole fabric might unravel. But if we simply cut it off, the thread is lost.

AN APPROACH TO COMMUNAL PREMEDITATED MERCY

How do we deal with conflicts that arise in community and family life? How do we handle those inevitable flaws we see present in each other? How do we heal the wounds caused by our faults or inflicted upon us by the faults of others? How do we mend the torn fabric of relationships within our faith communities? And how do we bring back to the fold those who are lost, re-connect with those who feel cut off, re-collect those who are scattered? These are some of the questions that were being addressed in the community to which Matthew was writing. And in response to these questions, he offers an approach to reconciliation that is radical in nature.

In trying to get a handle on this strategy for how premeditated mercy can be practiced in communities, I recall a simple story told by a camp counselor about a situation in summer camp in which the counselor practiced premeditated mercy in the manner of Jesus. It was an approach that fashioned not only forgiveness but friendship. The story concerns a small boy we'll call Timmy who receives a large package of cookies in the mail from his mother. He eats a few of the cookies, then places the remainder under his bed. The next day, after lunch, he goes to his tent to get a cookie. But the box is gone.

Later that afternoon, Timmy sees another boy sitting behind a tree with the missing box of cookies his mother sent him. Now, according to the strategy outlined by Jesus, Timmy's first step is to confront the boy who stole his cookies. If this doesn't work, he is to move to the next step, which would involve the camp counselor to serve as a kind of facilitator in the process of retrieving the stolen goods and reconciling the young thief into the good graces of the group. And if the camp counselor is unsuccessful in his efforts to convert the cookie thief, then the third step would be to bring the boy before the entire camp on criminal charges of stolen cookies with an intent to eat. If the boy still refuses to admit his wrongdoing, the final step would be to "treat him as you would a Gentile or a tax collector." This means, at least on the surface, that he would be expelled from the camp.

Now, that seems like a sound strategy to rid the camp of a known cookie thief. But doesn't it fall short of the kind of reconciliation by which Jesus lived throughout his life? Indeed, that fourth step of the strategy seems to give credibility to the practice of excommunication. So, maybe the point of this strategy hinges on our interpretation of what Jesus meant when he said, "treat him as you would a Gentile or a tax collector."

Let's imagine for a moment that in our summer camp scenario the camp counselor decides to try the spiritual exercises of premeditated mercy and treat the known cookie thief as Jesus treated the Gentiles and tax collectors, the outcasts and the castoffs of his day. Let's imagine that after Timmy has confronted the cookie thief but failed in his attempt to retrieve his cookies, Timmy brings his grievance to the camp counselor. The counselor says, "Timmy, will you help me teach him a lesson?" Timmy is puzzled. "Aren't you going to punish him?"

"No," the counselor says. "That would only make him resent you and hate everyone else in camp. No, I want you to call your mom and ask her to send you another box of cookies."

Timmy does as the counselor asks and a few days later receives another box of cookies in the mail. "Now," the counselor says, "the boy who stole your cookies is down by the lake. Go down there and share your cookies with him."

"Are you crazy?" Timmy protests. "He's the thief!"

"I know. But try it — see what happens."

Half an hour later, the camp counselor sees the two come up the hill, arm in arm. The boy who had stolen the cookies is earnestly trying to get Timmy to accept his jackknife in payment for the stolen cookies. And Timmy is just as earnestly refusing the gift from his new friend, saying that a few old cookies weren't that important anyway.

Well, that scenario might seem naive. Or it might work in summer camp but not in the boot camp we call the real world. But Jesus was not naive. What he proposes is a sensible, measured, mature process for reconciliation within the Christian community. If a person wrongs me, the first step is to confront the person, one on one. "Keep it between the two of you," he says. Don't blow it out of proportion. Make your case. Expose your wounds. Tell the other how the wrong has wounded you. Point out the fault but don't try to humiliate or embarrass the wrongdoer. Instead, do it in such a way that the fault line doesn't shake the foundation of the relationship. And since love is the foundation of any relationship that reflects the forgiveness of God, the first step in the process of premeditated mercy within the community is to name the pain while still claiming the love that forms the foundation of our relationship in Christ.

If the person listens and sees the wound caused by the wrong, the case is closed. But if the other fails to see how the wrong has caused a breach in the relationship, then Jesus advises a second step: "Summon another, so that every case may stand on the word of two or three witnesses." It seems this third person serves as a facilitator for forgiveness, a referee for reconciliation. This facilitator must be well versed in the process of pardoning. Listening with love, the facilitator seeks not just to point out the fault but to forge forgiveness.

However, if the facilitator is unable to bring reconciliation, the third step engages the entire camp, the whole community of the faithful. This third step brings the complaint out into the open. Now, while it appears the disagreement has taken on the look of a trial, there is no mention of judge or jury. Some might see this as the penalty phase of the proceedings, but there is no mention of punishment or condemnation.

If this third phase of the reconciliation process does not bring resolution, and the wrongdoer still fails to acknowledge fault, the fourth step of premeditated mercy that leads to reconciliation is the most radical of all. As we have seen, Jesus says the person at fault should be treated as a Gentile or a tax collector. This sounds like harsh punishment — it appears to mean excommunication. Since Gentiles and tax collectors were not welcome in the community, it seems the person at fault who fails to be reconciled is excluded from the table and expelled from the church.

And yet, if we think about this fourth phase of the premeditated mercy process in the context of Jesus' life and ministry, of how he treated the Gentiles and tax collectors, the radical notion of *reconciliation* comes into focus. Didn't Jesus say it was for such as these that he came into the world? Didn't Jesus welcome those outside the law to his table? Didn't he go out of his way to gather those who were lost or on the losing side of a dispute? Didn't Jesus practice a model of forgiveness that acknowledged the faults of those who followed him — and even if they did not acknowledge their own faults, did he not forgive them anyway? After all, reconciliation is for giving — for giving your life in love even for those who want to take your life.

While we look at the process of premeditated mercy that Jesus' outlines in Matthew's Gospel as a strategy toward reconciliation within the community, we need to remember that reconciliation is primarily a grace. It is a gift from God based upon the unconditional love of the Divine One. In the practice of premeditated mercy within the community, it is the grace of God that will help us gather the courage to confront the wrongdoer, name and claim the pain caused by the wounding, make our case as best we can, but ultimately, if all else fails, love the wrongdoer into doing what is right. This is the most radical recourse in the reconciliation process: to love the outcast, the one who has hurt us, the one who has wronged us. Whether the offender steals our cookies or steals our dreams, a spirituality of premeditated mercy always acts out of unconditional love and God's unlimited grace.

When we practice premeditated mercy in a group, we begin to see how with our faults — and maybe even through our faults — we are welcomed to the feast of forgiveness where there are more than enough cookies for everyone.

CARL: THE LOOSE CANON

In the summer camp scenario, the cookie thief was brought back to the table. But what happens when the person doesn't want to be reconciled with the community?

This is the story of a group known as the Canons Regular of the Round Table. One of the members of this group, however, had a reputation for being a loose canon.

The member of the round table often characterized as a loose canon was named Carl. While others followed orders, aiming only where they were told, and firing only upon command, Carl often dropped a bomb when it was least expected. He prided himself on having a mind of his own. Sometimes he would go off with no target directly in sight. He simply wanted to startle and shake the rest of the group from what he felt was their terminal state of sleep.

One day a good friend of Carl's invited him to lunch. "You know, Carl," this friend told him, "you have a reputation for shooting off your mouth and speaking your mind no matter whom you might hurt. The group is getting tired of the wounds you've inflicted. Though they admire your independence and respect your free spirit, they still very much want you to be part of the group. They want you to join us again around the table without worrying that you will shoot holes through every idea presented."

Carl appreciated his friend's concern and his invitation to return to the round table. But he told his friend that he enjoyed his reputation as a loose canon and felt that some of the rules and laws held by the group were unrealistic and unreasonable. He told his friend that too many of the other canons around the table were too concerned with aiming high — toward the sky — rather than setting their sights on targets closer to earth.

A few days later, this friend of Carl's invited him to a small gathering of other members of the round table. Because of Carl's reputation, the others were reluctant at first to accept the invitation. Finally they conceded when Carl's friend told them that he thought Carl was slowly coming around. But that night, Carl held his ground. Though the others made eloquent arguments in defense of the round table's strategy of aiming high, Carl kept focusing on what he felt the others were missing in their narrow view of truth. The others were astounded when Carl called them "narrow."

"Don't you see," they said, "that our vision includes everyone, even loose canons like you? Why else would we even bother to waste our time trying to convince you return to the round table?" But even though the group came to the meeting "loaded for bear" and released a full volley of ammunition in Carl's direction, nothing they said seemed to even dent his defenses.

Finally, a few weeks later, all the canons of the round table were called together for a meeting. There was only one item on the agenda: how to deal with this loose canon named Carl. Some argued that all relationship with Carl must be severed. "The time has come," they said, "for Carl to be dismissed. The time for talk is over; Carl must walk." So they presented a decree of excommunication, which meant, of course, that all communication with Carl from that day forward would cease. But others around the table pleaded with the group to give Carl another chance. "We can certainly work out our differences with Carl," this group said. "We just need more time to talk it through."

This group won the day, and Carl was summoned once more to appear before the canons of the round table. Carl appeared, fully loaded with his views and ready to unleash a barrage of his ideas. The canons of the round table also came prepared. Those who wanted Carl excommunicated were ready with documentation of every case they knew of Carl's smoking guns. Those who wanted Carl to remain as a canon of the round table also came ready with a battery of questions and a volley of the vision statements upon which the round table was founded.

The meeting began. All sides of every issue were placed upon the table. But when the smoke cleared, Carl was still not convinced that he could participate in the round table's plan. Those who were adamant about Carl's expulsion said that the time had come for Carl to be forever excommunicated from the Canons Regular of the Round Table. At this point Carl's friend stood and said, "That is not why we are here. We have followed the rules that have been passed on from generation to generation. We have allowed for due process to run its course. As canons of the round table, we are bound to one another in respect and reverence. We have come here today not for the purposes of excluding Carl from the round table but to try to include him in the vision to which we have been called. But if Carl freely chooses not to be part of this group, then he is free to go. The decision is his: to be bound by the vision that is larger than any of us and all of us or to be loosed upon the world to follow what he feels to be true." The others around the table nodded in agreement.

Carl looked at the faces of these friends he had known for years. For the first time he felt an insecurity inside. He'd always been so secure, so sure of himself. But after this friend had spoken, for the first time he felt wounded. His friend's words had penetrated his defenses. Yet, he couldn't stay. Deep inside he felt that if he stayed he would betray his very self. He was called to be the loose canon, and if he failed to live his call then his life would be over. With sadness in his eyes, he walked away. He left not with a final flurry of ammunition or with the kind of verbal assault of which he was so fond. Quietly, in silent retreat, Carl left the room where the canons of the round table were meeting and closed the door behind him.

The room seemed strangely silent. Even those who had passionately pursued Carl's expulsion seemed sad. For they knew that the whole point of the round table was that no one would be lost and that all would be welcome. They watched as Carl's friend went to the door that Carl had closed. He opened the door and then turned and said. "Now, my friends, let us pray that even though Carl closed the door behind him we will never close the door in front of him or anyone else."

SECURITY GUARDS FOR THE *KIN*DOM

As reconcilers of the round table, practitioners of premeditated mercy, we have a personal responsibility for the larger community. Our role as security guards for the *kin*dom of God means we are accountable to God and to the community that no person is lost. As security guards for the reign of God, we accept responsibility for checking the locks to the gates of our faith communities or houses of worship and making sure they are open for all. We walk the property and make sure there are enough holes in our security fences so that people can get inside. With flashlights pointing at the darkness, we look for any activity that might prevent the coming of the reign of God upon the earth. We search for any injustice, oppression, evil or indifference that lingers in the darkness and keeps the reign from reaching our house. When the light of this truth shines on the wickedness and holds it in the spotlight, we are responsible to correct it.

We cannot pass on this responsibility. We must respond. We do this quietly, personally. We don't make a federal case out of it. If any activity seeks to threaten the kindom, we confront it quietly but sternly. If the one engaged in this activity refuses to change, then, according to Jesus, we can call in another security guard for help. But if we fail to recognize and confront the evil, we will be held responsible. Now, there's the challenge! Instead of looking for others to blame, we embrace our responsibility to be security guards for sacred truth.

The motivation for being security guards for the kindom is that we are burdened by debt. We are so far in debt that we take this job as a security guard. Our debt is not financial but social. We owe a debt that binds us to "love one another." In our efforts to balance the budget, we can easily get into a pattern of "an eye for an eye, a tooth for a tooth." We can begin thinking in terms of balancing all our accounts — from friends to favors received: "I owe you one." But the fact is that we owe more than one; we owe our lives. This is the soul's standing debt. It is our motivation to be involved. We can never repay the love that God has bestowed on us. We can never crawl out of debt. We can never even the score or balance the soul's budget. We will always be in debt. But rather than being buried by it, we rise because of it.

I am not an economist, but my limited knowledge from the sound bites is that the larger the deficit the higher the interest rates. Lower the debt and interest rates go down. From the spiritual perspective this is certainly true. If we attempt to lower the debt of love by trying to repay the love others have showered upon us until we are even, then our rate of interest in the lives of others also goes down. We become satisfied. We think we have it made.

For interest rates to stay sky high, we must continue to add to the debt of love. This deficit spending includes spending time with those who have been left out of the spiritual recovery or have fallen through the safety (salvation) net. It means spending from our savings rather than holding on to our resources for our own security.

When we do this — when we focus our energies on finding those who are lost rather than on punishing them when we find them — we are reflecting the reign of God. And when we find those who, for whatever reason, have been going their own way rather than following God's way, we make every effort to win them over and bring them back to the table.

But what happens when we can't bring them back? What happens when — after we have exhausted all the avenues we know to show them the road of reconciliation that leads back home — they still go their own way? After we've made all the stops — of talking one on one; of bringing two or three others in to give witness and reflect their own faith stories; of bringing the one to the entire community in the hope that when that one senses love and not fear, pardon and not punishment, the desire for reconciliation and not the lust for revenge, the appetite for communion found in a piece of bread and not the hunger for vindication found in a pound of flesh — we hope the person will return to the community. But after all these steps have been taken and the person still feels he or she does not want to take part in this holy communion, then the person is "loosed" upon the world, free to go his or her own way. There is no binding arbitration here: If a person chooses not to participate in the unfolding of the reign of God, free will takes hold of the reins.

But even when the one runs away, the community is still challenged to gather and to pray. "For where two or three are gathered in my name, I am there among them" (Matthew 18: 19). The community never loses hope that the one who has chosen to walk away will one day return. The community never loses faith in the One who is present each time they gather to pray. The community never underestimates the power of this prayer to make even the loosest of ends meet.

As security guards for the kindom of God, love alone is our guiding principle. Love guards our open door. As companions at the round table we check the locks on the houses we call our hearts and make sure the doors are left open. We stop looking for scapegoats or others to blame and embrace our responsibility to be security guards who make sure each one finds a place at our round table.

FINDING COMMON GROUND

There are so many issues in society and in our communities of faith that seek to separate us and keep us apart. The Sufi poet and mystic, Rumi, offers a possible remedy for this sense of separation, an avenue by which we might find our common ground. He wrote in one of his poems, "Beyond the field of right-doing and wrong-doing, there is another field. I'll meet you there."

St. Paul put it this way: "In Christ Jesus you who were once far off have been brought near through the blood of Christ. It is he who is our peace, and who made the two of us one by breaking down the barrier of hostility that kept us apart" (Ephesians 2: 13-14).

Once upon a time, December, 1983, to be exact, I was a young priest assigned to parish ministry in Centerville, Iowa. The Cold War was still freezing the world as the nuclear arms race was lowering the temperature and the level of trust. The United States was deploying Pershing and cruise missiles in Europe. Pax Christi, a national peace organization, invited churches around the country to ring their church bells at noon on a particular Monday to protest this action taken by the government. And so, in the parish bulletin the Sunday before, I informed everyone that our parish would be participating and explained the reasons behind ringing our bells.

George, a very active and politically conservative member of the parish, ran to the rectory as soon as he read the bulletin. He confronted me about the church becoming involved in what he perceived to be a political action of protest. I knew George well and respected him because he was well-read and articulate about the issue. I had expected this kind of response. In fact, I would have been disappointed if I had not heard from George. We talked for an hour or so, debating the deployment of the missiles, the nuclear arms race and other social issues. Finally, I invited George to write a letter in the next parish bulletin, articulating why he felt I was wrong to ring the church bells.

"You won't print it if I write it," George said.

"George," I replied, "the parish bulletin belongs to you as much — even more — than it belongs to me. This is just the kind of discussion we should be having. Though we disagree, how will we ever reach any common ground unless we listen to each other? I only wish every parishioner had the passion you have to be so involved."

The next Sunday George's letter articulating his position appeared in the parish bulletin. In part, George wrote that "for the entire parish to be committed, by fiat, to a particular position, without discussion, and regardless of the opinions of many of the members, is wrong."

As a matter of routine, we sent our parish bulletin each week to *The Catholic Messenger*, the Davenport, Iowa, diocesan newspaper. A week later, *The Messenger* printed George's letter and ran it with their own editorial. In his piece, the editor wrote, "Discussion is crucial. The aim of discussion…is not unanimity. No action would ever be taken if it were. The aim is a fair airing and sharing of views so that the dignity of all involved is shown respect. Each person must be counted."

Though we disagreed on a number of social, political and ecclesial issues, George and I became friends. We respected each other's passion. We admired each other's courage in speaking out of his convictions. We challenged each other to see beyond our differences to the dignity, decency and devotion within each of our experiences. And every Sunday, we found ourselves standing on common ground: around the table of Eucharist.

As the editor of *The Catholic Messenger* pointed out, one of the tasks of premeditated mercy that leads to reconciliation at the round table is bringing peoples together, making sure that each and every person counts. No matter how divergent the views, how difficult it is to receive another's position on a particular issue, how wealthy one person might be or how poor another, how loudly one might be in expressing personal convictions or how quietly another, the challenge of premeditated mercy is to make sure all find a place at the table.

Jesus spent his life trying to gather the remnant, those on the fringe, those who had been left behind or set aside by society or synagogue. Because he was the embodiment of God's mercy, Jesus opened his heart to the wandering remnant. In our own lives, the practice of premeditated mercy raises the question: Who are the remnant in my life? Who are the people in my neighborhood, in my family, in my faith community, that I have pushed aside or left behind or given up on? Who are those with whom I find it most difficult to sit or stand at the table? Is it because of their ideology, their personality, their lifestyle?

At the round table, we are invited to meditate on the cup that is at the center of the table. When we premeditate mercy, we look into this cup of wine and see how we "who were once far off have been brought near through the blood of Christ" (Ephesians 2: 13). In lifting this cup, we celebrate God's mercy and go beyond the differences that might keep us apart to see the love that brings us near.

Though there are more than enough issues to keep us apart, the question the real presence poses for us in relation to reconciliation is, "How close do we want to stand with those with whom we disagree? How close can we stand to be?" When confronted with the people who are the most difficult to love, remember what Jesus' practice of premeditated mercy teaches: When all attempts at reconciliation fail, treat them as you would a Gentile or a tax collector. Welcome them to that round table which sits in the middle of the field beyond those other two fields of right-doing and wrong-doing.

I'll meet you there.

WHEN MENDING IS IMPOSSIBLE: A RITUAL OF ENDING

The approach we have outlined here reflects that the goal of practicing premeditated mercy in communal settings is to mend, not end, the relationship. After the impeachment process of President Clinton concluded with his acquittal, a debate arose on Capitol Hill about ending the Independent Counsel Law in the wake of the Kenneth Starr investigation. Those who were in favor of retaining rather than discarding the law talked in terms of "mending, not ending" the law.

Can the same be said for our relationships? Should we always strive to mend, not end, those relationships that have caused so much pain? If a trusted friend has committed "high crimes and misdemeanors" against you, justice may demand retribution or removal of the person from the "office" of friend. But mercy suggests that you mend, not end, the relationship.

Or does it? In the work of premeditated mercy, it is necessary at times to acknowledge that some relationships may not be recyclable — at least in their present form. When a relationship is beyond repair, when we have tried to fix the friendship but failed, when we have met in that field "beyond right-doing and wrong-doing" but are unable to find common ground and decide it's time to move on in different directions, to go our separate ways, we can celebrate the love we have shared but ritualize that our friendship is now in ruins. It can never be the way it was. We have changed. We are not the same people we were when the love was in its prime. Too much damage has been done; too many words have inflicted too many wounds. The love is ruined, beyond repair.

Some relationships are beyond mending; they must be ended. This is not an easy process. When we "clothe ourselves with heartfelt mercy" in a relationship that has worn out, is faded, torn or just full of holes, it is like an old sweater that has kept us warm on so many winter nights. This sweater has wrapped us with arms so calm and confident on long walks before the fall, when just a hint of autumn was in the air. This is the sweater we wore when we heard the news that a family member died. We felt the love of this friend reaching out across the miles to hold us and comfort us.

But since the betrayal, this sweater has not been out of the bottom of the drawer. We don't wear this sweater stained with betrayal anymore because we know it will never be "good as new." When going through our clothes at the change of seasons, we've been tempted to give the sweater to the Salvation Army Thrift Shop or to Goodwill. But the pain is so great — the heart still broken — that to give it away too soon would not be evidence of "good will" but rather "good riddance." In ritualizing that some relationships cannot be mended and must be ended, our intentions must be honest.

When the fabric of this friendship is caught on a nail of betrayal, the relationship is torn. Sometimes it's only a thread. We can keep pulling at the thread until the fabric unravels over months or even years. Or we can cut the string and be done with it. But either way there is no sense of sacred closure that reverences how important the relationship once was but will never be again.

When this nail of betrayal has damaged the fabric so deliberately and dangerously that ending not mending is the only alternative, ritualizing the loss may help us cross over to becoming a new creation. Once there was a woman whose husband betrayed her. He had an affair, and she asked for a divorce. After eleven years of marriage, the affair ended the relationship. Mending the torn fabric was not possible. When the divorce was final, this woman took a silk blouse from her closet, a blouse her husband had given her on their tenth anniversary. It was an expensive, beautiful blouse. As she held the blouse in her hand, she remembered how she felt that day. She remembered the joy she felt inside and the love reflected in the eyes of her spouse. But on this day, the day her divorce from her husband became the final nail in the coffin of their love, this woman took scissors and started to cut the piece of clothing into ribbons. She shredded the beautiful blouse.

But she did not discard the strips of silk that once was a gift from her former husband. Instead, she used the strips to tie her tomato vines to sticks to keep the vines from falling under the weight of the tomatoes.

This was for her a ritual of forgiveness. She knew she would never be reconciled with her former husband. They were divorced because of "irreconcilable differences." But in tying the vines to the sticks using the shredded gift of her former husband, she gave herself an image that helped her move on with her life. Like those vines drooping under the weight of the tomatoes, her life had touched the ground under the weight of her husband's betrayal. Now, using the strips of her silk blouse, she ritualized the death of the relationship symbolized in the divorce decree by signifying that her weight was lifted.

In tying those vines to the sticks, this woman who was betrayed by her husband discovered she was ready to move on and become a new creation.

Rituals of premeditated mercy that reflect how some relationships end and cannot be mended may be as simple and as sacred as going through the closet. We can find those clothes that connect us to or remind us of a person whose relationship was once held sacred and warm but now is cold, bringing only thoughts of betrayal instead of beauty. With heartfelt mercy, we take the clothes out of the closet and cut them into pieces. But rather than throwing out the patches and pieces of this relationship, we recycle the remnants of the relationship to create something new.

Like tying tomato vines to sticks in the garden.

In a ritual of ending, not mending, a relationship, mercy asks that I wish the other no harm, even when I do not wish to return to the way we were before the damage was done. I can pray the other will find success in future endeavors but acknowledge that I no longer desire to have that one by my side as a close and intimate friend. We reverence the other's path, bless each other's journeys and then turn and walk the other way with the prayer and the promise that we will meet again.

But not here. Not in the field we call friendship. We will meet instead at the place where justice and mercy meet: at the foot of the cross. We will meet in prayer, being brought to this place by a force beyond our power to resist: the blood of Christ. We give in to this power that draws all people near — the enemy and the enmity, the oppressor and the oppressed, the violent and the victim, the betrayer and the ambitious, the lover and the unloved, the forgiven and the unforgiven — until we stand again on the same ground, in the same field, at the crossroads of a relationship redeemed, if not recycled.

Prayer from the Crawl Space:
Celebrating God's
Extravagant Mercy

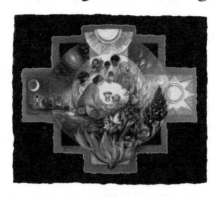

I wish I could live for a long time so that one day
I may know how to explain it;
if I am not granted that wish,
well, then somebody else will perhaps do it,
carry on from where my life has been cut short.
And that is why I must try to live a good and faithful life
to my last breath:
so that those who come after do not have to start all over again,
need not face the same difficulties.
Isn't that doing something for future generations?

— Etty Hillesum

The process of premeditated mercy makes us powerless before the awesome reality of another human life. But to paraphrase Paul's words, it is when we are the weakest that God's power and strength can flow through us. When we are weak and powerless, we begin to understand the great power of prayer and the grace of God that seeps through the cracks of our broken hearts. This prayer rises from our own experience of doubting that anything good might come out of a relationship that has been ruptured beyond repair. We have to trust that God will somehow, someway, deliver us. This brokenness with the other will tempt us to want to crawl into a hole and hide. Don't resist the temptation — at least if it means going into the soul's "crawl space."

Perhaps we have used the expression, "His words just stuck in my craw." According to Webster, the word *craw* is similar to the Greek word for trachea or throat. Indeed, this is where the words or actions of another get stuck, especially in our attempt to give voice to how we have been wounded by the other. But a second definition of craw offered by Webster is the stomach. The words or actions of another that cause us pain or make us angry can get stuck in the stomach. As we shall see later in this chapter, when this anger gets lodged in our stomach it becomes like acid that can damage us not only physically but spiritually as well.

With all due deference to Webster, I suspect the craw also has something to do with one's soul. So, when the words or actions of another get stuck in our craw, just add an "l" and call it your "crawl" space. The words that get stuck in our crawl space actually may not stay lodged there for long. They are like the mice that used to run under the floor of my cabin when I lived in the woods. They were looking for a hole or a crack to crawl inside to keep warm.

Words that have hurt us do the same. They run around beneath our soul's attention for awhile, but when it gets cold outside — when we don't feel the warmth of companionship either from friends, community, coworkers, family or spouse — these words look for an opening to come inside.

Once inside, the true meaning of these words surfaces through the cracks.

HONESTY: THE BEST MEDICINE

When the experience of betrayal comes inside our soul's crawl space, getting stuck, causing the acid of anger to bubble and boil inside, it is important that we name the pain. Honesty is the best medicine here. In order for naming the experience to lead to healing, we must be honest. For example, "He crushed my heart" seems to more honestly express the experience of betrayal than "He hurt my feelings." Betrayal is real, and the pain will last a long time.

How long? That is the question the prophet asked, "How long, O God?" (Habakkuk 1: 2). How long will I lick these wounds that scar my soul? Will I ever again feel comfortable in the presence of this person? Will I ever want to spend time in this person's company again? The answer is found when one spends time in one's crawl space. It's not a very comfortable place, but it could be a very sacred place if we use our time there to trace our wounds and discover the grace hidden within them. From this vantagepoint of the crawl space, one might also practice premeditated mercy and begin to look for some common ground.

In the silence of the crawl space of the soul, we might find a story or two that will help us enlarge this space and make us feel more at home. I discovered one such story recently when a small headline in the local newspaper caught my eye: "Ex-minister pleads guilty of murdering wife, will get life." The former minister pleaded guilty to second-degree murder to avoid the death penalty. And he received a life sentence. The intriguing aspect of this story is that the ex-minister lived with the parents of his dead wife for almost a year after the murder. She died while on a camping trip. The former minister was not a suspect initially. The mother of the woman who was murdered said, "We believed he was innocent. We loved him. We empathized with what we thought was his loss." As it turned out, they had harbored their daughter's murderer in their home for ten months. When he confessed and was sentenced, the dead woman's father offered a reason why the prayer of premeditated mercy that comes from the cracks of the soul's crawl space is so essential. "I refuse to get caught up in the bitterness and anger we feel towards him," the father said, "because it will make me an old man."

I suspect the father of the woman who was murdered spent a long time in his soul's crawl space to be able to resist the temptation to allow the bitterness and anger he felt to consume him. But he also had to be honest about the excruciating pain caused by the devastating loss of his daughter, and the subsequent betrayal of having the one who murdered his daughter live under his roof for almost a year after the crime. His statement revealed that he was not trying to seal the crack in the crawl space quickly or easily so he wouldn't feel the pain of his emotions. Rather, he knew the consequences if his anger and bitterness were to get the best of him. As we saw back in the first chapter, this is the danger when bitterness and anger get stuck in the crawl space and are not named for what they are: They get the best of us.

THE HEALING HANDS OF TIME

We discover the best in us when we find a quiet place in the soul's crawl space and listen for God's voice to whisper through the cracks, "You are mine." If we embrace the belief that we are God's beloved, that we belong to God, that God's image is imprinted upon our lives, we will find a safe place where God will confirm that reconciliation is different from mere forgiveness. I can forgive the friend whose words that betrayed a confidence or harsh words of condemnation left deep scars. But I also know that the place where the rupture occurred, though patched by pardon, will never be "good as new."

That's the fallacy about reconciliation in relationships: We're not trying to make it "good as new." Friendships are not furniture. Glue or patches will not work. The best we can do is arrive at a place of new understanding with the other, an understanding that comes from the grace of God's mercy. Here, the words of Rainer Maria Rilke serve us well: "Be of good courage, all is before you, and time passed in the difficult is never lost.... What is required of us is that we love the difficult and learn to deal with it. In the difficult are the friendly forces, the hands which work on us."

Are these the "hands of time," as in, "Time heals all wounds"? Or are these hands of the divine kind: the hands of God at work in the most difficult places in which we find ourselves, drawing forth from us a love we never knew existed within us. It's a love that holds even the one who betrayed us in our battered and bruised, but believing, heart. These hands, the hands of God, reach out to us in the darkness of the soul's crawl space. They massage our naked hope that even though we may never again be close to the person who hurt us we can learn to live in a more peaceful place with that person. We don't have to allow the bitterness and anger to make us old before our time.

Of course, the great danger in spending time in the crawl space comes with what we do with the time we find on our hands. Some people "mark time," a military term for marching while staying in place. We can keep ourselves busy without actually making any progress toward healing or reconciliation but simply fill up our time and space. Similarly, sometimes we kill time, wasting time in the crawl space until we become numb to the pain of our wounds. But remember what Henry David Thoreau once said, "One cannot kill time without injuring eternity."

So what do we do with this time on our hands in the soul's crawl space? We try to sit still and listen. We pay attention to the words that rise through the cracks. We sense the whisper of God gently breathing through these cracks to dislodge those words, those experiences, those events that are stuck in our crawl space. We allow the hands of God to work on our soul as we would let a physical therapist work on a muscle that has cramped. In the case of betrayal, of course, the muscle under attack is the heart muscle. Allow God to massage the heart in the silence of the soul's crawl space. For that is what betrayal is: an attack on the heart. The heart has cramped. We wonder if we will ever be able to love again.

When we are stuck in that crawl space, it may be helpful to write down what words we hear, what emotions we are experiencing. Writing may help to dislodge the pain stuck in the soul, but, again, we must be honest. Once, when I was confiding to my spiritual director an experience of betrayal that had left my heart broken and stalled, she asked if I was keeping a journal of my pain. Yes, I told her, I journal every morning, and often in these times I would write down my thoughts and feelings about the experience. I am right handed, so she suggested that I try using my left hand when I journaled about the experience. I was amazed when I followed her advice the next morning. Rather than writing with my right hand, trying to be neat, trying to stay inside the lines, with my left hand I wrote all over the page. I wrote down words that had been stuck in my crawl space for a long time. They tended to be words that reflected my anger over the experience of betrayal rather than just my hurt. With my left hand I was able to name the chaos caused by the betrayal in a way I had not been able to do with my right hand. When I finished, I looked at the page, and the words were not decipherable. But they didn't have to be read. They were now free from that crawl space. They were out in the open. The rage that had been stuck inside was now all over the page. I became unstuck.

Taking that page of raw rage from my journal, I went outside and set it on fire. I saw the words that had been stuck in my crawl space go up in flames. The smoke became like incense in search of a God who is merciful and kind.

Then, after ritualizing the release of words or events that have been stuck in the crawl space, it's time to enter the sanctuary of the soul and hold the image of the betrayer in prayer. Even if it's just for a moment, it may be enough. It may have to be enough. It's an attempt to find a way to get comfortable again in the discomfort caused by this relationship. You may recall how once you could slip into this friendship with such ease and calm. Now it will feel like an "uneasy" chair, an uncomfortable couch. As you sit down to pray, you might fidget and fuss, finding it difficult to be centered. It may feel like you can't sit still. But this is the soul suggesting you are feeling your way into another place. A more comfortable place. A place able to give you some comfort. A heart space where the brokenness creates a larger boundary. In the cracks of a broken heart, a few healing rays of light might seep in to warm the wound.

From that wounded place within your crawl space, you can begin to walk and to live again.

Turning Ourselves In

This crawl space within the soul is where true reconciliation and peace begins. Etty Hillesum, a victim of the Holocaust, wrote about this in her journal. "I really see no other solution than to turn inward and to root out all the rottenness there," she wrote. "I no longer believe that we can change anything in the world until we have first changed ourselves. And that seems to me the only lesson to be learned from this war." Her words ring with truth and power because they were written by one who experienced the absolute in evil that human beings can inflict upon one another.

There are times in our lives when we are confronted with so much evil, so much violence and so much suffering in our world that the words of Jeremiah must surface from the soul's crawl space and find their voice: "You duped me, O God, and I let myself be duped; you were too strong for me, and you triumphed" (Jeremiah 20: 7). These words rattle around like so many dry bones in the crawl space of our souls.

Jeremiah laments that God is too strong for him. Though he wants to quit, to give up and give in, still he remains faithful. Though he feels the sting of rejection, of being the "object of laughter," of being "mocked" for the positions he's taken and the words he's spoken; though he tried to "cry out" against injustice but found that God's word "has brought me derision and reproach" (20: 8), still, the prophet remains passionate about proclaiming this word. And he knows it is only through God's grace that he remains a prophet.

No doubt there have been many moments in our lives when we have felt like Jeremiah: "I say to myself, I will not mention God, I will speak God's name no more" (20: 9). There have been times when throwing in the towel, raising the white flag, turning ourselves in all seemed like reasonable responses to the experience of being duped.

But it is in the phrase, "turning ourselves in," that we might experience surrender to God's mercy, and God's grace might become a real presence in our fractured and wounded lives. When we surrender to God's will, when we turn ourselves in, we are caught in the glare of God's gaze and grace. It is at that moment of surrender, of turning inward, that God's word "becomes like fire burning in my heart, imprisoned in my bones; I grow weary holding it in, I cannot endure it" (20: 9).

This fire becomes too hot for one to hold inside for long. Turning oneself in, sitting too close to the fire, one's soul is singed. One begins to smell smoke coming from the caverns of one's crawl space. Yes, this prophet who has turned himself in and over to God is smoking! With nowhere to go but out, Jeremiah's words become like darts of fire that land on dry fields of grass or in bales of hay rolled and waiting to be picked up, setting them on fire. The world is afire because a prophet has turned himself in, surrendered to God's will and discovered the fire inside.

When one "turns oneself in," one becomes what Paul describes as a "living sacrifice, holy and acceptable to God" (Romans 12: 1). We become these living sacrifices, Paul writes to the Romans, "through the mercy of God." Only when we turn ourselves in will God's mercy get all the way through. But when it does, we catch fire. The body of one consumed by God's word, God's mercy, becomes suitable for grilling.

If we carry this image of grilling a bit further, we know how barbecue can be done on the outside but still rare, still unfinished, on the inside. Paul understands the spirituality of barbecue: "Do not conform yourselves to this age but be transformed by the renewal of your mind so that you may judge what is God's will, what is good, pleasing, and perfect" (12: 2). Paul encourages an inner transformation that can only occur when we "turn ourselves in."

People who proclaim God's mercy do not conform to the conventional wisdom of the day. In that *Newsweek* box that charts the conventional wisdom about famous figures each week, the arrow of reconcilers and prophets of premeditated mercy would always point down. That's because this is the "prophet's margin" — down and out. Conformity and acceptance in society's eyes — or even the eyes of the institutional faith community — is not the prophet's passion.

We can test our passion for being a prophet of reconciliation very simply, as simply as sticking a fork in a piece of barbecue to see if it's done. If we are still trying to conform, striving for acceptance and looking for applause, then we are not done. We are not finished. We have some more turning ourselves in to do. We have not taken enough risks for the sake of the truth. We have not held out for the only truth that really matters: the truth God has spoken to us in silence when we have turned ourselves in.

This is mercy's challenge: to turn ourselves in. Most of us are still on the loose, running free, hiding out, wearing various disguises, fugitives in search of a two-handed God. We are desperadoes who are desperate to be found, to be caught, to be turned in. Maybe that's why betrayal, as costly and painful as it is, becomes a metaphor for spiritual growth. If the fugitive doesn't turn himself in, a friend spots him and does it for him. This friend goes to the authorities with the whereabouts of the fugitive. The authorities surround the house where the prophet is hiding. "Come out with your hands up," the voice blares through the megaphone. This is the position of surrender: hands up.

It is also the posture for prayer.

If the fugitive prophet can't turn herself in, another can do it for her. And this betrayal will lead to that crawl space of solitude where, as Jeremiah said, the word becomes "imprisoned in my bones."

RESISTING ARREST: TURNING ONESELF INSIDE OUT

We have reflected on Jesus' experience of being betrayed by Judas. Though this is certainly his most dangerous and destructive experience of betrayal, since it leads directly to his death, it is not Jesus' only experience of being betrayed. Earlier in Matthew's Gospel Jesus experiences one of his closest friends turning his back on this messianic mission of premeditated mercy. Long before Peter, under the bright light of the campfire in the courtyard, denies that he even knows the recently arrested rabbi, his penchant for missing the point of Jesus' mission is revealed. Jesus tells his closest friends that he would have to go to Jerusalem "to suffer greatly there at the hands of the authorities." In Matthew's telling of this story (16: 13-28), Peter has just proclaimed Jesus as the Messiah and is publicly praised by Jesus as the "rock of ages" (See 16: 18). But the next moment, when Jesus spells out the implications of the messianic mission, Peter will not hear it. He takes Jesus off to the side and says, "No, don't turn yourself in." Peter wants to spare his teacher that dangerous journey to Jerusalem. "God forbid that any such thing ever happen to you" (16: 22), he tells Jesus.

If God forbids the fugitive Messiah from being turned in — either by himself or another — salvation remains out of reach. Peter is still following conventional wisdom about the kind of Messiah he was expecting: one who would overthrow the current regime, one who would expel the demons of oppression with the force of a mighty military campaign. Peter is still being a conformist in his attitude about the ways of the world, which say, "Never turn yourself in." Instead, Peter turns himself inside out trying to deny that Jesus must die.

So what does Jesus do? He turns on Peter. Jesus says, "Get out of my sight, you Satan!" (16: 23). Peter's fortunes turn immediately. The "rock of ages" begins to crumble. From being moved to the head of the class for his answer, "You are the Messiah," Peter is in danger of being expelled from the school of sanctity. "You are not judging by God's standards," the teacher says, "but by human standards" (16: 23).

Peter had not as yet embarked on the faithful footpath of the fugitive. He was still trying to conform his feet to the "one size fits all" model offered by the world. Though he started off well, leaving his fishing business and following in the footsteps along the beach, now he discovers how the tide has washed away those footprints in the sand. Instead of being the rock of ages, his bold proclamation of faith is nothing more than a sandcastle that collapses when the tide changes.

Nonconformity is mercy's call, and turning oneself in — or having others do it for you — is the way one becomes a prophet of premeditated mercy. Once Peter removes his conformist foot from his mouth, he will find his footing again. But first he must turn himself in and listen to what the prophet says: "If you wish to come after me, you must deny your very self, take up your cross, and begin to follow in my footsteps" (16: 24).

The fugitive's footsteps follow a path that contradicts conventional wisdom: "Whoever would save one's life will lose it, but whoever loses one's life for my sake will find it" (16: 25).

Turning herself in, the prophet of premeditated mercy learns to deny her gifts, her desires, her dreams, her very self while beginning to see all in the light of God's dream for her and the world. Steeped in the denial of himself, the prophet learns to lose — to be a good loser. Conventional wisdom tells us to win at all costs. But wise coaches will tell you that losing often builds more character than winning. Being a winner, so central to the world's view — in which all are divided into camps of winners and losers — teases the prophet into complacency. Being a loser, however, causes the prophet to turn inward, away from the applause and the awards, to look for the inner strength, that inner fire in the soul's crawl space that will burn away those conformist attitudes of the way things are.

Here is the prophet's margin of error: "What profit would one show if one were to gain the whole world and ruin oneself in the process?" (16: 26). There is nothing one can offer in exchange for one's very self. Mercy's challenge is to deny that self, turn it over to God, turn oneself in, and find the prophet's margin of victory.

This becomes the prayer of the prophet who practices premeditated mercy:

A Psalm of Turning Oneself In

Help me, O God, to turn myself in.
I give myself over to your will for my life.
I know how often I run from your love,
how I set off in a different direction
than the one you have in mind for me.
O God, give me the courage
to surrender my life into your hands,
to allow you to do with me what you will.
Help me to learn a new language
where every sentence begins not with "I will,"
but with "your will be done."
This is a life sentence
not a death penalty.
Denying myself leads not to diminishment
but to fuller life.
No longer feeling duped,
may I feel the fire of your love
and follow.

In these moments of prayer when we turn ourselves in, we discover the extravagant mercy and compassion of God that will give us the grace and the courage to love without limits.

EQUAL JUSTICE AND EXTRAVAGANT MERCY

We have already referred to some of the premeditation exercises that help to deepen this quality of mercy that teaches us to love without limits. When we practice these premeditation exercises on a daily basis, we will discover remarkable staying power — the ability to hold in prayer even those we find most difficult to love — and astonishing stamina — the ability to go the extra mile. We will find that when another has injured us, our first inclination is not to strike back but to forgive. When we experience persecution of any kind, our first impulse is to pray for those who treat us unjustly. When we identify another as an enemy, our first decision is to love that person. When someone asks us for a handout, we reach into our pocket without judgment or question. When someone asks us for clothes for the poor, we pick out our good coat.

This behavior seems foolish in the eyes of the world. That's why turning oneself in becomes so imperative. In an outer world where it seems cowardly to turn the other cheek, in our inner crawl space we develop a strength that holds the prayerful possibility of transforming the other. In an outer world where resistance to injury seems a precursor for appeasement, in our inner space our prayer for the persecutors seeks to touch the goodness in them, no matter how far beneath the surface that goodness is buried.

Jesus reflected this extravagant mercy of God in a parable about a king and a servant. This parable is told in the context of Peter trying to learn the mathematics of mercy. Peter asks Jesus, "How often shall my brother or sister sin against me and I still forgive them. As many as seven times?" (Matthew 18: 21). Jesus' response is, "I say to you, not seven times, but seventy times seven" (18: 22). Then, to explain this remarkable multiplication of mercy, Jesus tells the parable about "the king who wished to settle accounts with his servants."

This parable has long mystified me. We read how the servant who owes the king an incredible amount pleads his case before the ruler. He asks for more time to pay off the debt. But the king is so moved by the servant's plea that he writes off the entire debt. If the king had only given the servant an extension, one could understand the pressure the servant might be feeling and why he might be motivated to try to collect his own outstanding loans. But the king has written off the whole debt, and so the servant's motivation in the way he handles the one who owes him money — which is a "mere fraction" of what he owed the king — is baffling. No wonder the others are "badly shaken" (18: 33). He is totally free of all his debt. He doesn't owe a thing. He has a clean slate. So why does he treat his fellow servant who owes him a pittance with such disdain and disregard?

Could it be that the king's pardon is just too extravagant for the servant to comprehend? Could it be that the servant has incorporated society's standard system of debits and credits so deeply that he can't possibly understand the king's generosity? Could it be that he has learned the law so well, the legal system that views justice in the familiar line, "an eye for an eye, a tooth for a tooth," that he is only capable of operating out of this strategy of checks and balances?

"Seventy times seven" announces a new system of justice that is based on God's extravagant mercy rather than the ancient approach to justice that focused on equal exchange. Even though the servant has to be thrilled that the king forgives his debt, which in modern terms would amount to billions of dollars, he is still functioning out of the old model that says, "Pay back every cent you owe." Though his fellow servant only owes him what amounts to a day's wage, the forgiven servant is not capable of extending credit.

Since many of us still live out of such a strategy of justice, the servant's response should not surprise us. And because this new system of justice based on God's excessive mercy is still so difficult for most of us to comprehend, the actions of the forgiven servant toward his fellow servant is lived out every day in large and small ways. For many in our world today, revenge still tastes sweeter than reconciliation.

A few years ago, I was watching a special on television in which a reporter had spent a few days on death row with a man scheduled to be executed. It was an extraordinary glimpse into the eyes of a man who had lived on death row for fourteen years. All his appeals were exhausted, and his execution was imminent. The reporter interviewed the prison's warden, who had struck up a friendship with this inmate but would be the one to give the signal for the man's execution. The reporter also spoke at length with family members of the two people that this prisoner had been convicted of murdering. The murders had occurred more than fifteen years before, but the wounds inflicted by this felon were fresh in their minds and hearts. One man, whose father had been murdered by this man, met with the prisoner a few days before he died. He understood on a rational level that this prisoner had undergone some kind of conversion experience in prison. He had changed. The murdered man's son did not deny it. But he could not find it in his heart to forgive this prisoner for murdering his father. He kept reliving the horror of the crime committed against his father. And in his heart, the one who killed his father deserved to die. He demanded equal justice: a life for a life.

But the most gripping scene to me was on the night of the execution as the prisoner's family gathered outside the gates of the penitentiary where the man was scheduled to die at one minute after midnight. The convicted man's son, who was in his late teens or early twenties and who had been featured earlier in the day when the family gathered one last time with the prisoner on death row, now became engaged in a heated argument with an elderly couple sitting in lawn chairs just outside the gates of the prison. The reporter interviewed this couple, who said they traveled to every execution scheduled in the state to cheer the death of the prisoner. Since this was Louisiana, which has one of the country's highest number of executions, it had become almost a full-time job. Though this couple did not know the man about to die and only knew some of the circumstances surrounding the case, their involvement was very personal. More than ten years before, their only daughter had been murdered. They decided then to make it their crusade to see that every person convicted of murder pay for the crime committed with his or her own life. The anger they still felt over their daughter's murder was evident on their faces and clear in the words they shouted to the son of the man who would die that night.

THE ACID OF ANGER: BURNING A HOLE IN ONE'S SOUL

Someone once said that "anger is an acid that can do more harm to the vessel in which it stands than to anything on which it is poured." This acid was evident in the elderly couple whose daughter had been murdered. Their anger at the one who killed their daughter was eating them alive. Even the execution of their daughter's murderer did not satisfy their hunger for revenge. They felt the acid of their anger burn in their stomach every time they read about another murder in their local newspaper or heard about a crime on the evening news. Their appetite for revenge was insatiable. So they continued to feed their anger by attending executions.

In each life there arise situations of immeasurable loss, when anger seems the only appropriate response, when the desire for revenge blinds us to reconciliation as a possible remedy. These are situations in which the decision to nourish the anger or begin feeding on forgiveness can become a daily choice, a daily reminder of the acid that burns in the pit of our souls.

Certainly this couple's anger at the murder of their daughter was justified at the time of their devastating loss. But when that anger becomes the sole motivation, fueling an insatiable appetite for revenge, where does mercy have a chance to come in?

This is the point at which we find the new system of God's justice difficult to stomach. In telling the parable about the extravagant mercy of the king and the frugal forgiveness of the servant, Jesus is saying to his disciples that we are to extend God's mercy to others. But when we have been hurt so deeply, when our loss is so enormous, when the wound is so grievous, how it is possible to think in terms of excessive mercy rather than equal justice?

Indeed, there are certain crimes that turn one's stomach and maybe even one's soul. Hate crimes come to mind — crimes so cruel and vicious that when we hear the details of the violence, not only does our stomach turn but our heart begins to harden. When I first heard of the brutal murder of James Byrd, Jr. in Jasper, Texas, in June, 1998, I sensed this acid of anger within my soul. The viciousness of the crime made national headlines: Three young white men tied a black man to the bumper of their pickup truck and dragged him over a gravel road for almost three miles until he was decapitated as his head hit a drainage ditch. The testimony at the trial was gruesome. News commentators cautioned listeners that some of the details might not be suitable for some listeners — especially the young or the weak in stomach or soul.

Then, in early 1999, when the first of the three defendants, John William King, was found guilty of this murder, I felt some relief from the acid of anger. When the jury sentenced him to die by lethal injection, there was a part of me that applauded the decision. This surprised me because I am opposed to the death penalty. But if anyone should receive the death penalty, I thought, certainly it should be someone like King. His crime was so atrocious, so horrible, so heinous, and his attitude to the Byrd family following the verdict so vindictive, so vicious, so cruel, that King would certainly be the prime candidate for an exception to my opposition to the death penalty. As Lance Morrow wrote in an essay in *Time* magazine after the death sentence was given, "To object to putting King to death for the deed requires a saintliness I do not possess." Even John William King's body language — the kind of body language that was indelibly etched on the skin in the form of tattoos that covered his body — proclaimed without shame the hate this young man held in his heart.

In the pictures I saw of him on the television news or the reports and stories I read about him in the newspaper and magazines, John William King appeared to me to be the incarnation of evil. Is it possible that any one person is beyond redemption? Is it possible that a person is so filled with evil that not even a merciful and loving God can spare him? Are there people so filled with hate that there is no shred of decency and human dignity left? In King's case, it was his hate that fueled his anger and threatened to destroy the vessel of his life. And now the jury was taking the decision to live or to die out of his hands. They sentenced him to death.

As I was sitting at the kitchen table reading about the jury's verdict, a thought flashed through my mind. I don't know where it came from or why, but thinking about the crime committed by John William King, I thought of an incident in the Scriptures where another particularly vicious crime took place. A young man named Stephen, a deacon in the religious reform movement that began following the death and resurrection of the rabbi named Jesus, was taken outside the city and stoned to death (See Acts 7). As in the case of James Byrd, Jr., hate was the fuel that caused this crime. It was a hate sparked by fear and ignorance.

While the young deacon, Stephen, was being stoned to death, there was another young man standing by, holding the cloaks of those who were throwing the stones. He was not participating in the vicious crime by throwing the rocks that would kill Stephen, but he was surely an accomplice. He was complicit in the crime, no less guilty than a person driving the getaway car at a bank robbery or than one of the other young men riding in the front seat of that pickup truck that King was driving as James Byrd, Jr. was dragged to his death.

The accomplice in the murder of Stephen was a young man named Saul.

We know the rest of this story. Saul was so filled with hate toward this new movement that arose out of the Spirit of Jesus that he willingly participated in the violent death of one of the movement's early leaders. If he were caught for his crime of being an accomplice to this murder, would he not be liable to judgment, to imprisonment and possibly to a sentence of death?

Saul was caught, of course. Not by the authorities but by the Almighty. He was knocked from his horse by a bolt of lightning and his whole life began to change. The force of that thunderbolt began to change the contents of the vessel of his heart. Once filled with anger, rage and hate, a holy electrocution began to turn the contents of that vessel into love. The passion remained the same. The vessel remained full. But now the contents were changed.

God did this.

Is it possible that God can still do this even to the most vicious and evil people this world creates? Did God create John William King to be evil? Did God create Adolph Hitler or Slobodan Milosevic or Saddam Hussein to be evil? Do we believe that God can turn great hate into great love?

Or must we be satisfied that some people are beyond redemption and so deserve their fate, deserve to die? People like John William King, who is so full of hate that he would probably only kill again in prison if sentenced to life instead of death.

The hate crimes against James Byrd, Jr. and Matthew Shephard, the gay college student in Laramie, Wyoming, who was crucified on a fence post and left to die, leave me seething with anger. There is no question the perpetrators of these crimes should be convicted and sentenced to life imprisonment with no possibility of parole. But the death penalty in its present form and as it is practiced in the United States does not quiet the acid of anger in the loved ones of the victims of these vicious crimes, nor does it seem to deter future hate crimes. Capital punishment places life and death decisions not in the hands of God but in the hands of the state, in our hands, in human hands. We decide who shall live and who shall die. We decide who might be rehabilitated and who is beyond redemption. In doing so, the cycle of violence continues, and we become ever more what Pope John Paul II has called "a culture of death."

Imagine if we had been on the jury of those charged with the murder of the young deacon named Stephen. Imagine if one of those brought to trial had been a young man named Saul. Imagine if we had voted to convict Saul as an accomplice to this gruesome crime. In an "eye for an eye" legal system of justice, Saul would have to receive the same punishment he and the others had inflicted on Stephen: death by stoning.

But the conversion of Saul into the apostle Paul invites us to believe what we cannot understand: how a person like Saul, who displayed such remarkable passion in persecuting people, could be turned around to use that same passion in proclaiming to people the wonders of God's love. The Saul story challenges us to be open to what only God knows well enough to see: that within every human heart, no matter how vicious or evil, there is a faint glimmer of grace, which God can use to change a person completely.

Though on the surface the Saul story (See Acts 9: 1-19) suggests that some people change in the flash of a lightning bolt from the sky, as we read further into this story of conversion we hear that conversion — our own and others' — does takes time. When Saul was knocked from his horse, he wasn't converted right away. He went to a house in Damascus where he spent time in prayer, in the darkness of his soul's crawl space, trying to figure out what had happened to him on the road. Remember that he was still blind from the light he had experienced.

Remember, too, that God asked a man named Ananias to go to Saul and help him see the light. Because of all he heard about Saul's persecution of Christians, Ananias was not anxious to get involved. But he went anyway because God works like this — in mysterious ways. A reluctant Ananias helped Saul recover his sight. In the course of their conversation, the Scripture says, "something like scales fell from Saul's eyes and he regained his sight" (Acts 9: 18). Only after his inner heart was able to see what his eyes could not was Saul ready to accept baptism and receive the Holy Spirit. Then the Scripture says he "stayed some time with the disciples in Damascus" (9: 19).

The story says that our transformation in the real presence of the Risen Christ and our ability to premeditate mercy takes time. We have to be open to surprise from those in our lives we know too well. You never know when lightning might strike and when a person we find most difficult to love suddenly might become easy to like. It can happen, you know. It happened to Saul.

Remember, please, that this book is about mercy not justice. But justice, if not tempered with mercy, becomes only blind revenge.

And the acid of anger will then burn a hole in our collective souls.

A STEADY DIET OF PRAYER

When we have been injured by someone, when we have experienced a loss caused by another or a deep wound inflicted by another, when we have been betrayed by someone we trusted or felt the sting of rejection from someone we counted on as a friend, how do we respond? Each of us has known misunderstandings that have multiplied over time and left us fighting through a maze of regret and remorse. Likewise, each of us has spoken a word or done a deed that has injured another in some way and felt the need to be reconciled. When we pray the familiar words, "forgive us our debts as we forgive our debtors," we understand on a gut level what those words mean and imply. Yet we also know how strong the impulse is for revenge and how difficult it is to develop an appetite for reconciliation.

But each of us has also experienced on some level the mercy and compassion of our God and the forgiveness of our sins. As we see in the parable about the generous king and the miserly servant, we are not easily able to extend this mercy and compassion to those who have hurt us. Indeed, God's strategy of justice based on extravagant mercy is different from the system of justice based more on fairness than forgiveness. So how do we learn this very different system? How do we memorize it and memorialize it? How do we acquire a taste for reconciliation rather than an appetite for revenge? How do we develop a steady diet based on the forgiveness phrase in the Lord's Prayer?

The first step is to keep coming back to the table of the Eucharistic meal. Then, we might carefully look at the menu as we sit at the table in God's restaurant (a word, by the way, which means "to restore"). At this table of holy communion with God, we are not given many entrees from which to choose. As we've come to see in practicing the premeditation in this book, the main entree for this meal of memory is mercy. We remember how on the very night he was betrayed, denied and abandoned, Jesus came to the table, broke bread and poured wine. In doing these two actions, he inaugurated a new system of justice that reflects a spirituality of premeditated mercy.

In breaking the bread and saying, "This is my body," Jesus invites us to develop a taste for reconciliation even amid the ruptures we experience in our relationships with others. He is not just saying that mercy is the only cure for whatever is ailing in the body of Christ we call the church. He is also offering the only source of nourishment that can sustain us adequately in this practice of forgiveness.

In passing around the cup of wine and saying, "This is my blood," he invites us to drink the nectar of God, the sweet wine of mercy and compassion that alone can bring healing to those deep wounds that fester within our hearts and souls. He tells all of us to take this and drink because this new vintage replaces the old vintage that left a bitter taste in our mouths. This new vintage, he says, "is poured out for you and for all" — not just for the innocent but for the guilty as well — "so that sins might be forgiven." The forgiveness of sins is the point of Jesus pouring out his blood, offering his life, for all.

The practice of premeditated mercy acknowledges that reconciliation with those who have hurt us is a grace from God. With a steady diet of prayer, we stretch our souls to be open to this grace. It is only through the power of God's mercy that we will ever find the courage to be merciful. It is only through the power of God's grace that we will ever be able to develop an appetite for reconciliation and forever forego the taste for revenge.

But remember, it is a taste we must develop and acquire over time. The grace is always there, but because we have nibbled on junk food for so long it takes time. The only thing that is asked of us as we gather at the table is to try this new diet of God's mercy and forgiveness, and to pray for the grace and the courage to stick to this diet when we leave God's restaurant.

TRYING A NEW PLACE

We can ritualize this grace of reconciliation at all the tables of our lives. Let's say, for example, there's a favorite place where you and a close friend enjoy sharing a meal. Perhaps, it's a restaurant where the food is good, the service is great and the atmosphere is approaching intimate. You can have a conversation with this friend without the people at the next table hearing every word. You have met your friend at this place for lunch or dinner for several years. At the table, you talk about life, family, work and even faith. This is your place, a favorite place to meet.

But let's say you and your friend have a falling out. Notice the direction of the disintegration of relationship: falling and out. This distance could be caused by many things — something you said or something the other said, something the other didn't say or you didn't do. Or it could be something much worse, like a betrayal of a confidence that left you falling and out of sorts. This breakup — or is it a breakdown? — begins to settle into resentment. Instead of settling the feud, the feud settles into distance. You might wish someone would break up this fight because the breakdown in communication has caused a fracture in the friendship.

After spending sufficient time in the crawl space of your soul, allowing the wound to breathe and prayerfully listening for God's whisper, "You are mine," let's say you work up the nerve to call your friend. You make a reservation for lunch at the restaurant that's your favorite place to meet with your friend. But because this was the place where the friendship began to unravel, your friend says, "Let's try a new place."

Reconciliation is about restoring relationship by moving to a new place. It is not going back to the old place that held so many memories, though we must visit there now and then to name the pain that the breakup — or down — has caused in our lives. Reconciliation tries to bring us to this new place. In the practice of premeditated mercy, we try to move to this new place, experience a new integration, become a new creation.

In the stories of Jesus after his resurrection, he tried to restore relationship with his brokenhearted disciples at three different "restaurants": the upper room, where he said, "Have you anything to eat?"; the house in Emmaus where he took bread and broke it; and the place on the beach where he cooked breakfast for his disciples. In each of these encounters, he tried to move his friends to a new place, a place of restoration and reconciliation.

The prayer of premeditated mercy that rises from the crawl spaces of our souls invites us to believe that what Jesus did for his disciples after his resurrection God desires to do for us in all of our relationships. We can move to a new place where all peoples of the earth are invited in order to restore the broken spirits and souls of all humanity. The "special" at God's restaurant *each day* is mercy. It may seem too much for us; certainly it is more than we can digest at one sitting. But rather than pushing the plate away, we can take a small piece of bread and a tiny sip of wine, and know we can never go back to the old place. The old diet of revenge has only caused acid to burn in the crawl space of our stomach. But now a new fire is ignited in those depths as our addiction to anger is broken. From the crawl space of our soul we have moved to a new place where each day we try this new diet of premeditated mercy. With God's hands of time working on us, we begin to see a change. We begin to live healthier, happier and holier lives.

Drinking the Cup of Mercy:
Sipping Sour Wine
and Swallowing Hope

How well chosen wine was to stain our souls with remembrance.
He knew how it burst, vivid from the flushed skins of grapes
grown for this sacramental crushing:
a shocking red, unforgettable as blood,
a rich brew in the cup,
a bitter burning in the throat,
a warmth within....

— Luci Shaw

In the recipe for reconciliation we considered in Chapter Two, one of the main ingredients is a cup of blessing, a grateful heart. But we know from experience how that chalice of blessing can also resemble a cup of sorrow and suffering. The cup of our lives can hold more than its fair share of the sour wine of bitter memories, betrayals and broken dreams — those times when we realize that life is not fair. So at this point in our premeditation we need to ask: How do we drink from this cup of suffering and still swallow hope?

There is a prayer from the Sufi tradition that has become a favorite of mine. It reflects how this transformation can take place in the chalice of our hearts:

> O Divine One, to thee
> I raise my whole being,
> a vessel emptied of self.

Accept, O gracious God,
this my emptiness,
and so fill me with thyself —
thy light, thy love, thy life —
that these thy precious gifts
may radiate through me
and overflow the chalice of my heart
into the hearts of all those
with whom I come in contact this day —
revealing unto them the beauty
of thy joy and wholeness
and the serenity of thy peace,
which nothing can destroy.

This Sufi prayer echoes Paul's hymn to the Philippians, the song of Jesus "who, though he was in the form of God, did not consider equality with God a thing to be grasped, but rather he emptied himself, taking the form of a servant, being born in human likeness" (Philippians 2: 6-7). This hymn also resounds in the teachings of Jesus, who told his disciples to deny their very selves, take up their crosses and follow in his steps. The chalice of our hearts must be empty of all bitterness and ambition before it can be filled with the light, love and life poured out by God's mercy. So it seems that before we can become merciful, we must be empty. In the words of a prayer attributed to St. Romuald, "Empty yourself…and sit waiting, content with the grace of God."

In the twentieth chapter of Matthew's Gospel we taste and see how difficult this is for those who aspire to practice premeditated mercy. After their mother has pleaded on their behalf that Jesus find them a high place at heaven's table, Jesus asks James and John, "Are you able to drink the cup that I am to drink?" (Matthew 20: 22). There are three separate scenes in this story that illuminate how we learn to empty ourselves in order to become merciful — full of mercy.

In the first scene, Jesus tells the disciples that his destination is Jerusalem, where he must suffer and die. He says this after taking "the twelve disciples aside by themselves" (20: 17). Jesus is passing along inside information. He's telling them what is stirring inside of him. He's putting his heart on the table, his soul's secret on the line.

But in the very next scene, two of his disciples cross the line. The mother of James and John asks Jesus a favor. She believes that Jesus is the Chosen One who will initiate a new creation. Out of her devotion to her sons — who, remember, left her and her husband Zebedee "high and dry" when they followed Jesus that day on the beach — this woman of faith wants her sons to be taken care of when all this is said and done. But also remember that James and John's mom is not privy to the inside information about Jesus' destination. That is why Jesus says to this woman, "You do not know what you are asking" (20: 22).

But her boys do. Jesus has just told them about his impending suffering and death. So, more pointedly, Jesus now asks them, "Are you able to drink the cup that I am about to drink?" (20: 22). They say they are. This response, however, leads to the third scene when all ambition breaks loose and the disciples are so full of themselves there is no room for mercy.

CAN WE DRINK THIS CUP?

As we look into the chalice of our heart, we might be tempted to blurt out as James and John did, "Well, yes, of course we can!" (20: 22). But when we take this cup and really look into it, we might pause and ponder the implications of the question. When we look at this cup and see how it has caught our tears from sorrows we can barely name, from pain we can barely claim, from wounds we want to forget, we need to ask if we can really drink this cup.

When we see how this cup has caught our fear of loving without counting the cost, can we drink this cup? When we fear changes that are coming too quickly or too slowly, can we drink this cup? When we see how this cup has caught the shame we cannot help but embrace or our guilt that is so pervasive that forgiveness seems out of reach, can we drink this cup?

When we see how this cup has caught our indifference at another's suffering, or our blindness to the look of regret in another's eyes, or our silence in the face of injustice, can we drink this cup?

When we see how this cup has caught the words another has spoken that hurt us to the core, or the anger that simmers on our soul's back burner, can we drink this cup? When we see how this cup has caught the lack of appreciation we feel, or the want of encouragement we need, or the busyness that consumes our days, or the loneliness that lingers through the night, can we drink this cup?

When we see how this cup holds the courage to speak our truth though we know we'll be opposed, lose a few friends, distance a few relatives, unsettle a few superiors, rattle a few cages, see a few hands close into a fist, can we drink this cup?

Can we drink this cup when we know the vintage it holds will make us bold in living — and maybe even in dying — for what we believe? Dying not for ideas or an ideology, or even for causes no matter how just, but for the sake of real people. Can we drink this cup?

Can we drink this cup when a single sip might take us on a trip through killing fields marked with crosses, landscapes littered with losses, until we arrive at a lonely hill where we will be stripped and shamed, beaten and blamed, with nothing left to pray except, "Why? Why, God? Why have you forsaken me?"

Can we drink this cup after smelling its bitter bouquet? Rather than bristling at the steward for serving a vintage more like vinegar than wine, we know this one will have to do. For this cup contains all our suffering and sorrow, all our tears and fears, all our regrets and remorse, all our shame and blame. Can we drink this cup?

James and John say they can. But do they understand? Jesus had just told them of his destination and his destiny: Jerusalem and Calvary. We see the slowness of the disciples so clearly here. After just being told that the destiny of discipleship is crucifixion, they ask for a promotion! John and James want high places in the company, and the others reveal a similar bent. But in the company of disciples, there is no higher place to be sought than the lowest place. There is no one to wait on them, for they are to wait on God as they serve each other. Though they have experienced leaders who lust for power, privilege and position, Jesus tells his disciples, "It cannot be that way with you" (20: 26). Premeditated mercy is not about self-promotion but self-denial — a demotion that places the other's need before our own ambition.

Can we drink this cup?

We can if we know that in this cup is not an elixir that erases our wounds but a draught that causes us to experience them more deeply.

We can if we know that in this cup the Divine One we call Messiah is mingled with the mayhem and mangled promises of every person, the crushed hopes and shredded dreams of every generation.

We can if we know that in this cup, besides our self-emptying, we may just find a meaning that will raise us up "on the third day." For this cup holds the vintage wine of victory that causes courage to swell shrunken hearts, passion to pulse through paralyzed limbs and commitment to warm cold hands and cold feet.

We can if we know the risks we take when we drink this cup: That we will become intoxicated with redemption. And once we are inebriated with eternity, we will be inclined to take the lowest place, pick up the heaviest cross, endure the most grievous loss.

Can we drink this cup? We can if we know that in this company there are ultimately no slaves, only friends. And in this company of friends, all are equal, all are one. We become one in our desire to look out for the other's interests, one in our desire to serve the rest.

Can we drink this cup?

REAL PRESENCE: THE REAL THING

In this cup, this chalice of our hearts, brimming with God's mercy, is the real presence of Christ. With all due apologies to the soft drink company, this cup holds the *real thing*. But how often we settle for substitutes.

In our search for God, our images of God are no substitute for experiencing the real presence of God. In spite of our human nature to want to grab hold of images that try to help us get a handle on God, mercifully God is ever incarnating, always ready to reveal the divine presence. And so we have these images, these pictures of God etched in our souls, that might remind us of God's real presence. A red sky at night or the face of a child or of our beloved might illuminate for us the face of God. The shoulder of a friend when we are sad or brokenhearted might remind us of God's shoulder that catches our tears. The laughter of companions whose company we enjoy might capture for us God's joy. Though we have not seen God, we have seen glimpses of God's presence in very real and affirming ways. These glimpses, these benevolent glances, are so important to sustain our faith in the divine presence.

But sometimes our images of God become too small, too specific and too precise. Like a favorite picture hanging on the wall that falls to the floor and cracks when a door slams or the earth trembles, our images of God are sometimes smashed when the ground beneath our feet quakes because of suffering we cannot explain or loss we can barely name. We try to pick up the pieces of our picture of God in these times of incredible tragedy, but our images are never quite the same.

When I give parish retreats, I often spend some time visiting a few of the contemplatives of the congregation: the people in the parish who are shut-ins. I once met a husband and wife, Joe and Margaret, who had been married fifty-two years. Margaret was now suffering from Alzheimer's, the insidious disease that had stolen her memory. She couldn't even remember her husband's name and would look at Joe with such a vacant stare. Joe cared for her with such great compassion and love. I saw his tears as we prayed with Margaret and anointed her. Afterwards, in the living room, I saw the picture taken on their 50th wedding anniversary before the disease began to take its toll. Their smiles told a story of commitment and gratitude. It is a picture, an image, Joe obviously treasured. He remembered the good times even as he struggled through these very difficult times.

I met another woman, Theresa, a pediatric nurse about my age. Theresa loved her work. Every day she held newborn children in her arms. Is there a more profound image of God, of life, than this? But in her late twenties Theresa began to develop the symptoms of multiple sclerosis. For the last ten years, she had been confined to a bed, her body frail and useless. Those arms that had once held countless children were now not even useful to feed herself. The disease had affected her speech. She could barely talk above a whisper. After we celebrated the anointing of the sick and she had received Communion, Theresa asked me, "Has God forgotten me?"

I tried to assure Theresa that God had not forgotten her. But what evidence did I have? What images of God did I possess to give such an assurance? I held her hand and she smiled. I knew she wasn't expecting an answer. But it was a question she had to ask. And as we held hands in silence, I saw a beauty in her eyes I had not seen before because I was too distracted by the image of this woman in her early forties whose body had betrayed her. Held in the sacredness of that moment, held in the gaze of her eyes, I knew that Theresa already had the answer to her question: God had not forgotten. God does not forget.

When I left Theresa's room and walked back into the living room, I saw the pictures of Theresa before the illness had begun to make her body a hostage. There was one of those glamour photographs taken of her in her youth and health. How beautiful she was before this illness had imprisoned her. How beautiful she was now, even though her body was twisted and tortured. I saw the present beauty in her eyes that captured her faith. So, it isn't the glamorous picture of Theresa I will remember but the picture of Theresa in that bed, stretched out upon her cross. It is not a glamorous picture but a glorious picture of one woman's faith shining through inexplicable suffering that holds my attention and focuses my fragile faith.

In the echoes of Theresa's question, "Has God forgotten me?" I heard the question raised by another whose body was twisted and tortured: "My God, my God, why have you abandoned me?" In Theresa's anguished whisper, I heard the question, "Can I drink this cup?" echoing the plaintive plea Jesus whispered in the garden on the night before he died: "Let this cup pass me by." There is an image of God that in a strange yet sacred way gives me strength. For when we meet another in his garden of agony — when another invites us to spend some time in the garden of Gethsemane — we begin to see the real presence of Christ and the familiar face of God. For this ground where the garden of pain is located is holy ground.

In the practice of premeditated mercy, we come face-to-face with our images of God. Are they false idols that shatter when suffering overwhelms us, or are they images of truth that sustain and give us strength? Sometimes our images have to be shattered. But what remains may be the true image of a God who is so large that no pain, no suffering, no shame escapes the Divine Beloved's eye.

Besides the images of Joe and Margaret and Theresa, there is another image of God I cling to. A couple of years ago, a draft of wind slammed the door of my office and caused a picture of the founder of my religious community, St. Gaspar, to fall from the wall and shatter. When I picked up the remains, the two largest pieces that remained intact were of the face of the founder and the chalice he held in his hand.

When suffering slams the door on our lives and causes our images of God to shatter, I trust these two images will remain: the face of God that is stained with tears because God knows what we suffer, and the hand of God holding a chalice to collect all our pain and suffering. In this cup God collects the pain and suffering of every human being, lifts it up and drinks it all.

At the Eucharist, we see the tear-stained face of God, who holds out a divine hand and invites us to drink from the cup of mercy. In it we taste the bitterness of our own pain and suffering. We drink in the suffering and pain of others. We taste the memory of our God who does not forget. We taste the mercy of God, who knows our suffering and responds in the love of others, who by their presence in our pain reflect the face and the hand of God.

The Medallion of Mercy:
Forgiveness, Not Fairness

To drink the cup of life and swallow hope is not easy to do when we believe we have experienced more than our share of the ancient prayer "Life is not fair!" The bitter taste in our mouths intensifies when we hear Jesus tell a parable that seems to underscore the principle that life is not fair. But what makes the story about the laborers in the vineyard (Matthew 20: 1-16) even more difficult to swallow is that the moral of the story seems to be that God is unfair!

According to the parable, the workers toiling all day long in the scorching heat receive the same payment for their service as the ones who work only an hour. Not only does this story offend our sense of fairness, it seems un-American! From our earliest recollections of childhood, one of the basic lessons of life we've learned is to play fair. And though we've all had experiences that have reminded us that life is not always fair, when we hear Jesus saying it, it strikes at the heart of our understanding about fairness.

We've all been in situations like this. We wait in line at the grocery store and a person pushes through the crowd and goes to the head of the line. "I've only got a few items," she says. "Doesn't matter," we say. "Wait in line like the rest of us."

We stand in line at the division of motor vehicles, looking at our watch and holding number 53. The sign at the window says, *Now Serving Number 25*. We become more frustrated by the moment. Then someone comes along and doesn't even bother to take a number. The person moves right to the window, and the agent behind the counter renews his license without blinking an eye. My guess is our reaction would result in more than blinking an eye.

We're sitting in traffic. Signs have warned us for at least five miles that the two-lane highway will be reduced to one lane because of road construction. Left lane closed, the signs have warned us, merge right. Traffic slows to the pace of a parking lot. We edge ever closer to the spot where there is only one lane. We're just about there. In our rearview mirror, we notice a red sports car coming rapidly down the lane that in just a few feet will be eliminated. Our back bristles. "Oh, no, you don't," and we pull up as close as we can to the bumper of the car in front of us. "Not before me, you don't."

No, it's just not fair. Oh, Jesus' story is great news indeed if we're the ones who are last in line, or in last place in the standings, or languishing last in the polls. But if we're first in line, the news that "the last shall be first and the first shall be last" isn't good news at all. And it most certainly isn't fair.

So, perhaps what we need is a new perspective. The parables of Jesus seek to widen our perspective. They invite us to look at life, at God, at ourselves and at each other in completely new and fresh ways. Like the parable about the servant who was forgiven a huge debt and then immediately went out and throttled his fellow servant who owed him a small amount of money, the parable about the laborers in the vineyard is meant to stretch our minds about the radical nature of God's love. Whereas the parable about the forgiving king and the stingy servant reflects God's abundant mercy and how we are called to share that mercy with those who offend us, the vineyard story underscores even more forcefully the generous nature of God. The parable reminds us that fairness is not the standard for God's love of us, nor is it to be the standard in our relationship to others. Rather, forgiveness is the standard.

This parable is as difficult for us to digest as it was for the disciples. Recall that it was told in the context of the religious elite complaining about how much Jesus was mixing with the outcasts and sinners of his day. In Matthew's Gospel it occurs immediately before Jesus announces to his disciples that he must go to Jerusalem to suffer and die and then asks James and John, "Are you able to drink the cup that I am to drink?"

Those who heard this story for the first time were following the rules and keeping the letter of the law. They were frustrated that Jesus was not holding them up as models of sanctity but was rather focusing his attention on those who were breaking the law. In fact, Jesus was paying attention to some of the most blatant abusers of the law. This parable says clearly that all these pious people who had dedicated their lives to the service of God's law, who had worked all day in the vineyard, would indeed be saved. But so would those who spent most of their lives making poor choices or living scandalous lives. If they accepted the invitation of God to work in the vineyard, no matter how late they were in accepting the invitation to be employed in the reign of God, they would receive the same reward as those who toiled all their lives in God's service.

Jesus also directs this parable to his own disciples, who just a moment before were reflecting on how much they had given up in order to follow Jesus and wondering what would be in it for them. This parable reminds all his disciples that salvation is not based on merit but on mercy. Salvation is based solely on God's generosity, not as a reward for the good works we might do or the good lives we might live. Notice that those who were hired first received exactly what they agreed to when they began their day's work. That is why the question the owner asks at the end of the parable strikes at the core of our understanding about fairness and forgiveness: "Are you envious of my generosity?"

This parable is meant to shock us into a new way of thinking about justice and mercy, forgiveness and fairness. We spend a lot of our time trying to fit God into our image and likeness, our expectations about what is fair and what is not fair. We place God in a box and expect that God will act like we would in a given situation. If any of us was the owner of the vineyard, would we have paid the employees who only worked an hour the same wage as those who worked all day? Probably not. Wouldn't we be more likely to pay these stragglers by the hour? But even if we were so generous and had the money, wouldn't we feel compelled by our own sense of fairness to give to those who had worked all day even more than was agreed upon at the start of the day?

This parable seeks to let God out of the box we place God in and allow God to act like God. As we have already noted, our images of God are often too small. Like those first workers in the parable, we restrict God's justice by making God into something like a scoutmaster who hands out merit badges based on effort and results. And so we limit God's mercy, which is given generously, freely, unconditionally.

Do we really want to place restrictions on God's generosity? Do we really want to limit God's mercy? Do we really want God to treat us as we treat others? Do we really want God to forgive us in the manner that we forgive those who trespass against us?

The echoes of what we've heard and learned through the years about what is fair and just ring loud and clear. These echoes are stilled by the news that God's ways are not our ways, the news that the last shall be first and the first shall be last. The message is that we can't earn our way to being first in line, that we can't stack one good deed on top of another and expect that when we're finished we'll be sitting in God's lap. We will sit on the lap of God because God has lifted us up and put us there.

We do not practice premeditated mercy to earn a *merit* badge. We practice mercy because we have already received a *mercy* badge. Remember, the mark of Cain has been erased by the mark of Christ, who embodies the generosity and compassion of our God. Jesus did not spend his time hanging around the righteous, religious people who thought they had it made. Rather, he ate with the outcasts and walked in the company of prostitutes. Jesus stood around on the corner with those who, for whatever reason, were not working in the vineyard.

If this parable sounds foreign to our ears and our experience, perhaps we need to place ourselves on the corner. We might put ourselves in the place of those late workers who received the generous wage from the owner of the vineyard. We might put ourselves in the place of the people who came last and were paid first. How did they feel? How did they act? Maybe then the parable will make sense. Maybe then this parable that seems so unfair will yield some understanding to the words we say just before we receive the body and blood of Christ: "Lord, I am not worthy to receive you, but only say the word and I shall be healed." It's from this place and this perspective that we realize that we're already wearing God's medallion of mercy.

GOD'S WILL: AN INHERITANCE OF EVERLASTING LIFE

It's especially when life is unfair and we swallow more than our share of pain and sorrow that we need to know that the chalice of our heart is imprinted with this medallion of mercy. Inscribed on this medallion is the image of God that will sustain us and give us strength when life seems unfair. As we have reflected, the point of premeditated mercy is to become a new creation by allowing this image of God in ourselves to be seen. Contrary to all our images that seek to limit God's mercy, the image of God that transcends our labels is that God is love. We are God's beloved children. John writes about this divine initiative of premeditated mercy: "God so loved the world that God gave God's only Son, that whoever believes in him should not perish but have eternal life. For God sent the Son into the world, not to condemn the world, but that the world might be saved through him" (John 3: 16-17).

God's will is that the world not be condemned but saved. When we empty the chalice of our hearts, we leave ourselves open to God's will. This will, penned by the hand of God, offers us a remarkable inheritance from a most generous God. This inheritance is not in money, of course, but in mercy. God desires more than anything that we have life. We did not earn this inheritance. We did not win this inheritance. But it is our inheritance. Yet, when say yes to this great gift, we make the critical decision that reflects our core belief that we are made in God's image. We say that we will spend this inheritance, spend this gift, this life, in right relationship with God.

All the daily dilemmas and decisions that confront us are to flow from this basic orientation of life. Our core belief — that we are created in God's image and destined to become a new creation because of God's will that we be saved — shapes all that we do, all that we are. And even though at times we make some poor choices, as long as our core belief remains firm, we will have life within us. God will protect this life. God will save this life. God does not want to lose the divine inheritance given to each and every human being.

We remain faithful in spending this inheritance by embracing our identity as God's beloved. This is who we are: the beloved of God. This frames all the questions, all the choices, and all the decisions that we face. We look at the world and each other through this core identity of being the beloved of God. As we know when we are in a committed relationship, whether it is marriage or friendship, spending this inheritance of love is a daily decision, but the decision to love flows from the basic choice we made to love God and be loved by God.

There is a Hindu greeting, *Namaste*, which means: "I honor the place within you where God resides; I honor that place within you of love, of light, of truth, of peace; I honor that place within you where, if you are in that place in you, and I am in that place in me, there is only one of us." When we reverence the other, we reverence the image of God in the other. We are most fully human, most fully alive, most fully ourselves when we subject ourselves to God's will in all things, in all of creation, in all peoples. We see this in relationships that reflect sacramental union: the love of the two who become one flesh. The two become love, and the spirit of this love overflows the chalice of their hearts to flood their world with the very life of God.

When life is unfair and we are confronted with those daily choices to love or not to love, to believe or not to believe, to hope or not to hope, the basic question is: Am I saying *yes* to life, *yes* to God? In the silence of prayer before the altar, we ask ourselves: Does this decision confirm or deny my identity as God's beloved? When we recognize ourselves as God's beloved, we will spend God's inheritance, and the chalice of our hearts, emptied of self and filled with love, will spill out to refresh the lives of others with God's mercy.

MERCY'S ETERNAL LIFE INSURANCE POLICY

In addition to God's will that offers us an inheritance of everlasting life, we also are the beneficiaries of an extraordinary life insurance policy. If one reads the fine print on this policy, there is an astonishing addendum: "Whatever we ask God in Jesus' name will be given to us" (John 15: 16). Now, there's a life insurance policy that pays some extraordinary dividends. But though the premiums on this policy are out of this world, unconditional and eternal, promising a love that never ends and a joy that comes full circle, notice that the deductible is also very high. In accepting this life insurance, we deduct our very selves. The deductible is summed up thus: "Love one another as I have loved you. There is no greater love than this: to lay down one's life for one's friends. You are my friends if you do what I command you" (John 15: 12-14).

Now, that's not a catch or a condition, it's a command. The command is to love in the manner of Jesus. It's a love that is wide-open and expansive, a love that is mind-bending, heart-stretching, self-yielding and spirit-freeing. The question that surfaces in my mind when reading the fine print on this eternal life insurance policy is, "Do I really want to love like this? Or am I not more content with safe prayers rather than prayers that save; more content with guarded love than love without limits?"

As unconditional as this life insurance policy is, do I really want to accept the deductible: living as Jesus did without any conditions, loving as Jesus did without any limits, dying as Jesus did to make amends for the sins of others, rising as Jesus did to bring new life to his friends?

To drink the cup of life, to live as Jesus did, to love as Jesus did, is always a risk. To die as Jesus did demands the ultimate risk: to lay down one's life for one's friends. God was willing to take this risk, to make good on the divine insurance policy. But am I willing to take the same kind of risks for the sake of love?

There are, of course, various kinds of love with varying degrees of risk. There is, for example, the love a friend has for a friend that is deep enough to endure trials, wide enough to survive distance, high enough to know joy, strong enough to forgive mistakes, trusting enough to know vulnerability and open enough to speak and hear truth. Those are some extraordinary risks, but when we take them, when we know such a friend, love such a friend, we will understand the answer Charles Kingsley once gave to Elizabeth Barrett Browning when she asked him, "What is the secret of your life? Tell me that I may make mine beautiful too." Kingsley smiled and said simply, "I have a friend."

There is also the kind of love we see — perhaps some of us possess — that might be captured in that phrase ascribed to those who live and minister with the suffering, disenfranchised or marginalized, "He/she has a great love for the poor." This quality of love is expressed in compassionate presence and prophetic proclamation. Love as compassionate presence means standing in solidarity with those who are left out. Love as prophetic proclamation means challenging those structures that have left the poor out.

But the kind of love that demands the greatest risk is the love that cannot be measured by any human scale. This is the love for those who do not love us in return. This love is for those who hurt us or torment us or abuse us or ridicule us. This is the love that keeps on giving even when reason reminds us that no love is being received. This is the toughest kind of love because it demands the most tender of hearts. This kind of love can only come from a heart that is emptied of self and filled with divine mercy.

It is the kind of love to which the Scriptures give a name — the name of God. "God is love" (1 John 4: 16). And love is only possible "because God loved us first" (1 John 4: 19). This kind of love can only grow when we know God. But when we know God and know that we are loved by God, we can "love one another" (John 13: 34).

Harriet was one of those people who knew she was God's beloved. But it had taken a long time for her to realize it. She lived alone in a simple house just down the street from the church. One morning the pastor of the parish called Harriet to see if he could drop by for a visit. The priest was going through a difficult time, discerning whether or not he should remain in the parish or even in the priesthood. He had come to know Harriet as one of the "saints" of the parish, although to this point his only criteria for canonization were that Harriet attended daily Mass and that she made the best cinnamon rolls he had ever tasted.

When the priest arrived at Harriet's house, the aroma of the cinnamon rolls she had just taken out of the oven made his mouth water. When Harriet invited him to sit at the kitchen table, poured him some coffee and placed a cinnamon roll before him, the priest imagined that he was catching a glimpse of heaven's glory. They chatted about the weather and the success of the recently completed parish bazaar. But Harriet knew that the priest had something on his mind. Something was weighing heavily upon his heart.

"Harriet," the priest said finally, "when I came into the house, I noticed the pictures hanging on the wall in the living room. Would you mind telling me about your family?" Harriet smiled and went into the living room to retrieve three of the pictures. Pointing to the first, Harriet told the priest that her husband left her and their son shortly after the picture was taken. "He traveled a lot," she said. "Well, on one business trip he called and said he wasn't coming home. That was that."

At the risk of invading her privacy, the priest asked what had happened. "Oh, he just met another woman, settled down and lived happily ever after." She said this in such a matter-of-fact way that the priest was startled. Even more surprising was what she said next: "I still hear from him and his wife a couple of times a year." There was no trace of bitterness in her voice. The priest's first thought was this woman was incredibly forgiving, didn't care or was living in a land with which he was unfamiliar. Pointing to the second picture, Harriet said, "That's him, his wife and their children. They've all been very good to me. They were especially kind when our son died."

Now the priest's mind was working overtime. "Come on," he thought to himself, "you mean your husband left you to marry another woman and then your own son died, and you're not bitter or angry or resentful?" But instead of voicing this thought, he just looked at the third picture of her son's graduation and said, "He was very handsome."

"He was such a fine boy," Harriet said. "He died of a brain tumor when he was twenty-four. It was the most difficult time of my life. Even worse than when my husband left me. But I got through it."

"How?" the priest asked, expecting her to give the familiar formula he often used when confronted with a devastating loss: "I wouldn't have made it without my faith."

Harriet smiled. "Oh, I don't know exactly," she sighed. "It was a terrible time. I was very angry when my husband left me. For years, I was very bitter. I didn't speak to him the day he came to our son's graduation. And I carried that bitterness for years. I guess I know what hate is because I don't know what else to call what I felt toward him.

"And then when Jamie, my son, got sick, I just focused all my energy and attention on him and trying to get him well. I thought less of how bitter and angry I was toward my husband and spent all my energy on

Jamie. I loved that boy so much. His dad would come and visit, and since Jamie was his son too I couldn't stop him. Gradually, I guess I just let my anger toward him go. And especially when Jamie died, I could see in his eyes not just the terrible pain of losing his son but the guilt he had over abandoning us."

Now, the ground Harriet was covering was certainly unfamiliar territory for the priest, so he was very cautious in taking the next step. Finally, he asked, "So, your son's death brought some kind of healing between you and your former husband?"

"Oh, no!" Harriet said. "When Jamie died I was furious. I was angry with my husband for leaving us; I was angry with Jamie for dying so young, and most of all I was angry with God for allowing my life to become such a disaster. I kept saying, 'It's not fair!' And 'What in the world have I done to deserve this?' I stayed that way for a long time. I tried to pray and just couldn't. You probably won't believe this, Father, but I stopped going to church when my husband left me. But when Jamie got sick, I started going again. Every day I went to Mass and prayed for Jamie's healing. But when he died, I said, 'That's it.'"

"So," the priest asked, "What happened? Why are you now so accepting of all that has happened to you?" Again, he thought Harriet might offer some pious platitude that saints sometimes use, like, "Time heals all wounds." But she didn't.

"A couple of years after Jamie died, a woman from the parish came to see me. We had been friends for a long time, and she knew how I was hurting. We talked for awhile, and she's a good listener. Then, just as she was about to leave, she gave me a book, which she invited me to read sometime. Well, at first I didn't pay much attention to it. But one night I just started paging through this book and came across a line that made sense to me. The author wrote, 'I have learned not to confuse God with life.'

"I thought about that a lot. I had confused God with life. I was thinking that since God is supposed to be fair, life should be fair. But my life was so unfair, and, therefore, God was unfair. But the more I thought about it, God is not life, God is love. And that made all the difference for me. God didn't cause my husband to leave me. God was probably as devastated as I was when my husband ran off. And God didn't cause my son to get cancer and die. God wept as much as I did when Jamie died. I suddenly discovered that life is unfair but that God isn't life. God is love."

Harriet took the priest by the hand that morning and gave him a tour of the holy ground of her heartland where there were no longer boundaries. Through all the betrayal and bitterness, the pain and loss she had experienced in her life, a life that had been incredibly unfair to her, she had come to know God's love. She had experienced a love that is not measured in terms of fairness but by God's favor. Knowing this about God made Harriet aware of that ancient principle that love is a decision, a choice, a commitment. Harriet had to choose to keep on loving even when reason told her it was useless.

When the priest left Harriet's house that morning after listening to her story, he knew he had found a new perspective from which to make his decision about priesthood.

PROOF OF LOSS: A GRACE PERIOD

I am reminded how insurance companies have what is called "proof of loss." Those pictures of Harriet's son and her former husband offered proof of her loss. They were losses that ultimately did not deter her or keep her from loving. She realized that her life insurance policy was paid in full. All the premiums have been paid by Jesus, the Risen One, through the blood of his cross. By committing herself to love, no matter the cost her life had exacted from her, Harriet had come to recognize herself as the beloved of God.

God's eternal life insurance policy is written upon each of our hearts. When we read the policy closely, we notice there's nothing in it about promising that life would be fair. But it does offer assurance that no matter how unfair life is, God isn't life. God is love. And when we know God, we know love. It's a love that shows no partiality nor plays favorites, because all people are God's favorites. It's a love that is expansive, a love that exacts the awful price of commitment when confronted with catastrophe and chaos.

No, nothing in this insurance policy suggests that life will be fair. But it does insure that God is love and that we who abide in love, abide in God, no matter how unfair life becomes. We can accept this policy and sign our lives on the dotted line, or we can remain safe, if not secure, within the lines of our limited love. The choice is ours.

Like an insurance policy that gives us up to thirty days to pay the premium without a penalty or the threat of losing our coverage — insurance companies call this a "grace period" — God gives us an even longer grace period: the time of our life on earth. During this grace period, the practice of premeditated mercy stretches the parameters of our love. We take those we find most difficult to love, those who have hurt us or betrayed us, and place them in the chalice of our hearts. We place them in the presence of Love, whose other name is God. We place them there each day, every day. And through the grace of God, we learn a little bit more about this life insurance policy of love that not only has comprehensive coverage but eternal dividends.

Yes, at times life isn't fair. But do not confuse life with God, for "God is love and whoever abides in love, abides in God" (1 John 4: 16). Though at times everything we learned in kindergarten about playing fair doesn't seem to pay off, here's the payoff: If we empty the chalice of our heart of revenge and fill it with God's grace, then we will be able to drink this cup. If we empty the chalice of our heart of worry about what is fair and fill it instead with God's forgiveness, then we will be able to drink this cup. If we empty the chalice of our heart of fear and fill it with faith in the One who is merciful, then we will be able to drink this cup and swallow the sweet wine of hope.

Seeing Our Shadows on Mercy Street:
Finding Our Way in the Dark

*This is such an age
when madmen lead the blind.*

— William Shakespeare, *King Lear*

In the practice of premeditated mercy, we seek to establish places of remembrance and reconciliation in our world. We seek to remember and to create an environment which gives evidence that this residence where we live and work is a place of peace and of prayer, a place where memories are valued and reconciliation is practiced. No matter how unfair life seems to be, no matter the lack of care we see in ourselves or in others, no matter how often our prayer seems to rise and then fall on the Divine One's deaf ears, by remaining committed to the practice of premeditated mercy we seek to prepare a place for the real presence of God. It's a place of the presence of peace, the presence of life, wherever we pitch our tent in this world.

On a dreary, rainy July morning in 1987, I was on a train from Salzburg to Munich travelling with a group of Precious Blood priests and brothers. After our arrival in Munich, our plan was to take a ten-minute bus ride and spend the rest of the day visiting the Nazi concentration camp at Dachau. On the train, I was sitting next to Father Anton Loipfinger, who at the time was the leader of the worldwide Precious Blood congregation. He told me that as a young boy he had lived within a few miles of Dachau. Assuming that he had been to the concentration camp before, I asked him what it was like.

"I've never been there," he said.

He saw the look of surprise on my face. "I can't go there," he said. "The rest of you should go, but I cannot."

"Why?" I asked.

"It is a place of death," he said. "The memories of what went on there are still too strong in my mind. I cannot go there."

Father Anton went on to explain how as a boy he knew something terrible was happening inside that camp. He could smell the odor of bodies being burned. He was only ten years old at the time. What could he do? But as he looked out the window of the train, it was clear that the memory still haunted him.

Dachau. Auschwitz. Treblinka: These are names of places associated with death, with unimaginable suffering, with inexplicable evil. When we see any of these places on a map or read of them in a book, we immediately think of the Holocaust. We are just as instantly moved to memory and to prayer.

There is no escaping the blood that stains the map of our memory. In recent years, more places have been added to this atlas of evil and death: places in Bosnia, in Rwanda, in Cambodia, in the Middle East. These are places where indiscriminate slaughter has soaked the soil with blood and stained the name of the place forever. Take out a map of the United States and in the last few years of the twentieth century you will see similarly stained towns and cities with names like Jasper, Texas; Laramie, Wyoming; Oklahoma City, Oklahoma; Springfield, Oregon; Jonesboro, Arkansas; Pearl, Mississippi; Paducah, Kentucky; and Littleton, Colorado. These places read like a road map to death's dark valley. In Jasper, it is the blood of James Byrd, Jr., the black man tied to the back of pickup truck and dragged to his death by three white youths. In Laramie, it is the blood of Matthew Shephard, the gay college student brutally murdered by two young men. In Oklahoma City, it's the blood of more than a hundred men, women and children killed when a bomb exploded in the Federal Building on April 19, 1995. In Springfield, Jonesboro, Pearl, Paducah and Littleton, it is the blood of teachers and students murdered by other students. School was once a safe place. Now, it seems, there are no safe places anymore. There are no sanctuaries where people, even children, can feel safe.

With so many places in our world today associated with death, the challenge of premeditated mercy is to create more locations of life. As people of mercy, wherever we go, wherever we travel, wherever we pitch our tent, we are to prepare a place for the presence of God. When I recall the look on Father Anton's face as he said of Dachau, "It is a place of death, I cannot go there," I think of how the terrible memory of what took place at Dachau tormented him. But because of that memory he had committed himself to creating places of life. He carried the memory of that place of death and vowed he would never forget. In remembering the evil and death of Dachau, he committed himself to the practice of premeditated mercy by preparing a place for the presence of God wherever he went.

FOLLOW ME TO MERCY STREET

Mercy takes us by the hand to these places where we'd rather not go. As we travel this road of reconciliation, we rely on the map of God's word. In the Jesus story, the map continually points to one address: Mercy Street. As we have reflected often on Matthew's Gospel, it is appropriate to see how the story of this tax collector's call to discipleship (Matthew 9: 9-13) offers us the directions to Mercy Street.

The invitation is simple and direct: "Follow me." It means the one who says these words has a good idea where he is going. So we follow, thinking this one knows the way. But when we arrive at this place and our leader sits down, not to rest but seemingly to stay, at least for awhile, we say, "Why here?" We know *how* we got *here*! But *why*? We followed the leader. We trusted him. Now the question is, "Why of all places did you bring us here? We trusted you, and this is where you lead us? To the home of one of the most hated members of our community? To a house crowded with people who have sold out their religion and their nation to those who oppress us? To a table where people whose sins are known by all sit and drink and laugh and eat? There must be some mistake; our leader must have found the wrong address!"

But what if there is no mistake? What if our leader really does intend to stay and eat with people such as these? He doesn't seem to care that the reputations of the people with whom he sits and talks stain all our shirts in scarlet letters. Yet, it seems he hasn't made a mistake. This appears to be the address he intended to visit all along.

We think, "Some leader you are! If you don't think you've made a mistake, we are sure that *we* have. What fools we are to trust that you know where you're going! Look at yourself! Carousing with people who cheat and steal and disregard the law. What kind of teacher are you?

What kind of faith do you profess to practice?

"Follow you! Why, we wouldn't follow you if you were the last person on earth! We're getting out of here. Just being here makes us feel dirty, unclean. Just being in the same room, under the same roof, with this kind of people, these outlaws, makes us sick to our stomach. How can we eat in such a place as this? You've gone too far this time! You've taken us too far. We're leaving."

"Wait," he says. "Wait just a minute. Let me try to explain why I brought you here. Then, after I explain, if you don't agree, go. But, please, just listen."

We fold our arms and stand by the door. Our heads tell us to leave, but our hearts control our feet. We want to believe him. We want to know why he has brought us to such a disgusting place as this, though we can't imagine any explanation that will give us cause to stay much longer. But since we've already become ritually impure by being in such a place as this, we will stay to hear his explanation, certain it will never satisfy.

"When you are sick," he asks, "very sick, where do you go?"

We say, "To a doctor, of course. What are you getting at?"

"If you're feeling good and fit and healthy, do you visit a doctor?"

"Of course not. We don't need a doctor if we're not sick."

"Exactly," he says. "Now do you understand? It is mercy God desires, not sacrifice."

We've heard these words before. We know these words by heart. But until now, we didn't know what they meant. But they couldn't mean this. They couldn't mean dining with such despicable outlaws. This isn't what God intends by preferring mercy to sacrifice. After all, sacrifice means "doing that which is holy." And there is certainly nothing holy about this gathering of outcasts and castoffs.

As if reading our minds, he says, "Exactly."

"What?"

"You've got it," he says. "You understand."

"We do?"

"Absolutely. Now, let's eat. Supper is getting cold."

The one in whose house we are now standing shows us to our seats at the table. This one, this tax collector, who was one of us until he sold out to the oppressors and began taking our money and turning it over to our enemies, smiles as he pulls out some chairs. We want to wipe the smile right off his face. We want to run out of the house and race to the temple to offer sacrifice for being in the company of such a criminal. But for now we follow our leader and accept this outcast's hospitality as we sit at the table.

Yet how can we eat? How can we raise our glasses, as our leader suggests, to taste the wine of this enemy of the people? But we do. We drink. We eat. We even laugh once or twice when one of the outlaws tells a joke.

When the evening is over, as we are leaving, the one who led us here asks, "So, how do you feel?"

"Full," we say. And maybe a little lightheaded from the wine.

"Good," he says. "Follow me."

And we can't imagine where he will take us next. But from what we've gathered so far, this way he has asked us to follow has only one address: Mercy Street.

Finding Pink Flamingoes in the Dark

Finding our home on Mercy Street is difficult to do when it's dark inside. When darkness descends upon the landscape of our heart because of the betrayal of a friend or a sin that causes us to blame and shame ourselves, the darkness is deep. The possibility of light seeping through the cracks seems remote. The lights in the house on Mercy Street are turned out. We are lost in the dark.

A few days before graduating from college, four classmates and I decided to spend a few days at my brother Ed's place at the Lake of the Ozarks. Ed had just bought the place a few months before, and I had only been down there once. But not to worry — Ed supplied me with directions. They went something like this:

> Turn right at the Conoco station. Go to Lake Road 22 and take a left. Follow this road until you come to a row of mailboxes. Take a left. Follow this road until you come to the pink flamingoes in a front yard, turn right. Go about a quarter of a mile until you come to an orange cone, like the ones used at highway construction sites. Take a right....

Well, you get the idea. Finding the lost ark would have been easier. And since one of my classmates had a late exam, we didn't leave Kansas City until well after dark. But I told the other guys that it wasn't a problem since I had the directions. Besides, I had been there once before, I knew I'd recognize things when we got close.

We found the gas station — after passing it by two or three times because it was late and the gas station was closed so all the lights were off. We weaved our way through the Ozark hills and found the lake road. We even found the row of mailboxes. But after driving down narrow passages that could have been hiking trails for over an hour, we never found those pink flamingoes. So finally we drove back to the main road, found a roadside park and slept until dawn. Once the sun came up, we didn't have any trouble at all. The directions turned out to be perfect. How we could have missed those pink flamingoes was beyond us!

Except, of course, that it was dark. No matter how accurate the directions or clear the map, it's easy to lose one's way in the dark.

In seeking to follow the path of pardon and peace as mapped out by Jesus, we may at times experience the darkness of night, when light seems to have taken flight. This darkness descends in our lives and takes many forms that contribute to the fear, frustration and futility we feel in trying to find our way. But we need to remember the map — and to remember the one who drew this map. We need to remember what Jesus did when he was lost in the dark.

In Matthew's Gospel, after Jesus had spent time in his wilderness retreat to prepare himself for public ministry, he learned that his cousin John had been arrested. Upon hearing the news, Jesus went back into hiding: "He withdrew into Galilee; and leaving Nazareth he went and dwelt in Capernaum by the sea, in the territory of Zebulun and Napthali" (Matthew 4:12-13). Jesus had checked out the map of his mentor, Isaiah, who wrote: "The land of Zebulun and the land of Naphtali, toward the sea, across the Jordan, Galilee of the Gentiles — the people who sat in darkness have seen a great light. For those who sat in the land in the shadow of death, light has dawned" (Isaiah 8: 23, 9: 1).

In the darkness caused by John's arrest, the light of God's salvation is beginning to dawn on Jesus. And "from that time on Jesus began to proclaim, 'Repent, for the kingdom of heaven has come near'" (Matthew 4: 17).

As Jesus walked along the beach that day, the light was intense and caught four fishermen in its rays:

> As he walked by the Sea of Galilee, he saw two brothers, Simon who is called Peter and Andrew his brother, casting a net into the sea; for they were fishermen. And he said to them, "Follow me." Immediately they left their nets and followed him. And going on from there he saw two other brothers, James the son of Zebedee and John his brother, in the boat with Zebedee

their father, mending their nets, and he called them. Immediately they left the boat and their father and followed him (Matthew 4: 18-22).

These four fishermen were not blinded by this light but rather attracted to it. The light pierced whatever armor of resistance they may have been wearing to protect them from taking risks, and they left everything behind to follow the light.

What did Jesus see in these four fishermen? Maybe it has something to do with their enthusiasm about fishing that prompted Jesus to call them to be "fishers of people." That word, *enthusiasm*, literally means "to be inspired." It comes from the Greek, *en theos*, which means "with God." So to be enthusiastic about life, about what we do and who we are, means that we are with God. Jesus must have noticed how these four fishermen were "with God" — putting their heart and soul into what they were doing. He must have noticed how passionate they were about their work.

And what did these four see in Jesus? In the well-worn phrase of religious conversion, "They saw the light."

What is important to remember here is that the light came out of the darkness. Jesus had just endured a forty-day wrestling match with the evil one in the wilderness. When he left the desert, he heard that his beloved cousin was now in prison for doing what Jesus himself was about to do: preach the good news about the coming reign of God. This news might have placed a roadblock in Jesus' way right from the start. But instead, he retreated for awhile longer, took out the map of God's word and began to sense the light growing inside of him.

When we are lost in the dark, unable to read the signs of the times on Mercy Street because of the darkness around us, we are encouraged to step away, check our bearings and take out the map of God's word. Here we will sense how, even though we seem lost, we are on the right track. As we meditate on the word of God, as we take this word to heart, we will sense that we are not alone. This assurance of companionship on the road of reconciliation will ignite the light within us that will help us find our way to Mercy Street.

With that light glowing within us, we will also find others along the way. As Jesus realized when he walked on the beach that day, the work of reconciliation is not a one-person job. It takes more than one to be reconciled. And it takes more than a few to make reconciliation a reality in the world.

FOLLOWING THE MAP

As we seek to follow this map to Mercy Street, we might reflect on those moments in our lives when we have seen the light.

One of those experiences in my life occurred when I was on a leave of absence from my studies for the priesthood. After being in the seminary system since I was a freshmen in high school, through four years of college, a year of pastoral internship and almost two years of theology school, I took a leave of absence to work at a newspaper. One of the reasons I left was because I felt my religious community was adrift at sea, lost in the dark.

During my leave of absence, I received a letter from one of my professors at Catholic Theological Union in Chicago, Father Carroll Stuhlmueller. I was taking Carroll's course on the prophets when I left the seminary. As a requirement for the course, I was keeping a journal of how the Scripture was being prayed and played out in my life. Because my struggle over whether or not to stay at the seminary was at the center of my concern at that time, I often wrote about my discernment.

In his first letter to me, Carroll expressed his sadness and confusion as to why I had left the seminary. Then he challenged me in a way I will never forget. Carroll wrote that he could not see prophets like Isaiah, Jeremiah or Ezekiel taking a leave of absence from their work. It was precisely because of the tensions in their lives that they were driven deep into the mystery of God. They found their prophetic voice in the darkness of their discontent and discouragement. Carroll told me I would never find a community that would live up to my expectations, but that this is not the point of the prophetic journey. The point, Carroll wrote, is to love in such a way that we move the community closer to God.

What he said next made a light go on inside me. He told me to picture a boat full of people heading toward a waterfall. The boat was going along steadily, even happily, with the people in the boat seemingly unaware of the danger and the doom that was ahead. He said if one person jumped out of the boat because he or she was aware of the disaster that awaited the people on this boat, the boat would rock for awhile. But soon the ship would steady its course and continue toward the inevitable waterfall.

He noted that it takes more than a measure of courage to jump out of the boat, to abandon ship. But it takes even greater courage to stay in the boat, to rock the boat, to shake the ship, until the other people in the boat are awakened to the fact that the course they have charted is toward a waterfall and certain death. It takes courage to keep rocking the boat until the boat changes course, away from the waterfall and toward a new horizon of hope.

I had abandoned ship. I had jumped out of the boat. The challenging words of this wise professor were the light that gave me the inspiration to climb back into the boat and continue rocking that boat until we changed course.

In each of our lives, as we seek to follow the map to Mercy Street, there will be moments of darkness and doubt, fear, frustration and failure that will call into question our life's work, our relationships, our commitment. In those moments we are faced with the decision to jump ship or to continue rocking the boat until the course is changed.

For many in our world, in our neighborhoods, in our faith communities today, this is one of the moments. It is not unlike the situation Paul described in his first letter to the Corinthian community. He addressed a people in crisis and chaos. The community was fractured, split into factions, divided according to their allegiance to their favorite teacher. But Paul reminded them that there is only one teacher, there is only one light. And he prayed for them in their time of anguish and confusion to "be united in the same mind and the same purpose" (1 Corinthians 1: 10). It is the power of the cross of Jesus Christ, the light of the world, Paul wrote, that would bring the people together.

It is this same power of the light of Christ that will guide this ship, this Companion Ship, of which we are all crewmembers. Though our faith communities are divided at times, though there are divisions among the crew, Christ is the captain of this ship, and Christ is not divided. Christ is the light shining in the darkness of our disagreements, the light that will show us the way to the future. It is this light that will guide us through the storms to sail toward a new horizon of hope. There will be no mutiny on this ship of bounty and blessing so long as all of us continue to follow this light, rock this boat and listen to each other in charting the course and following the call. Maybe that was something else Jesus saw in the four fishermen he called that day to help chart the course to the reign of God. In addition to their enthusiasm, Jesus saw people who were willing to rock the boat. As fishermen they had experience in rocking boats.

When we are stranded in rivers of doubt or seas of discontent, the grace of God, reflected in the light of Christ, will guard us and guide us.

That grace, that light, was reflected to me by Father Carroll Stuhlmueller, one of the wisest and holiest people I have ever met. But it was also brought home to me when I was very young. There is a memory I have tucked away somewhere in the back of my mind that I retrieve every now and then, especially when life gets rough and relationships grow distant and work overwhelms me.

When I was four years old, my family was out in a boat on the Mississippi River with some friends. As evening drew on and darkness hovered over the river, we were ready to head to shore. But the boat's motor died and nothing our friend who owned the boat tried to do would work. So there we were, drifting in the middle of the river, without lights. In the distance, we heard a tugboat coming down the river. It drew closer and closer. Fear seized everyone in our boat. I was too young to know what was going on, but Dad has told me several times since that he was prepared to grab me, jump in the water and try to swim to shore. Frantically, our friend worked to get the motor going. With the tugboat unable to see us stranded there in the darkness, and drawing ever closer, our friend finally started the motor. We headed for shore and for safety.

That memory is a grace-filled reminder of how God is ever on the lookout for us. Like my father that night on the Mississippi River, God will show us the way to the shore. And when our ship safely docks, don't be surprised if the riverfront road is named Mercy Street.

As long as we have the map and trust the light in those who love us, those whose faces reflect this grace of God, we will not lose our way. But remember, it is much easier to find pink flamingoes in the light.

ME AND MY SHADOW

In praying with these images of light and darkness, there is a fascinating and dramatic story in Matthew's Gospel (8: 28-34), in which Jesus cures two men possessed by evil spirits. The two men, while they were possessed by evil, recognized Jesus as the Messiah. They called him "Son of God." But after the demons were expelled, there is no evidence in the story that these two men recognized Jesus as the Messiah and followed him. We don't know if they followed Jesus down the road or rushed home to be with their families and friends.

But we do know what happened to the evil spirits Jesus expelled. They took up residence in a herd of swine, causing the pigs to race to the edge of a cliff and perish in the sea below. (Might this body of water be nicknamed the "bay of pigs"?) I wonder what the swineherds thought when they saw Jesus perform this amazing feat with their pigs? After all, the direct result of Jesus' cure of the men possessed by demons meant taking away the swineherds' livelihood. (Now their pigs would never be "cured.") Did they take off to tell the rest of the town?

And what did the people see when they came from town after hearing this remarkable story about Jesus casting the demons out of the men and into the pigs who then committed mass suicide? The townsfolk who came out to see Jesus certainly had to be intrigued by this first documented case of humans giving pigs swine flu — a flu which made them so delirious that they jumped in the lake.

Seriously, though, what did the people expect to see when they saw Jesus? A glimpse of heaven? After all, evil had been expelled; good had triumphed. Light had eclipsed the darkness of the demons. No, it seems just the opposite is true. They begged Jesus not to come to their town. They pleaded with him to leave their neighborhood. What were they afraid of? Were they afraid of his power? Were they afraid that if Jesus came to town they would lose their livelihoods like their pig farming friends? Were they afraid of the light?

This is one of those Gospel stories that play with light and shadows, life and death. At the beginning of the story, the possessed men came out of the tombs and found life in the presence of Jesus. But at the end of the story, the light of Jesus was so bright that it blinded the people of the town to the presence of goodness in their midst. The story suggests that when the light is too bright, we go looking for the shadows. When the heat is intense, we seek some shade to cool our bodies and soothe our spirits. Is this what was going on in this story? The heat of Jesus' passion to cure the two possessed by demons was so intense that the people of the village didn't want him to come any closer. Perhaps they were afraid they might get burned.

Or maybe even healed.

What did the people of that town come out to see? My guess is that those people did what many of us do: They saw what they wanted to see. And when they saw the Truth, they wanted the Truth to flee, to leave them alone.

The presence of light always illuminates the shadows of our lives. When our shadows are exposed, we want to run and hide. The light always calls us to transformation, to conversion, to change. But most of us find transformation terrifying. We like to stay the same. We like to hold on to whatever it is that makes us comfortable. Would we have invited Jesus into our neighborhood after this startling account of a bay full of pigs? Would we have recognized Jesus' greatness and genius? Or would we have joined forces to run Jesus out of town, saying as we did, "You can't change me."

Since prayer is often described as illumination, we shouldn't find it frustrating or surprising if we find it difficult to pray. True prayer always calls forth from us some kind of conversion. True prayer sometimes illuminates our deepest, darkest shadows.

ON SPEAKING TERMS WITH DEMONS

When we walk down Mercy Street and see the shadow of the person walking ahead of us, we have cause to be careful. Some ancient cultures and modern-day mystics believe that if you step on another's shadow, you hold a certain power over that person. Maybe this is why the people begged Jesus to leave: He had stepped on their shadows, and they didn't want him to have power over them.

An early episode of the television series *Chicago Hope* reflects this ancient attitude about stepping on our shadow side and so gaining some measure of control over our evil impulses. Jeffrey Geiger, an expert but eccentric surgeon, loses his license to practice medicine. He is declared mentally unfit to do surgery following a near nervous breakdown after a difficult encounter with his former wife, Laurie. Dr. Geiger is a tortured man; his mother had pushed him to be a surgeon. Then, just as he was achieving his goal and was gaining a reputation as a world-famous heart surgeon, his mother died of heart failure. He wasn't able to save his own mother. The demon of failure begins to haunt him. He is also stalked by the memory of his wife drowning their son in the bathtub. Though his skill as a surgeon is beyond reproach, these incidents and others play in the dark corners of his soul, leaving his emotions frayed and his skills as a human being severely compromised.

As Dr. Geiger faces a medical inquisition that will determine whether his license will be revoked, his close friend, Dr. Adam Schutt, a brain surgeon, offers to the judge a summation as to why his friend Jeffrey should keep his license. At one point in his soliloquy, Schutt says: "Unlike most of us, Jeffrey is on speaking terms with his demons."

In the practice of premeditated mercy, we must be on speaking terms with our own demons. We fear communicating with our demons — it may cause frightening outbursts, eccentric behavior, venting and anger. All these point to possession. Yet, instead of *exorcising* the demons, we need to *exercise* the demons — giving them legs, taking them for a walk on Mercy Street. We may take them for a walk in the woods (a natural habitat for demons and such things in fairy tales and myths) where we hope the demons will get lost. But don't worry: they'll always find their way back home.

Are we on speaking terms with our demons? Or do we give them the silent treatment? Most of us don't give our demons the time of day. It's too frightening. We're too busy. We feel like we need to keep busy. But our demons don't seem to mind. They can't tell time by daylight anyway. They prefer the night.

Silence is the only treatment for learning how to communicate with our demons. Listen to them. Don't take their advice, but give them their say. They are here to inform us. Most of us prefer to lock our demons away in the cellar where they are secure, hidden. Little do we realize that when they are secure in the cellar they feed on our insecurities. Rather than wasting away for want of food, the demons grow stronger as they enjoy a feeding frenzy on the scraps we send their way. These scraps are the things we don't want to say or do in public for fear that others will think we are not normal. Demons have a taste for our undigested anger, our unresolved resentment, our hurt over a remark that maybe someone didn't mean to say, but the words stick in our crawl space all the same. Demons feast on our lack of forgiveness, both the forgiveness we fail to give others and that which we fail to accept from others or from God.

Our demons can grow quite large, so large that the cages in the cellar can no longer hold them. In the Scripture story when the disciples could not expel a demon from a child, Jesus says after healing the child, "This kind can only be driven out by prayer" (Mark 9: 29). Some demons become so accustomed to our place that they refuse to leave. No amount of forgiveness or pardon or psychological counseling or prayer can drive them out. They are adamant. They seem more tenacious than grace. They become part of us, initiated into our being, until death do us part. Only in death, when the spirit leaves the body, do the demons take flight too. Grace wins out in the end.

But there is a certain grace that also works on the most tenacious demons we encounter in this life: the grace of humility. For example, St.

Paul refers to this grace when he talks about his shadows. Though we have already referred to the sins of Paul's past life when his name was Saul and his hate was large, after his conversion Paul refers to a persistent thorn in his side that teaches him to be humble. We don't know the nature of this thorn, but its presence reflects how Paul was on speaking terms with his demons. This thorn taught him humility. When we are on speaking terms with our demons, we learn something about the grace of humility.

We all have our demons that dance in our darkness. They party on. We can close the door to the cellar and go about our business or try to get some sleep. The sound of demons is silenced when we're busy. And if we do drift off to sleep and are given the grace to dream, the demons can't find the space to make a nightmare.

But if we are quiet and stay awake, we will hear their music playing — the music of the night.

"Normal" people are oblivious to their demons. But as Dr. Schutt said of Dr. Geiger, "He sees and hears things most of us don't." We tend to label prophets and rabble-rousers of every sort as "insane" because they hear and see things we don't. They have a gift that tortures their souls. Because they hear and see too much, they are difficult people to meet at the corner bar for a beer or at the coffee shop for conversation. More often than not, we lock up our prophets because they are not normal. They are thought to be insane because they are on speaking terms with their demons.

When I lived in Kansas City, now and then I had coffee at a local hangout that caters to the eccentric. Here, the marginalized meet on the sidewalk. They smoke cigarettes and sip coffee and tell what they have heard. They wear earrings in the oddest places. But then maybe it's only odd to me; to them, since they are all ears, they wear the rings wherever they want. They hear the voices.

Sitting in the coffee shop one afternoon, I could barely concentrate on reading the newspaper because the elderly woman behind me was carrying on a conversation with her demons. I wondered, "Does she talk to herself, with her demons, because no one else — especially 'normal' people — will listen?"

Though I have no inclination to pierce various body parts with rings, I do want to be "all ears." When a friend wants to tell us something and the tone of the friend's voice is edged with anxiety, we stop what we're doing and listen. "I'm all ears," we say. And the person's story pierces our body, our soul.

Prayer makes us all ears. Yet when we are all ears, we need to beware. It gives the demons a stage, a platform, a podium. When we make friends with our demons, when we are on speaking terms with them, we provide them a safe place to vent, to scream, to express themselves. Spending time listening to our demons is not unlike Jesus spending his time with the disenfranchised members of society and synagogue in the Gospel. These demons represent the disenfranchised parts of ourselves, those parts of our lives that we have disowned or tried to hide because they represent our dark side. When we listen to them, we give them a chance to speak a truth we may be too fearful to face. It is only when our demons are neglected, pushed down deeper and fed with our anger, bitterness or resentment that they grow large and become very dangerous. They can become so large that they take over our lives.

When I write of these demon voices within, I am not speaking of mental illness but spiritual wellness. I'm not speaking of the voices heard by those who are mentally ill, who are diagnosed as schizophrenics. I have experience of these voices, and they are not friendly. They are deadly. I am convinced that my brother Ed, a paranoid schizophrenic, listened to one of these voices that told him to kill himself. But making friends with the dark side of our soul can lead to spiritual wellness as we realize how shadows only rise when there is light outside — and inside. Prayer brings the demons to light. That is why prayer is so dangerous. But like Paul in the famous story of his conversion on the road to Damascus, transformation implies that we have "seen the light." It may blind us for awhile, as it did Paul. And as we've seen, that flash of lightning certainly didn't exorcise all of his demons, as evidenced by the "thorn in his side" that never let him rest.

What I am talking about here are those little demons that dance and delight in the darkness of our lives. If we give them the silent treatment, they will possess us. But if we are on speaking terms with them, we can control the dialogue before the demons control us. By stepping on our shadow side, we can gain power over our demons.

If we go a step further and let God step on our shadows, then God will have power over us. Indeed, such close encounters with the Divine in the shadows of our lives can be terrifying because they challenge us to change. So, even if we think we have power over our demons, it is very tempting to stay in the shadows and away from the light and make sure God's feet don't step on our shadows. After all, we have livelihoods to protect.

Maybe the story about the "bay of pigs" is encouraging us to take a good, long look at the shadows that play when we take time to pray. Perhaps this story is inviting us to see what changes God is calling forth from us and our personal shadows. Maybe this story is asking us to consider that when we encounter the presence of the Divine One, instead of "taking to our heels," we take to our knees. We invite God into our shadowland, into our neighborhood. True, God may turn our neighborhood, our livelihoods, our lives, upside down. But then, that is the nature of God.

So, looking in the shadows, what do we see? What in us casts a shadow upon others? What are these shadows trying to teach us or tell us?

LOOKING FOR OUR SHADOW

We normally reserve questions about shadows to a particular day of the year: February 2, Groundhog Day. That is the day when we ask, "Did you see your shadow this morning?" Tradition holds that after hibernating all winter, the groundhog, not known to be a light sleeper, awakes from its long winter's nap, yawns as it rubs the sleep from its eyes, takes a deep breath and pokes its head out of the ground. The groundhog doesn't want to see the light because if it does it will see its shadow, become frightened and return to its hole in the ground to snatch six more weeks of sleep. This, of course, means six more weeks of winter. But if the day is cloudy and overcast, the groundhog will not see its shadow and takes this as a sign that spring is on its way, and so it's safe to stay above ground.

The groundhog is a good guide for those who practice mercy because if we see our shadow then we know it means we have seen the light. Another mentor for this shadow seeking is the patron saint we associate with February 2, the feast of the Presentation of Jesus in the temple: Simeon. He is an old man, a "just and pious" man, who is depicted in Scripture as someone always on the lookout for the light. The Gospel of Luke (2: 22-40) tells the story of Simeon the light seeker. Luke says Simeon was "inspired by the Spirit" (2: 26) to go to the temple on this particular day. Imagine if Simeon, after many years of looking for the light, had decided to sleep in that morning? Imagine if he had decided to stay in hibernation rather than poking his nose out from under the covers and saying to himself, "Well, who knows. Maybe today is the day."

Fortunately, as usual, he goes to the temple that morning and sees a young couple following the prescriptions of the law by presenting their firstborn son to God. He holds the child in his arms and declares him to be "a revealing light to the Gentiles" and the "glory of your people Israel" (2: 32).

In the presence of the light, Simeon had to see his shadow. But unlike the groundhog, who when it sees its shadow is fearful and returns to its hole in the ground, when Simeon sees his shadow caused by the presence of the Light of the World, he launches into a canticle that could light up Broadway. He is not afraid of seeing his shadow. Indeed, he's been waiting for years to see his shadow. He has been told that he would not die until he saw the light. And now that he has seen the Anointed One he rejoices that his time has finally arrived to be embraced by the light of everlasting peace.

What is our reaction when we see our shadows? Are we like the groundhog, afraid of our shadows, wanting to escape back into hibernation to sleep soundly — so soundly that we dare not even dream? Or like Simeon, do we welcome the presence of the light even though it illuminates the shadow side of our lives?

For Simeon, the temple became a lighthouse that day. After waiting out many a dark night, after many years of searching for the light, Simeon was humble enough, patient enough, awake enough to go to the temple that bright morning. And the lighthouse changed the direction of his life: He could now find his way to his true home. "Now, Master, you can dismiss your servant in peace; you have fulfilled your word" (2: 29). Though Simeon had been waiting for a long time, the old man's sudden encounter with the light in the temple that day made his years of patient waiting pay off. In the presence of the light, Simeon was refined and ready, purified and promoted to the place of peace for which he was longing.

But Simeon would have never seen the light if he had not kept his ear to the ground — the ground of his being — which inspired him to keep his hope alive. Unlike the groundhog, he was not afraid of seeing his shadow. Simeon didn't "hog" the ground — he was humble. Rather, he "hugged" the ground — he kept his hope alive by keeping his heart grounded in God's promises to him. Isn't that how we sometimes describe a person who seems centered and focused: That person is grounded. This pious, prayerful, patient old man believed that no matter how long the darkness of winter might linger on the landscape of his life, no matter how deep or steep the night, no matter how many years it might take to see the light, one day he would hold in his arms and welcome into his heart the Promised One of God.

If in the darkness of our lives we are able to keep our ear and our heart close to the ground, we might perceive the tiniest glimmer of light that will keep our hope alive. When Simeon saw the light that day, he knew God had not forgotten him. He knew that God had fulfilled the promise God made to him.

Simeon, the light-seeker, shows us not only how to stay "grounded," and so overcome our fears in seeing our own shadows, he also engages us in the ancient art of shadowboxing. After he saw the light, he did not pull any punches. He turned to the child's mother, Mary, and told her that this child of hers would be the downfall of many, that because of the brightness of his light the thoughts of many would be exposed. Then, he delivered what perhaps could have been the knockout punch in this shadowboxing: "You yourself will be pierced" (2: 35).

In the light of prayer, all our thoughts are laid bare. In the light of prayer, all those places where we've been pierced become clear. In the light of prayer, our wounds become visible. And only when our wounds are visible can the healing rays of hope rush in. In this ring where we box with those shadows of our lives, we discover how this child welcomed by Simeon was also tested by what he suffered. Because Jesus was willing to enter the ring of the world's regret and box with the dark shadows of our very human lives, he gives us the courage to stay grounded but not to stay down for the count. When all we see are shadows, the mercy of God reminds us that we wouldn't see these shadows if we had not also seen the light.

Simeon, the light-seeker, the heavyweight champion of shadowboxing, was not afraid of his own shadows. He had waited for years to see the Anointed One. But he kept his eyes focused on the light. He was aware of the shadows, but he lived in the light. In the practice of premeditated mercy, it is important that we see our shadows by keeping our hearts, our ears and our eyes close to the ground. As long as we're not afraid of those shadows that creep and crawl over us at times, we believe that through the grace of God we will come out of those shadows to see the dawn of a new day.

The Ministry of Mercy:
Finding Our Footing in the Shadow of the Cross

*Calvary was not a Church liturgy,
but an hour of human life,
which Jesus experienced as worship.*

— Edward Schillebeeckx

The shadows we experienced on Mercy Street pale in comparison to the shadows we encounter where Mercy Street ends and Independence Avenue begins. We know this intersection as Calvary or Golgotha. This crossroad is not a dead end but a lifeline. Here on this hill outside of Jerusalem, the cross casts the longest shadow over the landscape of our lives. But if we are willing to stand in its shadow, our feet will find the way to true freedom: the avenue to eternal independence.

Like long-distance runners about to embark on this cross-country course, the first thing we should do is check our feet. While on a retreat several years ago, Father Bob Ferrigan told about one of his first assignments in the inner city of Chicago. The neighborhood bore the scars of urban blight and decay. He went to the grocery store one day, walking over countless broken bottles on the sidewalks and streets. As he stood at the checkout line, a young boy from the parish who was behind Bob greeted him. The priest noticed that the youngster wasn't wearing any shoes. Bob asked him where his shoes were. The boy said, "At home." He told the priest that he preferred to walk barefoot. "Of course, my feet get bloody sometimes because I step on broken glass."

The priest summed up the story by saying, "I want to go to heaven with my shoes off."

In the ministry of mercy, this is what we do: We walk through the streets with no shoes. Nothing between our feet and the ground. With bloody feet from broken dreams, we find ourselves standing on holy ground. Ministry in the shadow of the cross means standing where the blood of the poor, the accused and the condemned has seeped into the soil beneath our feet, and knowing this is holy ground.

When someone asks us, "Where do you stand?" we often answer that question from an ideological standpoint. We say we are liberal or conservative, progressive or traditional. But in the shadow of the cross, we answer that question not from a viewpoint of ideology but from the vantagepoint of God's mercy. We stand with others under the weight of their crosses. When we do, we stand in the same place Jesus did. It is a place in the shadow of condemnation, accusation and rejection. It is a place that resembles a lonely hill outside the city of Jerusalem where tears are shed and hopes are shattered.

When we stand close to the cross, we see that the water and blood flowing like a stream from the side of Jesus form a reflecting pool of God's mercy. In water and in blood we are brought near: "But now in Christ Jesus you who once were far off have been brought near through the blood of Christ" (Ephesians 2:13). It is the power of this water and blood flowing from the cross of Christ, "who is our peace," that breaks "down the barrier of hostility that kept us apart (Ephesians 2:14)." In the water and in the blood that soaks the holy ground on which we stand, we find "peace through the blood of his cross" (Colossians 1: 20).

CROSS-COUNTRY: AN OBSTACLE COURSE

Those who stand in the shadow of the cross know the meaning of that phrase from the Apostles' Creed, "Christ descended into hell." They know because they've been there too. They have the scars on their souls, the wounds on their hearts and the ashes on their psyches to prove it. But this has taught them to keep striving, in Paul's words, to "know Christ and the power flowing from his resurrection; likewise to know how to share in his sufferings by being formed into the pattern of his death" (Philippians 3: 10).

People who are prepared to be cross-examined for their faith "give no thought to what lies behind but push on to what is ahead" (3: 13). Like Paul, their "entire attention is on the finish line" (3: 13). They see the cross not as a hurdle on this racetrack of redemption but rather as the way one must follow in order to reach the finish line. But remember what Paul writes, "It is not that I have already finished my course; but I am racing to grasp the prize if possible" (3: 12). This is "the prize to which God calls us — life on high in Christ Jesus" (3: 14). We run this race, this cross-country course, when we have the courage to examine the crosses of our own lives. We find our way to Independence Avenue when we are crushed by the crosses of our lives but have the courage to get back up again and continue on this cross-country course. Along the way, we stop and stand with others under the shadows of their crosses.

Followers of Christ find their footing at the foot of the cross. The cross engages our memory by reminding us how God chose to stand with us in the person of Jesus. So, when we stand at the foot of the cross, we do not stand alone. But though the cross is the primary symbol in the Christian tradition, we often view the cross as an obstacle course rather than the way of redemption. We see the way of the cross as an obstruction, not an invitation to be in a holy communion with a God who suffers with us, with a whole planet so often plagued with pain. We often move the cross out of our way. We hang the cross on the wall so that no one will trip or stumble or bump their heads on it. Or, we place it on steeples that rise toward the skies, putting the cross out of our reach.

In most places where I preach I have my back to the cross. Indeed, we often put the cross in the background of our activities because if we put it right before our eyes, it would be more than a distraction, it would be an obstruction. The cross would be in the way. But isn't that how we often view the cross in our lives: not so much as the way of the cross but as the cross being in the way? We view the construction of the crosses in our lives more as obstacles than opportunities. The crosses of our lives weigh us down rather than lift us up. Though our faith proclaims the cross is a triumph, more often than not we claim our crosses as tragedies. Of course, this is only natural. It's understandable. Would they be crosses if they didn't have the capacity to hold devastating pain? Without the presence of extraordinary grace it's not easy to embrace our crosses as opportunities for victory and rejoicing.

Think about how we speak of those crosses we carry. Don't we usually talk about them in the language of loss rather than triumph? When we suffer a setback, or are engaged in a struggle, or endure a relationship that is difficult, we say of the experience, the event, the person, "I guess it's a cross I have to bear." We speak of it as something (or someone) that tries our patience.

Reflect for a moment on how we use the word *cross* in our language. A parent says to a child after the child talks back: "Don't get cross with me." The boss comes to work in a foul mood, and the whispers in the office warn: "He's cross today." Or, "Better not cross him."

We use the word when there's a mix-up in communication: "She crossed me up." Or, "Our letters must have crossed in the mail."

We use it to write people off: "I crossed her name off the list."

In some disappointing relationships with people the cross is multiplied: the familiar double-cross.

In body language, we cross our arms, cross our legs, cross ourselves — and each gesture conveys a certain meaning: distance, lack of interest, a defensive posture, or a blessing, a prayer.

We cross the street to get to the other side. We come upon a hill with a yellow sign that has a black cross in the center and we slow down because just over the hill there's a crossroad. And we don't want to cross paths with an oncoming car and cause a crash.

We cross-stitch, cross-examine, cross over, cross-country. There are crosswinds, cross beams, crosswalks, crosswords. It's puzzling!

Have I crossed you up yet? Or is it down?

According to Paul's famous hymn in his letter to the Philippians (2: 5-11), the movement of the cross is both up and down. That's the direction of the cross. It takes us higher *and* deeper. But it also takes us to the east *and* to the west. In the darkness of our night, we look to the northern skies and see the Northern Cross; turn to the south and see the Southern Cross. This is what the cross does: It points to the north, pushes us to the south.

This is the direction of the cross: It is the way that leads to life. This sense of direction is captured in the Philippians hymn, which portrays a downward movement: Jesus did not claim equality with God as something to be exploited but rather emptied himself, taking the form of a slave. God came down to earth. Jesus humbled himself and became obedient to the point of death — even death on a cross. But because of this downward movement of Christ, "God highly exalted him" (2: 9).

The cross goes both ways. The cross goes all ways. The cross is the way. Except, for many of us, in the language of our lives, the cross is too often in the way.

When we look at our own lives and see the crosses we've carried, the experiences of suffering we've endured, and maybe even the people we've encountered whose personalities or ideologies have tried our patience, we begin to sense how these crosses have allowed us to go deeper into the mystery of suffering, and, thereby, into the mystery of life. When we look at those experiences, we see how we survived not by our own strength or talent or gifts, but because of an inner strength we never knew we had until our world came crashing in and the cross grew so large we thought we'd be crushed under its weight.

This is the quality of redemptive suffering that is traced upon the cross. Redemptive suffering brings people together; it does not divide. A powerful example of this occurred a few years ago when a frail, fragile little woman in India, Mother Teresa, died. There was an extraordinary outpouring of emotion from all parts of the world upon learning of her death. At her funeral, a true measure of what it means to be Catholic was in evidence as people from all faith traditions gathered to pay their respects and voice prayers of gratitude for this small woman who carried large crosses. It was because of her ability to see the tragic consequences of bearing the cross — the poor, the homeless, the hungry, the lepers — and still respond in faith that the world regarded her life as a triumph. Mother Teresa claimed the cross as her triumph. This was seen clearly at her funeral as national boundaries and religious barriers were crossed in paying tribute to a woman who consistently refused to be labeled as a saint and instead clung to the words, "as I have done, so you must do" (John 13: 15).

As Mother Teresa has done, so we can do. Unfortunately, for most of us, we are content to make people like Mother Teresa saints and let ourselves off the hook. But when we don't look away and see the cross for what it is, we see it at the heart of life. As painful as our lives are at times, there is the ultimate promise being spoken through this cross. As difficult as it is to bear at times, this cross will lift us free. As tragic as our lives become at times, God's faith in us, God's love for us, God's hope in us, makes it possible to claim our little lives as a triumph of the cross.

CONVERSATIONS WITH CROSSBEARERS

So where do we look to find the shadow of the cross we so often see hanging on our walls, so often feel strapped upon our backs, so often speak of in terms of tragedy in the language of our lives? More importantly, where do we look to find the call to service, the sense of triumph in the shadows of the cross?

I direct your gaze to a woman I met while giving a retreat a few years ago. On the first night of retreat, she walked into the room with great effort. Her body was twisted, contorted. She suffered from multiple sclerosis, making every movement a great effort. As she walked into the room, I caught myself thinking, "What a cross that woman bears." During the week, when she received Communion, she held on to my arm to keep her balance. However, when she came to see me later in the week, her physical condition was never mentioned. This wasn't her cross. When she told me her story, I learned her cross and caught a glimpse of true triumph.

She was struggling to come out from under the shadow of the cross after the tragic events of the previous two years. First, her brother died of a heart attack at the age of 44. Her dad was with him when he died. They were mending fences on their farm when her brother's heart stopped. His father held him in his arms as he took his last breath. She told me that her mother, when learning of her son's death, said, "His dad was the first to hold him when he was born and he was the last to hold him."

A few months after her brother's death, her mother suffered a stroke. Her mom was recovering slowly when her dad, who had been under stress with his wife's illness and his son's death, was advised by his doctor to get a checkup. They discovered some problems and recommended a heart catharization. Something went wrong in the procedure and her father stopped breathing. He was on a respirator when his wife and daughter came in to see him. This is what her mother said as she placed her hand on her husband's chest: "I give your heart, your soul, back to God." And her husband died.

This woman knows something about the cross. And as she spoke, and as she cried, I saw in this woman a faith so large and luminous that my own losses were caught in its glow. In the tragic circumstances of her life, there was a faith in this woman that magnified my own. The cross is at the center of her life. It is seen in her body, in the way she walks, the way she talks. It is heard in her story. She is one of those who has been humbled by life and now knows the power of the cross. Because this cross is at the heart of who she is, no matter the disability, no matter the loss, no matter the tragedy, she claims her life as a triumph. And though she has never been formally in the ministry, she is truly a living apostle; her life gives witness to the cross of Christ.

The ministry of mercy in the shadow of the cross is not about comparing losses, as when we hear about people whose crosses are so large that ours seem to shrink into insignificance. It is not about making comparisons. It's about making conversation with our own crosses. It's about feeling the weight of our own crosses, measuring the depth of our own losses and beginning to see them not as obstructions but as opportunities for God's ultimate triumph in our lives. For when we are in the depths, we cannot rely on our own resources. We can rely only on the One whose grace comes down from heaven and lifts us up again. When we are emptied by the suffering we have endured, we can only rely on the redemption won for us on the cross to fill us with hope again. We find our call to serve when we are weighed down by tragedy that teaches us humility — we don't have the answers. And yet, when we humbly stand under the shadow of our own losses, we sense the gift of faith growing inside our hearts. And only then will we be able to claim our cross-laden lives as a triumph.

If someone comes to me when I am sitting under the tree of the cross and says, "I know what you're going through," my first reaction is, "How dare you! How can you possibly know what I'm going through? How can you possibly know my suffering or my pain?" But when that person shows me his or her wounds, when I know a little of the story of what the other has suffered, I find the invitation to sit for a spell with the other under the shade of the tree of the cross. And I find that I can take up this cross and follow.

In the ministry of mercy our mission identity is to be carriers of the cross. The crosses we carry make us a priestly people of premeditated mercy. Yet, our mission of mercy will be frustrated and fraught with fear unless we allow our own experiences of suffering and sorrow to teach us how to stand with others in their pain, how to walk with others on the way of their cross, how to hold others in their time of need. From this common ground we can find the courage to go on.

This is what Jesus is saying to us: "I know what you're going through." And when God knows what we're going through, we can find the courage to continue.

In those times of great pain, we come to know that there are no earthly possessions we own that can heal the wounds of our own crucifixion. We come to know what it means to surrender to God even when we don't have an answer to the question, "Why?" We come to know what it means to walk this way of the cross and realize we do not walk alone. We come to know how to be truly free even as we are imprisoned by our pain.

When we spend time under the shadow of the cross, we sense the invitation that redefines relationship for this time, for the time of our greatest sorrow, and for all time: "If you wish to be my follower you must deny your very self, take up your cross each day, and follow in my steps" (Luke 9: 23). With arms stretched out on the cross, Jesus invites us to come and follow. With arms stretched out on the cross, Jesus says, "Come to me."

When we do, we just may discover our greatest gift in our deepest wound. Once while I was giving a retreat, a woman who was in her 70s came to see me privately. The first thing she did was to show me her hand. In the palm of her hand there was a deep hole. She told me that when she was nine months old she had burned her hand severely. The doctors told her parents that as soon as possible they should give her piano lessons so that her hand and fingers would develop some flexibility. Otherwise, her hand would be forever clenched into a fist — the fingers would be useless, except to cover the wound. So, at a very early age, she learned to play the piano. She became an exceptional organist, playing in churches and cathedrals all over the world. She earned a doctorate in music and taught music for years at a major university in Texas. She told me that she discovered her gift of music in her wound.

When we heed the conversation of our crosses, we hear the wisdom of the wood — a wisdom the world considers foolish. These planks of wood, once living, were cut down and tied together to hold the body of the crossbearer. From this wood, the voice of the dying one gives life to the living, the compassion of the crucified one gives comfort to the grieving, the suffering of the innocent one gives forgiveness to the guilty.

THE CROSS AS A LIGHTNING ROD

The ultimate meaning of the cross is found in the forgiveness of our sins. This instrument of violence becomes the symbol of salvation, the sign of pardon and peace. As Paul reminds us, it is through the blood of the cross "that we have been redeemed and our sins forgiven" (Ephesians 1: 7). Yet, we don't often appreciate the full impact of this faith statement.

One summer evening when I lived in the woods at a contemplative house of prayer in Kansas, a violent storm moved into the area. The skies looked ominous as streaks of lightning cut jagged lines across the darkening heavens. With every bolt of lightning and every drum roll of thunder, I picked up the pace as I walked the two hundred yards from my office in the main building to my cabin. This was no meditation walk! I didn't mind getting wet; what I was most mindful of was my intense fear of getting struck by lightning! My heart raced; my pace quickened.

Shortly after I reached my cabin, the tornado warning sirens sounded. It was the first time I had heard them since moving to the forest. I knew what they meant: Take cover! Go to the basement! But, of course, I was aware there was no basement under my cabin. There was a crawl space but that prospect seemed about as promising as walking in the woods with the lightning, since my fear of being bitten by a brown recluse spider is on par with my fear of being struck by lightning. Yes, I was the wimp who lived in the woods.

As the tornado sirens roared, I lit some candles and grabbed a beer. I decided just to ride out the storm by watching Mother Nature's light show. What else could I do? I know I should have been on my knees in prayer as I remember doing when I was a child and the tornado warnings would sound and Mom and Dad would parade us down to the basement to say the rosary. But, instead, I stood at the sliding glass doors of my cabin, sipping on a beer and watching with amazement as the lightning illuminated the dark forest. If any prayer did come to my lips that night as I marveled at the violent, ragged edges of lightning, it was simply this: "Hosanna in the highest!" Imprisoned by the storm, with the lightning looking like so much barbed wire strung haphazardly across the skies, that prayer, "Hosanna," which means "Set us free" or "Save us," may be the most primal prayer that rises from a fearful heart.

Though the storm passed that night, its images of lightning stay with me. Fear of lightning is a healthy kind of fear because we know that a person who is struck by a bolt of lightning can be killed, or a lightning bolt can strike a tree and can cause a forest to go up in flames.

Meteorologists tell us that lightning is caused by an electrical current very much like what is produced in the sparkplug of a car. The difference is that one stroke of lightning can measure more than fifteen million volts! Lightning that creases the skies cannot cause damage or destruction to us or to the earth. But when an electrically charged cloud comes too close to the earth and overcomes the resistance of the air that normally serves as an insulator between the clouds and the earth, a lightning strike can be deadly.

To protect property and human life, the ever-curious inventor and founding father, Benjamin Franklin, developed the first lightning rod in 1752. This was sometime after George Washington, in the midst of his sometimes stormy relationship with old Ben, had told his friend to go fly a kite. Franklin constructed an iron rod on the roof of his house and extended it five feet into the ground. That metal rod served as a conductor, which caught the lightning bolt and allowed it to dissipate into the ground without causing any harm to Ben's house or property.

Even today, we see lightning rods in rural areas to protect homes and barns. But it's important that the ground rod should be planted at least ten feet or more into moist earth. The ground must be soft, not rocky or hard, in order to receive the electrical charge from the lightning.

Many, many years before Benjamin Franklin invented the lightning rod, a device was invented that would protect us from the lightning storms of sin and death, violence and oppression that cause us to take cover and hide in the basement of our soul. For followers of Christ, the cross has become a lightning rod that saves and sets people free. As Jesus told Nicodemus in John's Gospel, "Just as Moses lifted up the serpent in the wilderness, so must I be lifted up, that whoever believes in me may have eternal life" (John 3: 14-15).

Moses lifted up the bronze serpent in the desert because the people were dying from a plague of snakes. He used the very symbol of the evil they were experiencing to free them from the evil. In effect, he was drawing the poison out of their lives. It is no wonder that the medical profession uses this symbol of a snake coiled around a pole to capture their desire to heal.

In the same way, the cross, which in Jesus' day was an instrument of execution, torture and death, becomes the lightning rod that saves people from the poison of sin. Like Moses lifting up the bronze serpent in the desert, Jesus is lifted up on the cross. And in this action of being raised up on the cross, Jesus would draw to himself all the pain and suffering, all the violence and injustice, all the sin and death the world has to offer. When Jesus was lifted up on the cross, he became God's lightning rod to divert the sin that seeks to strike us, damage us and even destroy us. He took our sin, and what dies inside of us because of our sin, and took it upon himself.

The practice of premeditated mercy invites us to keep our eyes focused on the cross. But just as a lightning rod must be planted deep into moist ground to protect us, so this lightning rod of the cross must be planted deep into the moist soil of our souls in order to save us. This cross must sink deep beneath the surface of our moist and holy hearts. For if our hearts are hard, this cross will not be able to reach the ground of our being.

MOIST HEARTS: MEMORY AND MERCY

So how do we keep the holy ground of our hearts moist? We again return to the first ingredient of our recipe for premeditated mercy. Memory saturates the soil of our souls with the tears we have shed because of what we have suffered. Memory holds the stories of who we are, who we have loved, who we have hurt, who has hurt us. Memory soaks the holy ground of our hearts, causing them to break open and become moist, and so allows the lightning rod of the cross to find its meaning.

During those storms when I was young, we'd go down into the basement to pray the rosary. Depending on how long the storm lasted and how quickly we prayed, we often would also remember. We'd ask Mom and Dad questions about our ancestors, questions that would often launch them into stories. In the basement, in the midst of the storm, we would listen to stories.

Memories are important to keep the holy ground of our hearts moist. When Jesus was conversing with Nicodemus, he began by telling the story of Moses lifting up the serpent in the desert. He used this story so familiar to Nicodemus to describe God's plan of salvation. We need to remember our own faith stories and family stories to keep our hearts and souls moist. We need them to understand who we are, where we've been and where we're going as people saved by the lightning rod of the cross.

One of the most important memories we need to keep our minds, hearts and souls moist is that of mercy. Paul helps us remember the mercy won for us in the blood of Jesus' cross when he writes: "God is rich in mercy; because of God's great love for us God brought us to life with Christ when we were dead in sin" (Ephesians 2: 4-5). Under the shadow of the cross, we spend time remembering the mercy God has shown us in our lives. We seek to name the pain and sorrow of our lives caused by our sin and to remember how God is with us to bring us healing. We seek to name the sin that keeps us divided and apart, and we believe we are brought near through the blood of the cross. When we are beaten down by the injustice we so often see and feel, the cross lifts us free, lifts us higher to touch the hand of God.

It is God's forgiveness that makes the soil of our souls, the holy ground of our being, rich with deposits of mercy. When we experience God's mercy, we are moved and motivated to pardon those who have hurt us. We all know how the ground of our hearts can become hard when we cling to resentments too long. God's mercy seeks to break open this harsh and hard ground by helping us to remember our own actions of infidelity, our own words that have wounded another, our own actions that have caused others to suffer or our inactivity that has allowed injustice and oppression to continue.

The mercy of God kindles within us memories of love, of forgiveness and faith, and inspires us to live in the light. We live in this light when we become a lightning rod for others, offering protection and peace to those trapped by the terrors and tragedies of their lives.

When the storms of life force us to take cover, when the forces of evil batter the houses of our hearts, causing us to flee to the basement, when we are surrounded by lightning strikes of anger and vengeance that frighten us half to death, we are invited to take courage because we have a lightning rod that will protect us and save us. In those dark and stormy times of our lives, may we huddle close to this lightning rod of the cross, tell a few stories filled with memories and mercy, break some bread and pour some wine and discover we have already been set free. We have not been struck by lightning, but we have been lifted up and struck with something called salvation. Our prayer, Hosanna, in front of the window has been answered: We have been saved.

ESCAPING THE SHADOW OF THE CROSS

When we fail to become a lightning rod for others because of our fear, we flee the shadows of our own cross. This escape will lead us to hide behind barriers of indifference and walls of neglect. The more we escape due to our fear of engaging in the suffering of others — because we are afraid to look honestly at our own pain — the easier it will be to miss each other. And the more likely that we will inflict even deeper wounds by our indifference.

One day as I was opening my mail, I recognized the return address on an envelope. The letter was from a friend in a parish where I used to serve. I hadn't heard from her in awhile so I was anxious to read what was going on in her life. I missed this friend, but when I opened the letter and began reading, another sense of "missing" her became apparent.

Her letter was a response to something I had written about how important it is to pray and play in the remnants and ruins of our burned-out dreams to discover true healing and hope. My words had obviously opened a deep wound that I had inflicted upon her soul many years before. She wrote of a time when I had missed her pain and failed to see her anguish. At that time I had failed to stand with her in the place where she found herself: a place of worry and hurt and fear. And because I had failed to stay in that place with her and had walked the other way, I'd inflicted a wound that remained for years.

She reminded me of a day in 1986 when she came to me and told me that her son was going through a very difficult time and she was worried about him. This letter now charged me with brushing off her concern like "leaves blowing in the wind." I showed an incredible lack of compassion that day, she wrote.

My first reaction was to defend myself. Her son had been a student of mine in a religion class studying death and dying. I remembered her son very well. I was aware of some of the pain he carried in his heart. But it was evident from the tone of her letter and the words she wrote to me, that I had missed her concern and her pain that day. Finally, now, she was unleashing an outburst of anger against me.

She concluded her letter by saying, "Maybe you can't do anything, but perhaps my writing this letter will bring healing to me. I hope I can read your writings with an open mind, a burden lightened, open hands and a forgiving heart."

To be indicted with the crime of indifference to her suffering, to be charged with lacking compassion, struck a chord so deep that it shook my innermost convictions and caused me to question everything I believed about faith, about priesthood, about life. But this friend was right to indict me. Whether or not the charges were blameworthy didn't really matter because I knew there was truth in what she said. Though I remember trying to reach out to the young man in class, I had obviously not reached out to his mother that day she came to me with her concern.

I had not taken time for her pain. I don't remember why. Maybe I was in a hurry. Maybe I missed her pain because I was fleeing my own. Or maybe I failed to stand with her because I was too preoccupied with my own sense of loss. But whatever the reasons, they all come down to the same cause: I missed her because I was too preoccupied with myself.

Her indictment raises an important question for us as ministers of mercy: What do we do with our suffering? Do we allow it to remove us from the scene, to put on blinders to others in need, to nurse our wounds at the exclusion of others? Or do we allow it to deepen our sense of solidarity with others, to open our eyes to the suffering we see all around us, to reach out to the wounded ones we encounter along the way of our life?

Once my friend sensed me not being concerned about her son, the words I wrote or preached from that time on became like weapons that wounded her. My inability to see her suffering that day left such a vicious scar that she was not be able to put the wound into words until many years later.

The struggle to have my witness measure up to my words, to regard equally my wounds and others', continues. But there is a way to personal integrity through this struggle, a way to see Christ in the other, a way to stop missing each other. It is a way that can only be seen when we have the courage to walk our own path of pain, to go through our own wounds, to stand under the shadows of our own crosses. Only when we have touched our own wounds can we reasonably expect to see — let alone touch — another's wounds. Perhaps I hadn't responded to my hurting friend with the kind of care demanded by the situation because I didn't know enough about my own pain. But by the time I received her letter, I knew a little more about touching my own wounds. Because my brother Ed had ended his own tormented life, I certainly knew all I wanted to know about suicide and the effect it had on my family and me.

After taking a couple of days to allow the words of her letter to sink in, I wrote this friend a letter in response. I don't remember exactly what I wrote, but a week later I received another letter from her. And in between the lines of what we wrote to one another over the next few months, there was an attempt at reconciliation. It was a reconciliation that became more real when I went back to that parish a year or so later and presided at the wedding of her son.

Silent Witness: A Humble, Contrite Heart

The initial letter from my friend indicting me for my lack of compassion left me speechless. In Matthew's passion account, there is a subtle movement from words to silent witness that reflects how when we stand in the shadows of the gallows, words lose their meaning.

In the first part of the story of the passion, Jesus has much to say to his disciples at the table and in the garden. We've reflected on some of these words — for example, the words of Jesus in the garden, "My Father, if it is possible, let this cup pass from me" (Matthew 26: 39). Three times Jesus falls to his knees and prays for God to remove the cup of suffering. Three times he asks God to let this cup pass him by. Three times he says, "Thy will be done." When we are weary and afraid, wounded and not wanting to continue the journey, we fall to our knees and pray as Jesus did in the garden. Where does he get his courage to carry the cross if not on his knees in prayer before God? When we are weary, his words "Thy will be done" can empower and rouse us, allowing courage to swell in our fearful hearts, giving us strength.

Or when a friend betrays us, we carry these words: "See, my betrayer is at hand" (Matthew 26: 46) and "Friend, why are you here?" (26: 50). How painful this word must have been for Jesus to speak: "Friend." Betrayed not with a stab in the back but a kiss on the cheek. A friend betrays him with a kiss. Jesus' fate is sealed with a kiss. For thirty pieces of silver, the price of a male slave in Jesus' day, he is arrested and taken into custody.

But after his arrest and his appearance before Pilate, Jesus stands silent under the shadow of the cross. When he is brought before the high priest, his words are gone. Standing before his accusers, Jesus loses his voice. The Word made flesh is silent. As people spit in his face and slap him, Jesus empties himself of all words and remains silent. Sometimes words are redundant when the witness is so eloquent. Words just get in the way.

Jesus doesn't speak again until just before he dies. Hanging on the cross, Jesus says the prayer of the crucified, the prayer of the condemned, the prayer of the victim, the prayer of the oppressed, the prayer of the dying. This is the prayer before dying, the grace before death: "My God, my God, why have you forsaken me?" (Matthew 27: 46). It is, of course, not an original prayer. Jesus is reading the words of Psalm 22 etched upon his heart. He gives voice to the words that will rouse the weary, words that will give voice to the voiceless, words that will speak to those who don't know what to say in situations of extreme suffering, excruciating pain or unimaginable injustice: "Why have you forsaken me?" According to Matthew's account, these were Jesus' last words. Jesus' last words are a question, not an answer. These words form an inquiry that becomes a declaration of faith.

A prayer of inquiry was the prayer on the lips of George del Vecchio on the night of his execution. He asked for forgiveness from those whom he had hurt. He was humbled and contrite for what he had done, deeds for which he would pay with his life. George also asked that those who lied about what he was accused of would hear his words of forgiveness. Then he said, "Mom, I have to go. They're here for me."

His mother, Yvonne, told him, "I love you."

"I love you, Mom."

Then, at 12:01 A.M. on November 22, 1995, George del Vecchio was executed by the State of Illinois.

Now, Yvonne, a tall woman who walks with a cane, visits prisoners on death row to honor her son's memory. She travels from her home in northern Illinois to Chester, a town that sits on the banks of the Mississippi River in southern Illinois, where she spends a week every couple of months visiting prisoners on death row at the Menard Correctional Facility. She is known on death row as "Mama D."

I spent one evening listening to Mama D's story. It is not an easy story to hear. For a mother talking about her son, it is an excruciating tale to tell. George was a troubled young man. He became involved in drugs as a teenager. At 16, he ran away from home with two other boys. High on drugs, they killed an old man. George was tried as a juvenile and sent away until he was 21.

It is odd to hear the mother of an executed death row inmate say, "I was so proud of George." She wasn't proud of him for killing another human being. She only became proud of him when she saw what he became within the prison system. George experienced a conversion. He became a spiritual advisor to many men on death row.

Yvonne said that during the sixteen years George spent on death row, his cell became like a chapel. Bibles and books on spiritual matters crowded his cell. Though he never graduated from high school, "George had a way with words," his mother said. "He had a way to make difficult concepts simple." Yvonne said she always had a deep faith, but the man George became in prison "put my faith to shame."

Some might suggest that this mother's pride was misplaced. They might say that George was a man only his mother could love. And they would be right, at least at first. "The man he became in Christ," Yvonne said, "any mother would be proud of." That is why Yvonne continues to stay connected with the prisoners in Menard on death row. She feels a commitment to these men because her son was so committed to them. Yvonne said her son saw these death row inmates as his community. They were bonded together by blood — the blood of Abel. The blood of the innocent victims of their crimes. Like Cain who killed his brother, George and his fellow death row inmates were marked with the blood of the people they had killed.

George had the blood of a six-year-old boy on his hands. He was charged and convicted of cutting the boy's throat. George did not remember the murder. He was so strung out on drugs, he did not remember murdering this boy. In recounting the events of that fateful night, December 22, 1977, Yvonne recalls how George's defense attorney tried to point out that there was blood all over the room, but the only blood on George when the police arrived to arrest him at the scene was on his arms. George remembers carrying the boy when he discovered the boy's body in bed. But he does not remember killing him.

George spent two years in Cook County Jail and almost sixteen years on death row. The chronology of events is striking: George was married on June 11, 1977. His dad died of a heart attack on November 29, 1977. George was arrested and charged with murder less than three weeks later.

As a young man, Yvonne said, George was filled with rage. "God must be a monster," she remembers him telling her one day. "Why does God allow so much evil?" This was George's question, and he became a violent answer to that question, an incarnation of the evil he couldn't understand. There is no denying George died with blood on his hands. But not only the blood of his victims — the old man and the young boy he'd killed — but also the blood of Christ. He changed in prison. He became a disciple in his cell. And his mission became one of bringing Christ to other death row inmates.

On the morning of his last day, as his mother, family and friends gathered to pray with him, the devotional book George used for his prayer had this passage from John's Gospel: "It is finished" (John 19: 30). George had become in prison what God wanted him to be from the moment of his conception. Now that he had become a new person in Christ, Yvonne said, "it was time to go." Through the eyes of his mother, George was a modern-day Dismas: the criminal crucified at Jesus' right side, the one who defended him at the time of their torture, the one who heard the promise, "Today, you will be with me in paradise" (Luke 23: 43).

Yvonne's tears touched me, but she was not looking for sympathy. George is dead. He paid the ultimate price for what he did. According to polls, most would say that justice was accomplished when George was executed. Most people in this country — even in the pews of churches — believe in capital punishment. But George's story is not about justice, it is about mercy. If a man is changed from seeing the blood on his hands, can we be changed from a vindictive society thirsty for revenge to one that seeks reconciliation? This is the place where justice and mercy meet: the place of reconciliation. Justice and mercy come together on the cross of reconciliation where Jesus paid the ultimate price for our sins by experiencing capital punishment.

The final word, "My God, my God why have you forsaken me?" was a scream that echoes through the ages. It was a shout that caused the earth to quake, the temple curtain to tear, the tombs to open, the rocks to roll, the saints to rise, the dead to wake. It was the final word and the first word: the Word that rouses the weary, wakes the dead and shakes loose the faith of the centurion who says, "Truly, this was the Son of God" (Matthew 27: 54). A new creation was erupting. This new creation, begun in the wilderness, was now forged in the crucible of Christ's suffering on Calvary.

"In the beginning was the Word.... The Word made flesh" (John 1: 1, 14). But in the end, under the shadow of the cross, there is nothing more to say. In the beginning was the Word. In between, there were many words. In the end, there were no more words. The Word is dead, but the witness is alive. After the Word made flesh is dead and buried, two women named Mary sit in silence "facing the tomb" (Matthew 27: 61). There is nothing more to say. The tomb is sealed, like Jesus' fate, like our lips. Our lips are sealed. There is nothing more to say. The Word is locked away in a tomb. The language inside us is dead. Words are buried within us. There is nothing more to say.

Under the shadow of the cross, as we await this new creation, we pray in silence.

There is nothing more to say.

Psalm of the Lightning Rod

Blessed are you, God of all creation,
God of heaven and earth.
We give you thanks for the endless evidence
of your divine power and promise.
We are most grateful for the gift of your Son, Jesus,
who was lifted high upon the cross
to take upon himself the pain and suffering of the world.

As Jesus stretched out his arms on the cross,
he brought all peoples near to your divine love.
When sin and death threaten to divide us,
when storms of suffering cause us
to seek refuge underground,
when guilt haunts us or shame binds us,
Jesus brings us all to his very self
through the blood of the cross.
In the face of whatever strikes at our soul's life,
that seeks to destroy our dignity
or damage our dreams,
the cross of Christ becomes our lightning rod
of protection and peace.

God of compassion,
fill our minds with memory,
and make our hearts moist with mercy
as we seek to live under the shadow of the cross.
May your justice roll like thunder;
may your peace fall like gentle rain
as we await a new creation.

Waiting Tables and Washing Feet:

Seeing Inside
and Seeking Out the Lost

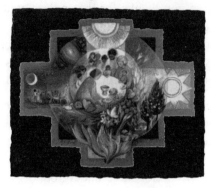

Our task is to see with eyes of love
all that is good, all that is wounded,
all that is marred, all that is beautiful.

— Mary Evelyn Jegen, SND

When we spend time under the shadow of the cross, we sense a call gathering momentum within us, the call to extend God's mercy to others. This momentum of mercy fuels our desire to serve others. In the experience of God's mercy filling the chalice of our hearts, our hearts cannot hold all the divine love we have known. Divine mercy spills out of the chalice of our hearts in very human acts of service and compassion.

In the ministry of mercy, then, the vestment we might wear is a simple apron. The apron that hangs behind the kitchen door is not only for cooking up a meal of memory and mercy. It can also be used to wait on those who gather at the table. Waiting tables is an act of hospitality that reflects how premeditated mercy is not only an attitude that results in inner healing but an action of service that extends divine healing to others.

This is what Jesus did when, on the night before he died, he got up from the table, put on an apron and washed the feet of his disciples. When he had finished, he said, "As I have done, so you must do" (John 13: 15). In John's Gospel (13: 3-20), this action of washing feet replaces the action of breaking bread and pouring wine. This symbol of service is our summons to serve the reign of God by waiting on each other around the tables of our lives.

I have great respect for those who spend their lives as waiters and waitresses. When a good friend left the ordained ministry and religious community a few years ago, his first job was working at a restaurant. He often told me how difficult the work was. I told him he probably felt more like a priestly servant waiting tables at a restaurant than he felt at times at the altar in a church. Certainly he came face-to-face with the demands of service: from the grueling hours to the grumbling customers. He knew immediately if his service was satisfactory by the size of the tip. Of course, the change on the table might have reflected more the mood of the customer than the quality of his service.

In the practice of premeditated mercy, we stand and wait and seek to serve. And in this standing and waiting and serving we learn that meditating on God's mercy must lead us to make this mercy known in actions of loving service.

FINDING MEANING IN THE MESS

For those of us who like order in our lives, in our work, in our relationships and in our worship, the act of washing feet makes us squirm. At that last meal in the company of his friends, Jesus does the unexpected. It's not part of the plan. The ritual doesn't call for the rabbi, the teacher, the leader, to wash feet. He should be the first to have his feet washed. He should be sitting at the head of the table. He should be the first served. Instead, he takes the lowest place and washes the feet of his friends.

Jesus puts into practice everything he preached and taught all those years. Yet, in one simple, sacred act of service, Jesus profoundly turns the tables of our expectations by becoming the waiter, serving his friends, waiting tables.

By washing the feet of his friends on the night before he died, Jesus extends the ritual celebration of the Passover by adding a new ritual. But to fully understand and comprehend the impact of this radical act, it is important to remember the first Passover.

For those of us who like manicured lawns behind freshly whitewashed picket fences that separate us from our neighbors, the story of the first Passover from the Book of Exodus (12: 1-14) makes us blush. For here the white picket fences are brushed with blood; the doorposts of our houses are splashed and stained with the blood of the Lamb of God. Neighbors come scurrying across our lawns to find a place at our crowded table. There's not enough room; there's not enough food. Yet everyone finds a place, and there's enough lamb left over for a sandwich or two for the journey ahead.

This meal also makes those of us who like a sit-down supper — quiet and paced, with lengthy intervals between each course — suffer a bout of indigestion. As the story goes, the Passover meal is eaten in haste, "like those who are in flight" (Exodus 12: 11). We have miles to go before we get to sleep. Eat and run. There's no time to lose.

But lose we do — not time, but friends. For those of us who only feel comfortable sharing a meal in the company of those we like, Jesus' final Passover meal makes us more than a little uncomfortable. For we remember that Jesus shared that supper with friends who would betray him, deny him and abandon him. Still, Jesus waited on tables and served a memorable meal, a meal of memory: "Do this in remembrance of me." Breaking bread and pouring wine, washing feet and challenging expectations, Jesus says, "Whenever you do this, remember me."

The Eucharist, which reflects the Passover ritual of our Jewish ancestors and the meal of memory Jesus celebrated on the night before he died, is about finding meaning in the messiness of our lives. It is about sensing the fragrance of forgiveness in the foul odor of betrayal. It is about tasting the bread of life in the dark hours just before death. It is about savoring the wine of compassion made from grapes that have been crushed. It is about finding courage on one's knees.

On the night before he died, Jesus did the unimaginable: The teacher washed the feet of his students. His audacious act of humble service inaugurated a new revolution of love that will stand so long as we are willing to kneel in reverence before other human beings. In the messiness of life, waiting tables and washing feet are rituals of remembrance that reflect the ministry of mercy that dares to change our lives.

BLOOD ON HIS HANDS

For the past couple of years I have been corresponding with a man named Michael, a man who has blood on his hands. He is in prison in Oklahoma, serving a life sentence for murder. In his letters, Michael has told me some of his story. He has spent most of his life outside the law and on the fringes of society. He described how this experience turned his heart into stone: "I never cared much about others or their feelings.

And I never had great respect or concern about their lives, their problems, their concerns. I concerned myself only with my own hedonistic desires, wants and demands. Satisfaction of those things that I desired came most often at the expense of others. I was a substance abuser, thief, con-artist, deceiver of others, embezzler, liar and ultimately a killer. I had no conception of myself as one of 'God's beloved' and, in fact, saw myself more closely aligned with the evil one."

Michael saw himself lurking in the shadows with Judas. In the Gospel of John we read how "the devil had already put into the heart of Judas, son of Simon Iscariot, to betray" Jesus (John 13: 2). Michael saw himself as a betrayer, but he never considered himself a killer — until that night in 1987 when he committed murder. "Of all the things I believed about myself — that I was a liar and a thief, I could still not conceive of myself as a killer. I always felt that somehow I was above killing another human being; I could just never stoop to those depths. But there I was. I found myself in jail. I could not help asking God, 'What happened? How could I have done such a thing?'"

The night of his arrest, Michael asked God to show him the way back, to show him what it was that God wanted him to do. When he was sentenced to life in prison, he remembered that prayer in the county jail. "I opened my eyes and began looking for the 'doors' that God would open before me."

But these doors didn't open right away. The only doors Michael saw and heard were the steel doors of a jail cell slamming shut. For the first five years of his incarceration he continued to live as he had outside the stone walls of his prison cell. He was a loner, an outcast within the prison system. But then a religious sister from the Adorers of the Blood of Christ reached out to him. In conversations and prayer with Sister Elizabeth Determan, he came to a place where he began to believe that God was watching over him and was opening the doors he needed open.

There was still blood on Michael's hands from his murder, but now he also began to see there was blood on the house where he lived. The blood stained the door of his prison cell. And the door that led to his heart. He felt a liberation, a freedom to love, that he had never felt before. He felt God passing over him, opening doors for him, inviting him to follow.

One of these doors opened for Michael on December 24, 1996. A very close friend of his was diagnosed with terminal lung cancer. This friend, Brad, came to Michael, as he often did, for advice and comfort. "All I could think of to tell him," Michael wrote, "was that I would help him in any way I could. I would do whatever I could to make him more comfortable. In my mind, I wanted to run; I really was not ready to take on this type of burden. I wasn't ready to take on his suffering."

Though Michael and Brad were friends, Brad's illness would now cause their relationship to become more intimate — if Michael chose to be present to Brad through his dying process. This prospect raised great fear in Michael because Brad was openly gay and was serving a life sentence for child molestation, a crime not at all well tolerated in prison. "While our relationship was one strictly of friendship," Michael wrote, "I worried what others might think."

But Michael overcame his fear, and for the next year he accompanied Brad from life to death. At one point, Brad asked Michael to become his cellmate. Until this time, Michael wrote that he "was still somewhat insulated from the full impact of Brad's condition. I was striving to be present to him in whatever way I could; I was trying to help him with daily life and trying to do for him those visible things that said I cared for him and loved him." But now, Brad was inviting him, in Michael's words, "to join him on his journey to Jerusalem and to put my own life and needs to the side. I would have to meet him in his suffering right where he was, and together we would need to join our suffering with that of Jesus."

Michael became Brad's cellmate in September, 1997. He tried to be as hospitable and helpful to Brad as he could — running errands, doing laundry, cleaning the cell. One evening, near the end of Brad's life, they were sitting in their cell. Brad turned to Michael and said, "Mike, I would really like to soak my feet. Maybe they would feel better." Here is how Michael described the experience:

"I retrieved the foot basin from the corner, filled it with warm water and Epsom salts and placed it at his feet. I removed his socks and raised his pant legs, and then carefully lifted one foot and then the other into the basin. I was shocked at how large his feet were — he was retaining water and his legs and feet were very swollen and painful. For reasons that are still vague to me, I reached into the basin and began gently rubbing his feet. He was somewhat surprised, but he told me that it was the most relaxing feeling he could remember having in a very long time. His head leaned back, and he closed his eyes. I sat on the floor of the cell for close to an hour just rubbing his feet with warm water."

Michael writes that the Gospel of John flooded his mind and heart. "I found that place within me that allowed me to be humble enough before God to do God's work completely," and with the kind of love Jesus showed on the night he was betrayed.

The experience that night in that prison cell as he washed the feet of his friend changed Michael's life. The humility and love he had learned at the foot basin carried him through the rest of Brad's illness and his death. Just as the heart of a convicted murderer, a man who admits his heart was like a stone, could break open and show compassion and love to a dying friend, so our practice of premeditated mercy means our hearts can be broken open. And when our hearts are broken open, we can get down on our knees and find the courage to wash the feet of others.

At his last meal in the company of his disciples, Jesus needed to wash the feet of his friends. He needed to show them that love's service begins and ends on our knees. He needed to give them an example of how our communion with God implies our holy communion with one another. In washing the feet of his disciples, Jesus reminded us that ministry and service mean messiness, inconvenience and risk. But when we wash another's feet, we welcome Jesus coming to us in unexpected people and unexpected ways.

The ministry of mercy means pouring out one's life in love's service. It means being humble, open and empty enough to drink in the experience, the compassion and the care of another. In washing the feet of his friends, Jesus showed us that it is in our common need that God finds us and we find our way to each other. Waiting tables at the last suppers of our lives — on our knees, washing feet — we begin to understand and maybe even believe what the German poet Goethe wrote: "In a dark time our eyes begin to see."

OUR TABLE IS WAITING

What do we see when we wait tables? Do we see meaning even in the mayhem of personal tragedies and cosmic catastrophes? Do we see how methods of premeditated mercy, love and service are the only ways to meet the madness of violence and vengeance? Do we see ourselves as servants of love who are called to get down on our knees to wash the soiled hopes of those too fearful to believe?

The ministry of mercy invites us to see love in the messiness of betrayal, hope in the messiness of despair, life in the messiness of death. In order to see, we need only to look. This vision is captured in a story about Bishop Desmond Tutu visiting a women's prison in South Africa. He went to the prison to celebrate Eucharist because he said he wanted to have communion with people who knew pain. In his homily, which focused on the image of Jesus as the Good Shepherd who leaves the ninety-nine sheep on the mountain and goes in search of the one who has gone astray (Matthew 18: 10-14), Bishop Tutu stood before the women and said, "I am so glad that there is no picture on the wall of the Good Shepherd. So many churches have the Good Shepherd on the wall, and the shepherd is dressed in a white, pressed gown, and he holds a clean, white, bright-eyed lamb in his arms. The picture is wrong. A shepherd who has been out all day or night looking for a missing lamb would come back a mess. His face would be dirty, his clothes torn, his body exhausted. And the lamb? The lamb would have briars in his wool and would stink even more than a clean lamb does."

Bishop Tutu, who had fought steadfastly for years with nonviolent and reconciling means to overturn the apartheid regime in South Africa, looked at these women who had failed, who were lost, who had scarred arms, scarred faces, scarred souls, and he said softly, "That lamb was the worst of them all. And the Good Shepherd wanted that lamb the most." Then, holding the bread and the cup of Communion, this priest of God, a compassionate shepherd who knew more than most about suffering, looked with kind eyes at his broken, lost church and said, "Is anyone not hungry? Then everyone come." These left-for-lost women, with their broken hearts and bruised souls, recognizing their hunger, came forward to be fed.

If we have been on the receiving end of divine compassion, as those women in the South Africa prison were the day Bishop Tutu invited them to the table, then we know that life ultimately doesn't make sense unless we see our lives and the lives of each person we meet on Mercy Street not simply through the mind's eye but also through the cracks of our broken hearts.

That is how God sees us. That is how Jesus sees us. This is how the Eucharist invites us to see: beyond our fears, through our tears, beneath our scars, to the divine image etched upon our heart. And when we do, we sense the hunger in those hearts and hear the invitation, "Is anyone not hungry? Then everyone come."

SEEING BY HEART

When I see people come to the table to receive the Eucharist with a blank stare in their eyes or frowns on their faces, I have to wonder, "Why?" But, of course, looks can be deceiving, and I am learning from experience to pause a moment, or maybe even a millennium, before passing judgment. I remember a sister attending a retreat I was giving several years ago. This woman had the sourest expression on her face throughout the entire retreat. Early in the retreat, I noticed that she wasn't laughing at any of my jokes. She rarely made eye contact, and when she did, her eyes seemed to reflect a distance my feeble words could not bridge. So I decided that this woman would be my "project" for the week. I would focus all my energy, all my passion in preaching, on this one sister who was sitting in the front row and who, though she was physically present, seemed to be very far away.

Well, I failed. By the end of the retreat, this woman had not cracked a smile. Her eyes had not sparkled in the slightest. I felt as if I had failed to reach this woman. She had not come to see me privately, so I did not know her story or why she seemed so distant. But as we gathered for the last meal of the retreat, there she was standing behind me. She tapped me on the shoulder and smiled. She told me how much she enjoyed the retreat and how much the conferences meant to her.

I wanted to say, "You could have fooled me!" But I simply thanked her for her presence on the retreat. Then at the table, she told me her story. She had been diagnosed with cancer the year before. After treatment, the doctors told her she was cancer-free. But she was worried that the cancer would return. I had completely missed this concern about her health when I looked into her eyes. I had tried to read her face and saw only boredom and distance. In reality, her soul was in anguish at the ordeal she had gone through the past year. Her look spelled concern about her health and the prospects for her future.

Though I had completely misread the look on this sister's face, when she shared with me her story about her health I committed to memory the poem of her pain. I can't say I've memorized all the details of her story, but she reminded me how dangerous it is to just see the look on a person's face and fail to see the poem of pain written upon her heart.

We memorize a poem and we say we know it by heart. We remember the words of a song and we say, "I know that song by heart." We visit a place where we've been before, perhaps lived before. We have spent much of our lives in this place — we know where every piece of furniture is, where every picture hangs, the way the morning sun catches the dust on the dresser — and we say we know the place "by heart."

But what is our experience of knowing another person "by heart"? Does it mean we have memorized that person's features and can pick the person out of a crowd? Or does it mean we have memorized her moods and know exactly how she will respond in a certain situation? Does it mean we've known his story, known her gifts and her limits, touched his wounds, heard her cry, seen his joy, held her pain?

Is it memory that shapes this knowledge of another's heart? When we have memorized our own poem of pain, then we can better read those verses written on the faces of each other. When we know our pain by heart, we can learn to see others "by heart."

Memory is often associated with the mind. We might say, "I can't remember names." Or, "Your face looks familiar, but where did we meet?" As we grow older, we may complain that our memory is not as good as it used to be. And yet, the experience of knowing a person, a place or a poem by heart reflects the truth that our hearts are also shaped and sustained by memory. The heart knows, and this knowledge reflects a basic truth about God: God knows us and our pain by heart.

When we are seen — and see each other — by heart, we recognize real presence.

THE EYES HAVE IT

The story is told of the day the disciples James and John were having lunch on the beach when they saw Harold, an old fishing buddy of theirs. Harold noted that he hadn't seen them around the docks and boats recently and wondered what had happened to them. James said that they had been on the road with the rabbi from Nazareth. "You've really got to hear this guy, Harry," James told his friend. "He sees human beings as they really are, not as they pretend to be."

Harry expressed some interest in hearing Jesus speak, so the brothers agreed to take him along to Jesus' course on miracles that night. But John warned him, "Harry, not everyone is ready for the honest revelations taught by Jesus. He teaches that we must see our own faults, and not just find faults with others. You can come with us, but your reaction to his teaching will determine whether or not you're ready to find your true self."

Well, that night Jesus presented the teaching about loving your enemies, doing good to those who hate you, blessing those who curse you, praying for those who abuse you. He explained this teaching by using the following parable:

Can a blind person lead a blind person? Will they not both fall into a pit? A disciple is not above his teacher, but every disciple when he or she is fully taught will be like the teacher. Why do you seek the speck that is in the other's eye, but do not notice the log that is in your own eye? Or how can you say to the other, "Let me take out the speck that is in your eye," when you yourself do not see the log that is in your own eye? You hypocrite, first take the log out of your own eye, and then you will see clearly to take out the speck that is in the other's eye.

For no good tree bears bad fruit, nor again does a bad tree bear good fruit; for each tree is known by its own fruit (Luke 6: 39-44).

As they were leaving Jesus' course on miracles that night, James asked his friend Harry what he thought about the teaching.

"Oh, you guys were right!" Harry said. "That man sees straight through human hypocrisy! He described several people I know!"

Poor Harry just didn't get it. He was still blind to the teaching of Jesus. Harry had a blind spot. His inner eye was not yet open to the truth of Jesus' message.

So what do we see? Do we notice or are we even aware of any blind spots in our living out the message of Jesus? Though I'm far from being an optometrist, as I understand it the term "blind spot" refers to a condition in which there is no photoreceptor at the place where the optic nerve passes through the retina. This means that the eye is literally blind to any images that fall into that place. Jesus spoke the truth in images, but his images fell into Harry's blind spot. At the same time, of course, Jesus wasn't just speaking to Harry. He continues to speak to each of us. And since we all have our blind spots, the important thing according to Jesus is to recognize them. If we don't, and if we try to lead others from that blind spot, we will become like his first image: the blind leading the blind.

The second image Jesus uses also has to do with the eyes, though admittedly in a less direct way. Jesus says that a student is not above the teacher, but all students when finished with their studies will be on par with the teacher. Now, maybe it's a little stretch, but students are often called pupils. The pupil in our eye is that dark spot in the very center of the eye. It is surrounded by the iris, which makes the pupil grow larger or smaller in response to light or strong emotions. In a sense, what the iris does for the pupil, the teacher does for the student. Good teachers enlarge our vision, enabling us to see more clearly. Wise teachers encourage us to see things we never noticed before. Holy teachers help us to adjust our eyes when it is dark, whether the darkness is inside or outside, and so guide us through the night. If you've ever had your pupils dilated in an eye exam, you know how sensitive you are to the light for several hours after the procedure, because the pupil has been expanded and enlarged. As a good teacher, Jesus often dilated the eyes of his pupils. He tried to make them sensitive to the light. From a spiritual perspective, it's good to have our pupils dilated every now and then: not only to check for diseases that might linger inside, but also to make us more sensitive to the light of Christ in our midst. When we are sensitive to this light in others, we will tend to walk more carefully, be less critical, be less in a hurry to pass judgments and ultimately to see more clearly. By having our eyes dilated every now and then, we may even be able to detect some of our blind spots.

A third image Jesus uses in the teaching is the familiar one about recognizing the plank in our own eye before trying to remove the speck in another's eye. Again, some spiritual insight might be gained from looking at the physical eye. For example, I have a condition in my eyes known as *muscae volitantes* — or what my eye doctor, after I told him my Latin was a little rusty, translated as "floaters." Now, these are not planks, but they are specks floating in my eyes. According to my optometrist, these specks are harmless — just dead blood cells floating perpetually before my eyes. The danger would come if they ever stopped floating and became stationary.

Jesus warns that specks like these can become planks that prevent us from seeing the goodness in others. There's no question that at times in my spiritual life these specks have grown in size and have blinded me or caused me to see the specks in another's eyes while missing the plank in my own. The only known cure for this spiritual disease known as hypocrisy is to get my own eyes checked, to look within and see my flaws before trying to play spiritual doctor and remove the flaws from someone else. As Jean Vanier writes, true community recognizes that

the evil is inside — not just inside the community, but inside me. I cannot think of taking the speck of dust out of my neighbor's eye unless I'm working on the log in my own. Evil is here in me. Warfare is inside my own community, and I am called to be an agent of peace there. But warfare is also in me and I am called to see wholeness inside of myself. Healing begins here, in myself. Wholeness and unity begin inside of myself. If I am growing toward wholeness, then I'll be an agent of wholeness. If our community is an agent of wholeness, then it will be a source of life for the world around it.

Seeing how other eye conditions might apply to us can yield further *insight*. For example, some of us suffer from myopia — the ability to see close up but not far away — while others have hyperopia or farsightedness which allows us to see things far away but not close to us. Some of us suffer from astigmatism, which distorts our vision, especially affecting our peripheral vision — our ability to see those who are on the fringes of our lives. Some of us may even have cataracts, which cloud the lenses of our eyes, thus dimming our vision. But whatever eye condition we experience that may reflect some spiritual condition, our Eye Doctor advises that we look within. The more we look within and see those floating specks and planks or acknowledge that at times our vision is blurred, the less likely we will be to see the flaws of others. The more we notice our inability to see at a distance or recognize what is closest to us or pay attention to those on the fringe, the less likely that we will see the faults of others.

In the ministry of mercy, our eyes are dilated and we become sensitive to the light of Christ within us. Our hearts are dilated, and so they grow large and expansive, allowing us to see the light of Christ in each other.

AN EYE-CATCHING EXPERIENCE

So, what do we see? What experiences catch our eye? What new glances of God's grace have we seen? What "eye-catching up" do we need to be about as we engage in the ministry of premeditated mercy? When I think of all the catching up I have to do, the sign that the former provincial of my religious community had hanging in his office comes to mind. It read: "Oops, there they go again! Since I am their leader, I'd better catch up with them!"

I am reminded of the story about Jesus' healing of the two blind men (Matthew 9: 27-31). What strikes me about this story is how the blind ones had a lot of catching up to do. The Gospel describes Jesus on the move and the two blind men "came after him crying out, 'Son of David, have pity on us!'" (9: 27). The indication is that Jesus didn't stop to hear their prayers until he arrived at the house where he was going to stay. At that point, the Gospel reports, "the blind men caught up with him" (9: 28). Only then does Jesus respond to their request. Notice that they don't have to ask him again. Jesus has heard their cries. But instead of healing them immediately, he poses a question, "Are you confident that I can do this?" (9: 28).

It would seem their confidence in Jesus' ability to heal them had already been proven. After all, they had been walking in faith, not by sight — sometimes running in faith — trying to catch up with Jesus. They had to be confident that Jesus would answer their prayers, or they would have stayed in the same place where they were before, confined to the darkness. Their confidence led them out of confinement. Their faith was fueling their desire to catch up to Jesus. "Because of your faith," Jesus tells them, "it shall be done to you " (9: 29). And the blind men recovered their sight.

What catching up do we need to do to practice premeditated mercy? Where are the blind spots in our lives that need to be touched by God? How confident are we that we will one day catch up to this one who lights the way for us but who sometimes seems so far ahead of us that we lose hope that we will ever catch up? And so we stay in the same place, our blindness slowing our pace, our growth in holiness. The longer we stay in the same dark space, our blind spots securely in place, the more accustomed we grow to the face of the earth scarred by violence and injustice. The longer we are content with the confinements imposed by our blind spots, the more our confidence will weaken.

After all, our eyes adjust to the darkness. When we walk into a dark room, we are blind at first. We pause; we stop in our tracks, until our eyes adjust. After awhile, we can move again because our eyes have grown accustomed to the darkness. Our confidence in our ability to move around in the darkness grows even as our confidence in finding the light that will illuminate the darkness dims. It seems this is what has happened in our world today, and perhaps in our own personal lives as well: We've grown accustomed to the face of violence and evil and death. We learn to cope with the dark, even if we sometimes stumble — or even as others often falter.

Our night vision improves the longer we stay in the dark. But the 20/20 vision statement of mercy's mission is captured in the words of the poet Rabindranath Tagore: "Faith is the bird that feels the light and sings when the dawn is still dark." This is the faith playing in the hearts of the two blind ones who cried out to Jesus. They had some catching up to do. But because of their faith they sensed the light within them, and this gave them the confidence and courage to catch up to the light and to witness the dawn.

For many in our world, the dawn is still dark. Confidence grows thin as the forces of darkness gain strength. In time, many lose hope that we will ever catch up to the light or that the dawn of peace and justice will ever break across the horizon. It is reminiscent of a story I often used when I was on the circuit to promote the bishops' peace pastoral. It's the parable about the time the disciples came to Jesus and asked him, "Lord, how can we tell when the night is over and dawn has arrived?"

So Jesus, being the good teacher, asked them how they would answer that question. Andrew said, "Could it be when one looks in the distance and can tell a cypress tree from an olive tree?"

"No," Jesus said.

"Well," Philip suggested, "could it be when one looks in the distance and can tell the difference between a cat and a dog?"

"No," Jesus said.

So, finally Peter tried, "Could it be that the dawn has come when one can look in the distance and tell the difference between a canary and a cardinal?"

"No," Jesus smiled, "that is not the answer."

"Then, what is it?" the disciples cried out in unison.

"You will know the dawn has come when you can look into the eyes of any man or woman and see your brother and your sister. Because if you can't, then it is still night."

By that standard, I know I have a lot of catching up to do. But then, that is why we premeditate mercy: to allow God to instill within us the vision that no matter how deep the darkness becomes inside of us or around us, faith is the bird that senses the light and sings through the night, proclaiming our belief in the dawn.

As long as we resist the temptation to allow our eyes to grow accustomed to the night, as long as we stay committed to catching up to the light, this vision for which we long, this light which we seek, will one day catch up to us.

THE PRINCIPAL OF COLUMBINE HIGH

In the dark time, the seemingly endless night, following the massacre at Columbine High School in Littleton, Colorado, on April 20, 1999, there were many stories told of anguish and terror, of courage and compassion. As the families buried the dead, as doctors and nurses treated the wounded, as experts assessed the tragedy, as people of all ideological, religious and political persuasions wrote letters to editors or raised their voices on talk shows about how to stem the violence, most of us were trying to make some sense of such a horror happening in a high school.

There were many opinions about who was to blame for this bloodbath. Some blamed the parents of the two young suspects. Some blamed the school administrators for not being more vigilant, for not having tighter security at the school. Some blamed the police and SWAT team for not responding to the crisis more quickly. Some blamed the easy access to deadly firearms. And, some blamed society, which includes all of us, for the erosion of values and the lack of reverence for human life, echoing what Pope John Paul II has called "a culture of death."

There were so many voices raised in anguish, in assessing blame, in looking for answers, in crying out for an end to violence, but there was one voice I heard a few days following the tragedy that still echoes in my mind. It was the voice of the principal of Columbine High School. He was being asked about the Trenchcoat Mafia, the gang of outcasts at the school who were being held responsible for the shootings. The interviewer asked the principal whether he knew the two young men who were the suspects in the suicide mission and about the security at the school. The principal seemed too sad, too devastated, to be defensive or to take offense at the suggestion that he could have provided more security, could have done more as principal to create an environment where such cataclysmic violence could never have occurred. He simply said, "I love these kids. I would take a bullet to save these kids if I could."

If the image Bishop Tutu used with the women in the prison — the image of Jesus as the Good Shepherd — is difficult for us to see or to identify within our modern, urban culture, then try this one drawn from the terrible events in Littleton, Colorado: "I am the principal of Columbine

High. I love these kids. I will take a bullet for my students." For this is precisely the image that Jesus was conveying to the people of his time when he spoke of himself as the good shepherd. He is saying to us: "I will protect you. I will take a bullet for you. I will go to the cross to save you."

Many of us have trouble with the image of Jesus as a shepherd because, by implication, we are sheep. And our experience of sheep is that they are so innocent and dumb and seemingly helpless. But if we had not lost our innocence in the wake of the violence at other schools around the nation in the sixteen months prior to April 20, 1999, then most certainly in the aftermath of the massacre at Columbine High we were no longer innocent. Most of us were dumbfounded by the sheer horror of the events. How could boys so young carry so much hate in their hearts? We felt helpless, like sheep that had fallen and were lying on their backs, unable to get up without the help of a shepherd. Though we may not appreciate being called sheep, don't we, in the aftermath of so much violence, suffering and bloodshed, sense a need for a shepherd?

If the image of Jesus as a good shepherd is too archaic for our modern minds to understand, then think of the principal of Columbine High School. And think of Dave Sanders. He was the teacher who took two bullets in the chest and lay dying for three hours during the siege as his students tried to staunch the flow of blood. It was reported in the newspaper that at one point he asked the students to show him pictures of his wife, children and grandchildren he had in his wallet. And just before died, he said to the students, "Tell them that I love them."

In chapter ten of John's Gospel (1-8), Jesus identifies himself not only as the good shepherd but also as the "sheep gate." He says, "I am the gate. Whoever enters through me will be safe" (10: 9). During Jesus' time, shepherds protected their flocks literally with their own bodies. They were the actual doors to their sheep pens. The sheepfolds were very simple, very primitive enclosures made of stones loosely piled upon one another. There was a single narrow opening to the sheep pen, and that is where the shepherd would sleep at night. The shepherd would sleep in that opening so that any sheep that wanted to wander out would be stopped, or any thief or wild animal that wanted to get into the pen would have to go through the shepherd first. The shepherd's own body was the only protection from a violent attack on his sheep.

This is the quality of love, the quality of relationship, that Jesus longs for us to hear and to embrace in the ministry of mercy. We need to know and to believe what lengths Jesus is willing to go to protect us and to save us. It is the willingness of the shepherd to lay down his life for us that gives us hope in times of great sorrow. It is our faith in the wounds on the resurrected body of Christ, the wounds by which we are healed, that offers hope in the midst of so many wounds, so much death. What Emily Dickinson wrote about deer, "the wounded deer leaps highest," also applies to lambs and sheep. The wounded Lamb of God leaps the highest.

We hear just how high at the celebration of Eucharist when the presider holds up the bread and wine and says, "Behold the Lamb of God who takes away the sins of the world." Jesus, who identified himself as the Good Shepherd, is now identified as the lamb. Jesus is both the shepherd and the sheep. He is the one who goes out looking for the lost sheep, the lonely lamb separated from the flock, distant and quite likely in danger. He is also the one who so identifies himself with the lost sheep that he becomes the lamb — the Lamb of God who through his sacrifice on the cross takes away the sins of the world.

Jesus is also the lamb mentioned in the Book of Revelation (7: 9-14) who sits on the throne when peoples of all tribes and nations, races and religions, cultures and creeds, languages and ways of life come before the slain lamb to do their laundry. They wash their robes, their hopes and their dreams in the blood of the lamb and thus are made clean.

MEMORY DETECTORS

In the ministry of mercy, our mandate is to become good shepherds for one another. We are called to see how all of us are responsible for one another because of our commitment to one another. We know that whatever happens, whatever violence we inflict upon one another, we can always point fingers and place blame, yet beneath it all we know that all of us are responsible. All of us. We know that to be a shepherd is to be committed, deeply, passionately committed to one another. If one of us is wounded, all of us are wounded. We feel each other's pain. We celebrate each other's joy. When one of us strays, we seek each other out. When one of us is betrayed, we look for ways to forgive. We carry each other in our hearts, on our shoulders. We are responsible.

Whether or not that responsibility will ask of us to lay down our lives for each other, we cannot say. We will never know if or when we will be called upon to take a bullet to protect those we love. When Dave

Sanders woke up on Tuesday morning, April 20, 1999, kissed his wife and children good-bye and went to Columbine High to teach and coach as he had been doing for more than twenty years, do you think he had any idea what he would be called upon to do that day? But he took two bullets in his chest to protect his students. Instinctively, he responded because he knew he was responsible to protect his flock, his students, from bullets ricocheting off lockers, from gun-wielding, bomb-throwing terrorists who the day before were simply other students sitting in his classroom.

In the ministry of mercy, we know we cannot save ourselves. We need a shepherd. We need a savior. We depend on God's grace. We need each other. We need to know we are not alone. But we also need to embrace the truth that because we have a shepherd who saves us, and who saves us as a flock, we are responsible for one another.

So, as we seek to be reconcilers in a wounded world, in those times when we are feeling helpless about what to do with all the violence and pain, the anguish and anger we see in this world that resembles "a culture of death," we realize that there *is* something we can do. In response to the shootings at Columbine High and at so many other schools in recent years, there has been much talk about putting metal detectors at the doors of all schools to increase security. But as people who desire to be merciful, we can install "memory detectors" at the doors and gates of our hearts to detect the Spirit of God in every human being. These memory detectors were invented by Jesus at the Last Supper when he said, "Do this in memory of me" (Luke 22: 19). After washing the feet of his disciples, including his beloved and his betrayer, Jesus said, "As I have done, so you must do" (John 13: 15). Memory detectors will alert us to another's anger or anguish, making an alarm go off in our heart and enabling us to reach out to one who is carrying so much ammunition that may be used to kill another's spirit.

After excruciating experiences of violence and evil, there is always more than enough blame to go around. But premeditated mercy suggests that instead of placing blame on others — which only tries to lighten the weight of responsibility we feel on our own shoulders — we might instead install memory detectors at the gates of our hearts. Such devices that are calibrated to the Spirit of Jesus can help us to be aware of each other a little more, to detect another's pain, to hear another's anger seething in fuming silence, to see another's tears, to touch another's wound. Instead of placing blame, we can place the names of those who are the victims of the violence in the temple of our hearts. But we also need to place on the prayer table of our hearts the names of those who inflict the violence. Like a good shepherd we can place all of these names upon our shoulders.

In the ministry of mercy, our challenge is to see each other by heart, to wash each other's feet, each other's hopes, each other's dreams. Our task is to carry each other, shelter each other and be for each other shepherds and guardians of each other's souls.

Is anyone not hungry? Then everyone come. Our table is waiting. The washbasin, water pitchers and towels are ready. The ministry of mercy that serves a new creation has begun.

Becoming a New Creation:
Feeding the Multitude with Mercy

When death, the great reconciler has come,
it is never our tenderness that we repent of,
but our severity.

— George Eliot

God was hungry to abide with us, so God sent Jesus to become the living bread to nourish the deepest hungers of the human heart. God was hungry for community, for connection, for stories told around a table as wine is poured and bread is broken. God was hungry for us to connect with one another — to extend the tables of our common lives, to open doors into our private pain and to welcome God as a guest at the banquet of our belonging.

What are we hungry for? Are we hungry to make connections with those who have been pushed away from society's table? Are we hungry to make community with those who have been left outside the doors of our awareness?

Are we hungry to make the ministry of premeditated mercy a daily practice, an ordinary occurrence? Do we satisfy this hunger by breaking the bread of friendship with someone who has fallen out of favor, by sharing the wine of our compassion with someone who longs to make connections, by washing the feet of someone who stands in the dust under the shadow of the cross?

The ministry of premeditated mercy that proclaims a new creation is about making such sacred connections. The following story reflects mercy's natural inclination to connect.

MAKING CONNECTIONS: EDNA AND LOUISE

Edna ran into Louise at the supermarket. Literally. They crashed their carts together in front of the frozen foods. These two old friends hadn't seen one another for months, and they laughed until they cried. They caught up on one another's lives, on what had transpired since they'd last seen one another. And they caught up on who had expired. You see, Edna and Louise were of that age when the first section they turned to in the morning paper was the obituaries.

As they were talking, each sneaked a peek into the other's shopping cart. Louise couldn't help but notice that Edna had five bottles of wine braced against a brisket that could feed a multitude. "Are you having a party, Edna?" she asked.

"A party?" Edna replied. "Why do you ask?" Louise motioned to the wine with her eyes. "Oh, the wine! Yes, well, I'm having a few friends over on Saturday night. Say, if you're not doing anything that night, why don't you come over?"

Louise was tempted to accept Edna's invitation. Since her husband Frank had died about a year ago, Louise hadn't ventured out of the house very much, except, of course, to attend Mass every morning. But, then, Saturday night was not a good night for her. *Dr. Quinn, Medicine Woman* was on television, and she didn't like to miss her favorite show. "Maybe another time," she said.

"Well, then, come over for lunch some day. I'll call you." They traded a few more stories they had heard via the grapevine — which of course was the major conduit of communication until the internet came along — and then Edna repeated her invitation for Saturday night and pushed her cart toward the fresh vegetables. As she did, she couldn't help but feel sorry for her friend, Louise. She really hadn't talked to her since Frank's funeral, and she felt a little guilty about losing touch with her. But what struck Edna as she checked the tomatoes was what she had seen in Louise's cart. Nothing but single-serving microwave meals. How sad, Edna thought to herself; poor Louise probably eats alone every night.

As it happened, Edna and Louise arrived at the checkout lines at about the same time. Louise was poised to go through the ten-items-or-less line, while Edna, whose cart was overflowing with food and drinks, waited patiently in the regular line. "Think about Saturday night," Edna called out.

Louise smiled but did not respond as she began to spread her nine single-serving microwave meals and a bottle of Geritol on the counter.

"I see you're still swilling that Geritol!" Edna laughed.

"Oh, I have to! Iron poor blood, you know."

On Saturday morning, Edna couldn't get Louise out of her mind. So she called her and insisted that Louise come to the dinner party that evening. Since Louise had checked the television listings and discovered that her favorite show was a rerun, she was more inclined to accept. "But only if I can come over early to help you prepare," she said. Edna was delighted and told Louise to come over whenever she wanted since she would be in the kitchen most of the day.

When Louise arrived around two o'clock, the awkwardness she felt in somebody else's kitchen quickly disappeared in the warmth of Edna's welcome. As soon as she walked into the house, the smell of fresh-baked bread brought back memories of her own bread-baking, an art she discontinued when her children grew up and moved out of the house. Though she still cooked when it was just Frank and her, she stopped baking. When Frank died, she lost her desire to cook altogether. "Cooking for one is such a chore," she told Edna. "It's just so much more convenient to pull something out of the freezer and pop it in the microwave."

But as she became more engaged in conversing with Edna while they worked side-by-side at the kitchen counter, Louise remembered how much she missed cooking. She missed the look on the face of her husband Frank when he'd taste a new recipe and would wink his approval. She missed the smell of fresh-baked bread. But rather than getting lost on her stroll down memory lane, she changed the subject. "So, who are all the people coming for dinner tonight?"

"Well," Edna said as she wiped her hands on a dishtowel, "I haven't a clue. You see, every Saturday night one of the volunteers at the homeless shelter brings eight people who are staying there to my house for dinner."

Louise was stunned. "You mean you invite strangers into your house?"

"Oh, Louise," Edna said, "they're only strangers until they come inside. When they sit down at my table and begin telling stories of who they are and where they've been, it almost seems like they're old friends.

Some are pretty shy at first, of course, but once they've had a glass of wine you'd be surprised how friendly everybody gets."

"So that's why you bought all that wine," Louise said with more than a hint of sarcasm in her voice.

Edna smiled and said, "Oh, no, dear, those five bottles of wine will last for five Saturday evening meals. It's just a way to celebrate at the table. Most of the people who come have really had some rough times, and though they get a fine dinner at the homeless shelter, it's kind of nice for them to have a sit-down meal served on real china with a glass of wine."

"Aren't you afraid these homeless people might steal your china?" Louise asked, still shocked by the thought that Edna was hosting a dinner party for people from the street and that she was unwittingly being an accomplice.

"Hasn't happened yet," Edna said.

She went on to explain how she got started inviting the homeless into her home. As Louise knew, Edna never married, so she didn't have children or even any close relatives — but she always had a number of friends. Edna told Louise how one morning while reading the obituaries she noticed that a woman she used to work with but hadn't seen in awhile had died. She began thinking how she had lost touch with so many of her old friends — some had died, some were in nursing homes, some had moved to Florida or Arizona. She found herself eating alone so much that nothing seemed to taste very good anymore.

Then, Edna saw a notice in the paper about the homeless shelter needing volunteers, and she signed up. After serving at the shelter for awhile, she got the idea to host a few people every once in awhile at her home. She told the coordinator of the shelter that she loved to cook and would enjoy the opportunity to host a dinner party for some of the people who came to the shelter. Thinking that Edna was naive, the coordinator was skeptical and told her it wouldn't be feasible.

But Edna persisted. "Feasible?" she said. "Feasible is a word for bureaucrats! I can just see a 'feasibility of a feast' study! I'm not talking about feasible; I'm talking about feasting! You know as well as I do that there's something sacred about sharing a meal in a place that at least feels a little bit like home. I mean, these are homeless people. For them, life is a daily grind. It might give them a little hope."

The coordinator of the shelter was concerned about the logistics —

how the homeless people would be transported to Edna's house, how many she could handle at a given time. Edna waved her hand as if swatting flies. "Logistics are not a problem," she said, "because there is nothing logical about this! Do you think Jesus was concerned about logistics when he fed the multitude on that mountain? We can figure out the logistics later. Just give me your okay, and I'll get the ball rolling."

By the time Edna concluded her story by saying, "This is not about logistics, it's about love," Louise saw a spark in Edna's eyes she had not seen in years. Moreover, it was a spark she once saw in her own eyes when she looked in the mirror. Now Louise understood. Yes, she understood. Though she knew that Edna had never been much of a churchgoer, Louise suddenly realized that every Saturday night Edna provided Eucharist in her home for homeless people. The spark she saw in Edna's eyes and heard in her words ignited a feeling in Louise's heart that she had not felt since her husband Frank had died. Her fears about this dinner party seemed to melt away in that kitchen that now seemed very warm as she asked Edna what she wanted her to do next.

After the eight guests from the homeless shelter had left that Saturday night, as Louise was helping Edna put the dishes away (which the guests had helped wash before they went on their way), Louise said, "You know, Edna, I go to Mass every morning. And every morning after Mass a group of people go out to McDonald's for coffee. They've invited me often, especially after Frank died, but I never went with them. But you know what, I think Monday morning I'll go have coffee with them."

Edna smiled. "Good for you," she said. "And maybe, if you want to, you could come over here now and then to help me with dinner. That is, unless you're busy most Saturday nights."

Louise thought for a moment and smiled, "Well, yes, most Saturday nights I have a doctor's appointment — with Dr. Quinn, Medicine Woman! But Edna, I think you might be the best medicine woman I've ever met. So, do you need any help shopping for next Saturday night's dinner?"

AN APPETITE FOR GOD:
FALLING IN LOVE AGAIN

There is something about a meal in the company of friends that helps us make connections with others. In the wilderness of our sometimes very routine lives, when we break some bread, pour some wine, tell some stories and make some new friends, we capture the essence of the real presence reflected in the Eucharist.

Microwave meals in front of the television set can feed an empty stomach, but they don't fill an empty soul. Until that Saturday afternoon in Edna's kitchen, Louise didn't realize how hungry she was. Even though she felt her appetite for God was nourished each morning at Mass, it had become more of a private devotion than a communal celebration. Though it certainly was a good way to begin her day, it was just God and her; it didn't really include anyone else. Spending that day with Edna and gathering at the table that evening with folks from the homeless shelter had changed that. Experiencing Edna's friendship and seeing the homeless people savor the chance to sit down in a home to share a meal and a story or two had taught Louise that Eucharist is about making connections, making community. She realized that Eucharist really is a holy communion with God and with other people. It's about having a large appetite for God, who is love.

The ministry of premeditated mercy calls us to reverence the real presence of Christ we celebrate in the Eucharist, a real presence that reveals the reconciliation God desires for us as we remember what Jesus did on the night before he died. It then invites us to make a connection between that Eucharistic real presence and the real presence of Christ in the world. With every connection we make between our worship of God in the sanctuary and our works of mercy in the streets of our world, the more our appetite for God grows. We begin to recognize the presence of God's image in people and in places where we thought God had been absent for a long time. We premeditate mercy when we practice reconciling with the one who has hurt us or whom we have hurt before offering our gifts at the altar. We also engage in premeditation when we make the real presence of God's mercy we receive at the altar a reality in our world through our works of mercy. For we are to extend the tables of our worship space to our workspace. We are to remember God's presence not only on the ground on which pray but also on the ground on which we play.

Remember how in Matthew 25 — the last chapter before Jesus' passion begins — the works of premeditated mercy are placed in the context of the Last Judgment. As God separated the just from the unjust, notice that the just are those who practice mercy: "I was hungry and you gave me food, I was thirsty and you gave me drink, I was a stranger and you welcomed me, I was naked and you clothed me, I was sick and you visited me, I was in prison and you came to me" (Matthew 25: 35-36). These are the works of premeditated mercy that reflect the real presence of Christ in the world.

In the telling of this story, the just are not even aware that they were ministering to the presence of God when they fed the hungry, gave drink to the thirsty, clothed the naked, welcomed the stranger, visited the sick and those in prison. "When did we see you?" (25: 37), they ask. And the judge replies, "Truly, I say to you, as you did it to one of the least of my brothers or sisters, you did it to me" (25: 40). The perception is that even though the just did not recognize the image of God in the people to whom they ministered, they had made a real connection between their worship of God and the works of God.

On the other hand, the unjust are those who failed to make this connection. They ask the same question, "When did we see you hungry or thirsty or a stranger or naked or sick or in prison, and did not minister to you?" (25: 44). They receive the same answer as the just. The judge says, "I was there in the faces of all those you met along the way, but you failed to reach out to me" (See 25: 43).

Notice that the judge doesn't say, "I was in church on Sunday, and you failed to worship me." Though this is obviously one of the "Top Ten" according to the Mosaic Law, in the Last Judgment parable Jesus does not refer to it as a prerequisite for redemption. Maybe it's a given. Or maybe Jesus is more concerned about making the connection between worship of God and recognizing and serving the presence of God in all peoples of the earth. Perhaps Jesus is warning us not to become complacent because we worship God every Sunday and support the parish with our financial stewardship. Jesus was about making sacred connections and, as we have reflected on often in these pages, warned about becoming complacent. The attitude of "We have it made because we follow the rules" decreases our appetite for seeing God in one another.

In the Book of Deuteronomy, Moses, the prophet and guardian of the "Top Ten List," also warned his people as they were about to enter the Promised Land not to become complacent, not to become too satisfied or content. Remember, Moses tells them: Remember the desert (See Deuteronomy 8: 2-3). Remember the hunger that humbled you. Remember the manna. Remember the One who fed you in the wilderness and quenched your thirst with "water flowing from flint rock" (8: 15).

Remember how God "led you through the desert" to the land of your dreams.

Once again, memory plays such an important part in the ministry of premeditated mercy. It is important for us to remember our hunger — for food, for friendship, for love, for peace. It is good for us to remember our own desert, the wilderness of our daily routines — to remember how thirsty we get at times, the cravings we have for true companionship, the yearning we feel for compassion. All of these contribute to increasing our appetite for God. It is an appetite based on the awareness that God will provide for us if only we remember how desperately God wants us to depend on the divine presence in our midst.

Jesus takes this real and divine presence even further by identifying himself with real food, real drink, with bread and wine (John 6). Why? Because God, Jesus says, wants to abide in us in an intimacy that defies logic. This is not about logistics; it's about love. He tells the people, "I am the bread of life. Your ancestors ate manna in the wilderness, and they died.... I am the living bread that came down from heaven; if any one eats of this bread, that one will live forever, and the bread which I shall give for the life of the world is my flesh" (John 6: 48-51). When the people hear this, they say, "Is this guy crazy? How can he give us his flesh to eat?" It doesn't make any sense.

But in identifying himself with this bread, this wine, we sense how hungry and thirsty Jesus is to make connections. He is hungry for our redemption, thirsty for our reconciliation. "Those who eat my flesh and drink my blood abide in me, and I in them" (6: 56). Now this makes sense: abiding with God. And, God abides in us, making us feel and think and act like God. So, sharing this meal in the company of friends, abiding with one another in our hopes and our hungers, evokes the presence of God who abides within each of us. We thus become what we eat, the body of Christ. We become what we drink, the blood of Christ.

This common union, this holy communion, is a feast of forever, in which we share the cup of blessing and break the bread of friendship. Rooted in the experiences of our ancient ancestors in faith, who received manna from above as they journeyed across the wilderness, the Eucharist provides us with our bread from heaven, our communion with God through Jesus. This bread not only feeds us, it comes into our bodies, creating an appetite in our hearts, a longing for love, for unity, for joy as we continue our pilgrim way across the daily desert of our routine lives.

Jesus, the bread of life, fell down from heaven to nourish the deepest hungers of our very human hearts. He fell in love. In falling in love with the world, Jesus invites us to fall in love again with one another.

Falling is the movement of the soul's joy and the soul's anguish. Falling in love is bliss beyond words. But falling out of the arms of the beloved is pain beyond description. In Psalm 130, the poet prays: "Out of the depths I cry to you, O God." When we have fallen from grace, this prayer rises from deep within our souls. Yet when we are in the depths, we are in the place where premeditated mercy begins to take shape. When we fall from grace, God gives us space to become a new creation. In this sacred space of the soul, before offering our gifts of love at the altar of our world, we explore a land of wounds, wonders and wide, wide mercy. Here we examine the hurts we've caused others and the walls that are still in place, walls that hold people beyond our arm's length.

It is in this place — beneath the surface in the wide-open spaces of the soul — that true, living worship begins. This is the place where a new creation begins to take shape.

VISION 2020: BLINDED BY PASSION

Sometimes, though, it is not our sin that builds the walls that keep us apart. Sometimes it is our passion that can create obstacles on the way to embracing this new creation. Sometimes we feel so strongly about a particular issue that we are blind to the positions held by those with whom we disagree. Sometimes we are so sure about the rightness of our cause that we exclude the views of others who might have something to teach us.

It was an early spring morning, cool but very calm, without even a brush of a breeze. The members of the board of trustees and representatives of various ministries from the congregation gathered in the upper room of the church office building to spend the day in discussion and discernment about the future of the church. Each member of the board and each leader in the various ministries had been working on his or her own individual draft of a project known as "Vision 2020." Each had submitted his or her plan a few weeks before so that everyone attending the meeting would have a chance to review the material.

The first few people who arrived opened the windows of the room where they were meeting because the room seemed stuffy. As each board member came into the room, greetings were exchanged and comments about the weather circulated. Just before the meeting was called to order, all those present reached for the pile of position papers that they had carried in briefcases and tote bags. The table was weighed down with all these stacks of paper. "I hope this table is strong," one of them joked. Another said, "I wonder how many trees gave their lives to produce all this paper."

The meeting was called to order with a moment of silent prayer. As the pastor of the church looked at the faces of the people gathered around that table, he was struck by how blessed this church was. "What a gifted group of people," he thought to himself. "What a remarkable range of enthusiastic, passionate and prophetic people!" He closed his eyes to whisper a prayer of gratitude. He wanted to say something about how awestruck he was to be with such a group of faithful people who were so obviously favored with God's grace. But he decided instead to offer a simple prayer invoking the presence of the Holy Spirit. "Come, Holy Spirit, enkindle the hearts of your faithful and fill us with the fire of your love." Everyone present answered, "Amen."

And through the open windows, a cool breeze gently brushed the faces of those around the table.

As the meeting began, each one was given the opportunity to present and to clarify his or her particular vision for the church. The principal of the school spoke eloquently about the importance of educating the children who are, she said, the future of the church. The director of social services quoted Scripture verses and the church's mission statement to underscore that concern for the poor and social justice should receive primary consideration. The director of worship strongly suggested that since the vast majority of people who belonged to the church only surfaced at weekend services, liturgy should be the top priority in the vision for the parish. The religious education coordinator pointed out how many children in the parish did not attend the parish school but were very active in the Wednesday evening CCD program, the confirmation classes and the other sacramental preparation programs. Injecting just a hint of dissent, she wondered how such a large percentage of the parish budget could be given over to the school while the religious education program had to hold car washes and bake sales to supplement its budget. The principal became just a little defensive about this remark and was about to speak out when the youth director interjected a real concern about how the church doesn't seem to care for its teenagers, how single adults don't feel welcome at the church because there isn't anything for them to do.

At this point the director of ministry to the elderly spoke up and asked those in the group if they knew how many shut-ins there were in the church? "Talk about nothing to do," he said, "these people are left alone with no one to visit them except for a few people who bring Communion to them on Sundays." That's when the coordinator of the divorced and separated group spoke up and said, "If you want to talk about not feeling welcome," and proceeded to reflect the attitudes and concerns of the people she represented.

By now a stronger breeze had begun to blow through the open windows, but none of the board members seemed to notice. A few of the loose-leaf papers on the table began to move, but everyone was so intent on making sure that his or her voice was heard — that his or her constituency was represented — that no one observed the fluttering of a few papers.

As the meeting wore on, the director of finance and stewardship told the group that unless the level of giving increased all the programs would experience some cutbacks. And then the coordinator of buildings and grounds mentioned with great severity that unless more attention were paid to some of the structures so badly in need of repair, all the points made by the others would become moot because there would be no buildings to house all these programs. To this statement the director of evangelization emphatically asserted that the church is about people not buildings.

Now the battle was on, the lines were drawn. One after another, oftentimes several speaking at the same time, as if they were auditioning for a part on *The McLaughlin Group* or *Crossfire* — they filled the room with accusation and innuendo:

"You don't care about the children."
"You don't care about the elderly."
"You don't care about the young people."
"You don't care about the poor."
"You don't care about the unchurched and the alienated."
"You don't care about..."

The litany of accusations of indifference reached a crescendo as the words became more heated and the faces more flushed and the fingers more pointed. Because everyone seemed to be speaking at the same time, no one noticed that now the wind was howling outside and sweeping through the open windows. Just as the pastor, who all this time had been sitting back listening to all the arguing, got up to close the windows, a mighty blast of wind came rushing into the room. All the papers on the table were swept up in the sudden whirlwind. The papers swirled around the room as the roar of the mighty wind silenced the voices of those around the table. Everyone looked around in awe at how all the papers, even those secured in three ring binders, were caught up in what seemed like a tornado. Not a single piece of paper remained on the table. The papers filled the room as a few board members dived under the table for protection. Some tried to make it to the windows to close them, but the wind was just too strong. The force of the mighty blast sent them scurrying to join the others under the table.

Suddenly, the wind died down. All the papers caught up in the gale-like force began to float gently downward to cover everything in the room. When they felt it safe to come out from under the table, the people in that upper room were knee deep in paper.

"My God, what a mess," one said.

"I've never experienced such a windstorm," another remarked.

They all looked at one another for a moment and then seemed to focus their common gaze on the pastor, who was the last one to come out from under the table. He cleared his throat and said, "Have I ever told you how gifted I think you all are?" Then he smiled and said, "Now, where were we?"

EXCEPTIONALLY GIFTED, SPIRITUALLY CHALLENGED

Does that parable sound the least bit familiar? Does it touch upon any of what we have experienced regarding what it means to be a community of faith? The Holy Spirit bestows on us extraordinary gifts and exceptional talents for the building of God's reign upon the earth. This Spirit ignites within us a fire of desire that we might live with great passion, using the gifts the Spirit has given us in the service of others.

But the great paradox is that this Spirit creates more challenges than cures. Rather than erasing the boundaries of our turf mentality or burning down the barricades we've constructed around our own passionate preoccupations or knocking down the fences of our private pursuits, the Spirit of God creates a people we might call spiritually challenged. Often, these boundaries, these barricades, these fences are constructed precisely because of the fire of our passion for a cause. And the greater the gifts, the greater are the temptations to believe that my gifts and my passion are the most important. My role in this reign making and kingdom building seems the most vital. My responsibilities to my constituencies seem the only ones that matter.

Like sin itself, our gifts can get the best of us, the best *in* us. When they do, those tongues of fire that came to rest on the first followers of Jesus huddled in the upper room are turned inside out. Our tongues then flash flames that scorch the interests, gifts and passions of others as we seek to protect our own interests and gifts and convert others to our point of view.

How often do we experience this in our own communities of faith today? How often do we sense it in our own places of ministry and community? How often do we get knee-deep in the paperwork of presenting our own position?

I believe Pope John the XXIII had it right. It is said that shortly before he opened the windows of the Roman Catholic Church by calling for the Second Vatican Council, he got down on his knees and prayed, "God, would you ever give us another of them Pentecosts? Because we blew that last one."

As we begin a new millennium, a millennium of mercy, may we not blow this one. Instead, may we commit ourselves to breathing in this breeze of a new creation by recognizing the extraordinary gifts of those who gather around the table with us. May we unleash our vision rather than protect our turf. Rather than reminding ourselves of our differences, may we allow the Spirit of God to revive our desire for unity. May we get knee-deep in prayer rather than paperwork or position papers. May we allow the Spirit of God to enkindle fire in us again, but a fire that will burn away the barricades and allow us to fuse our visions, to incorporate the dreams of those with whom we disagree.

Let's return for a moment to that upper room in the church office building that had become a wind tunnel. As the people sat amid the piles of windswept papers — after the pastor asked, "Where were we?" — the religious education coordinator, without saying a word, stood up and went to the school principal. She stretched out her hand and the principal did the same. Taking her hand, the religious education coordinator said, "May the spirit that is within me reverence the spirit that is within you." And then she gently breathed upon the hand of the principal. Around the table, each one did the same.

After they had breathed on each other's hands, hopes, gifts and wounds, the pastor looked at those who surrounded the table and said, "You are a most gifted people."

AN OPEN DOOR POLICY: THE PRIVILEGE OF BELONGING

Membership does have its privileges, and the first privilege is this: We are all members of the human race — a race where there are no limits as to how fast we go or how slow, how we walk or how we talk, what we believe or how we see. What limits us is our blindness to the image of God in ourselves and especially in the one we find most difficult to love. Our belief in the new creation means we can remain open and passionate, faithful and focused without having to close the door to another's point of view or religious tradition.

I once met a man who was joining the Catholic Church, and I asked him about his motivation for that decision. In reply he simply said: "The door was open." Nick was a delightful man, a 77-year-old native of Holland whose words dripped with a Dutch accent. One day he was out for a walk and came upon an interesting looking church. "The door was open," as Nick said. Because of his interest in the architecture of old churches, he just went in to look around. He met the music director, who was practicing the organ. The music director introduced him to the pastor, and the pastor ushered him into the community. Nick found warm and friendly people in a place that felt like home.

Nick told me he was very happy at the other churches where he had worshipped through the years, but there had always been a gnawing feeling that something was missing. "Now I know what was missing," he said. "It was the belief about the real presence of Christ in the Eucharist." But it's interesting that his newfound belief was sparked by a community of faith that lived that belief. This community of faith had welcomed him with open arms. This community had put into practice their belief and now became very real and very present to Nick.

This may be the best metaphor for a new millennium of mercy: The door is open. When we practice premeditated mercy, we leave the doors of our hearts open. As a community of faith, we open doors when we practice hospitality, minister joyfully, pray reverently and love intensely. Such open doors make real the connection between worship and works of mercy. In turn, this quality of living worship reflects the goal of premeditated mercy expressed by the prophet Isaiah: "I am about to create new heavens and a new earth" (Isaiah 65: 17).

We see this living worship where all people are welcome to receive God's mercy in the story of Jesus feeding the multitude on the mountain (Matthew 15: 29-33). The context for this Eucharistic story is important because it reflects how Jesus' "open door" policy is inspired by a woman who has spent her life locked out of the faith community. Before feeding the four thousand with a few loaves of bread, Jesus encounters a Canaanite woman who cries out for a favor: "Have mercy on me, O Lord, Son of David; my daughter is severely possessed by a demon" (Matthew 15: 22). This woman is one of the many outsiders who came to Jesus to experience God's mercy. At first, Jesus pays little attention to this woman from the wrong side of the religious tracks. But she is persistent; she keeps coming after Jesus. The disciples try to close the door in her face: "Send her away, for she is crying after us" (15: 23). Jesus finally stops and, in what could be interpreted as an apology, says to the woman, "I was sent only to the lost sheep of the house of Israel" (15: 24). This response certainly is consistent with the many stories from Matthew's Gospel about Jesus seeking out the lost. But this woman is not a member of the "house of Israel." Nor does she accept Jesus' "apology." Instead, she is determined to find help for her daughter. "Lord, help me," she says stubbornly.

Now, it seems, Jesus loses his patience with the woman and is ready to slam the door. At the very least, he puts her down by saying, "It is not fair to take the children's bread and throw it to the dogs" (15: 26). But in "slamming" this woman with a slur, in calling her a dog, Jesus actually gives the woman an opening for one of the most profound and prophetic professions of faith in all of Scripture: "Yes, Lord, yet even the dogs eat the crumbs that fall from their master's table" (15: 27). Jesus is astounded by this woman's response. "O woman, great is your faith! Be it done for you as you desire" (15: 28). With the instantaneous healing of her daughter, the boundaries of God's mercy extend not only to the lost sheep of the house of Israel but to all people in need.

At first Jesus wrote this woman off because she did not belong to the house of Israel. He had crossed her off his list of those he could help. But this woman's persistent and passionate faith attracted Jesus' attention and affection, and so stretched the boundaries of who would be saved.

This new open door policy continues in the next scene in Matthew's

Gospel when Jesus climbs a mountain "and great crowds came to him, bringing with them the lame, the maimed, the blind, the dumb and many others, and they put them at his feet, and he healed them" (15: 30). Jesus is evidently so busy healing this multitude that there is no time to eat. So, after a long weekend of teaching and healing, he says to his disciples, "I have compassion on the crowd, because they have been with me now three days and have nothing to eat, and I am unwilling to send them away hungry, lest they faint on the way" (15: 32).

The disciples immediately turn down the heat on the idea that seems to be cooking on Jesus' front burner. But Jesus serves up the idea anyway. He commissions his disciples to be the waiters and waitresses for the reign of God and cooks up a meal for the masses — and for the ages. Notice how close is the connection between the real presence of Jesus and reconciliation. Before baking some bread in his warm hands — hands that became like an oven fueled by the fire of love that blazed in his heart — he shows God's mercy by causing the mute to speak and the maimed to be made whole; the lame began to walk and blind eyes could see for the first time. Then, "he took the seven loaves and the fish, and having given thanks he broke them and gave them to the disciples, and the disciples gave them to the crowds" (15: 36). As the disciples serve up the meal, they don't even ask for a tip.

These incidents in the daily life of Jesus are sacramental moments. They reflect a living worship that makes presence of reconciliation very real. These stories of the Canaanite woman and the feeding of the multitude on the mountain are also earthly reminders of Isaiah's heavenly vision of new heavens and a new earth. Since the feeding of the multitude takes place on a mountain, it recall Isaiah's vision of God's holy mountain where "the God of hosts will provide for all peoples a feast of rich food and choice wines, juicy, rich food and pure, choice wines" (Isaiah 25: 6). The prophet's image of heaven is not a health club where we have to sweat off the pounds of flesh or the weight of sin that has made us heavy, but a banquet where it's "all you can eat" for free. Obviously, Isaiah wasn't concerned about calories or his cholesterol count. Heaven's banquet is not for the lean and mean but for the plump and pleasing. And what pleasures we will see at this feast on God's holy mountain: a feast with enough food to weigh down the sturdiest folding tables at a country parish picnic. Large quantities of the most delicious foods and the choicest wines. No worries about waist lines. All weight watchers are welcome.

And remember: God's breakfast buffet is all you can eat for free!

Like that day when Jesus fed the multitude on the mountain, the guest list for the eternal banquet feast on God's holy mountain will include peoples of every race and nation and way of life. Just as Jesus invited "the crowd to sit down on the ground," so the feast at the divine restaurant atop Mount Holy will also be a sit-down meal rather than fast food — with silverware, not plastic knives and forks; fine china and crystal, not paper plates and Styrofoam cups. I imagine soft candlelight instead of glaring, gaudy spotlights — and linen napkins, of course. When we look around at the folks at the table, we will notice there are no more veils, because "on this mountain God will destroy the veil that veils all people" (25: 7). There will be no more need for masks, no more misconceptions that entangle us in webs of misunderstanding. Truth, honesty and joy will rule the day and laughter will linger well into the night, because on this holy mountain "God will destroy death forever" (25: 8a). The most fascinating feature of this feast is that in addition to the napkins at every place, the waiters and waitresses all will carry handkerchiefs. These waiters and waitresses, some call them saints, will stand by, ready to "wipe away the tears from all faces" (25: 8b).

When Jesus multiplied the loaves and fishes to feed the multitude, he was offering an appetizer to the feast on God's holy mountain. Every time we gather at the table of Eucharist, we whet our appetites for this feast at the divine restaurant on the top of Mount Holy, a feast that God "will provide for all peoples." At the table of Eucharist, the Divine Host desires to wipe away our tears and our fears, to sprinkle us with the grace that makes us salt for the earth, to flavor us with the spice of compassion and love. Even as we gather at table, we realize that some of us are crippled by carelessness, lame with indifference, paralyzed by fear, blamed and blinded with guilt. But like the huddled masses that gathered around Jesus on the mountain, we are all hungry. God, the Gourmet of all Goodness, desires that all people feast at the table where the dream of new heavens and a new earth comes true.

REMEMBERING MARK: PROCLAIMING THE MYSTERY OF FAITH

This vision of the eternal banquet beckons us to believe that the final doors that are left open for us in the ministry of premeditated mercy are the gates of heaven. Our belief in eternal life reflects the sacred connection we have with those who have died and now reside on the other side, those we love who have taken their place at the eternal banquet of heaven. In this communion of saints, we embrace the belief that time and space cannot separate us or keep us apart. We believe that the spirits of those who have died are closer to us now than when they were alive. For now they are not confined by the limits of their bodies or by the illnesses or accidents that claimed their lives. Now they are free to join us at the table of our memory and our hope. Here we find them present, very present, with a real presence that transcends the limits of our imagination.

A few years ago, I was giving a retreat at a church with a parish cemetery close by. One day I went for a walk through the rows of stones. I stopped by one of these tombstones and read the name *Mark* and the dates *1965-1991*. Underneath was a simple verse, "May your song never end." As I stood there wondering about the story behind this name, this man who died so young, I was startled by the presence of a woman standing a few feet away. I recognized her as the sacristan of the parish, Clara. Each morning during the mission, she set up for Mass.

"That's my son," she said softly. We stood there in the damp, early spring air, and she told me the story.

Clara remembers the night her son told her about a dream. "He visited me," Mark told his mother.

"Who?" she asked.

"Jesus came and told me he wasn't ready for me yet. There were still some things I had to do. But he told me he would come back for me."

Clara told me that this dream gave Mark the courage to die because he knew everything would be all right. One of the last things he did before he died was to sing the *Exultet*, the great anthem of praise that announces Christ's victory over death, at the Easter Vigil. Since moving back to this small farming community after he had been diagnosed with AIDS, Mark, who was a gifted singer, sang at the parish Masses.

Clara and her husband welcomed their youngest son home and cared for him until the night he died at the age of 26.

Clara's eyes often filled with tears as she told me Mark's story. He died on a steamy June night. The summer heat filled his bedroom. At one point during the night, Clara went into Mark's room to check if he was okay because from her bedroom she could hear his breathing was becoming more labored. When she walked into the room, she felt a chill.

She thought to herself that the night had cooled down considerably, so she turned off the fan. She went back to bed. When she tried to wake Mark around 9:00 the next morning, her son was dead.

"Now I know," Clara said to me, "that the chill I felt that night was Mark's spirit leaving his body." She said that every now and then she dreams of her son. A smile creased her face. "He always looks so happy, so healthy in those dreams. It gives me some peace to know he's okay. Though I miss him terribly, I know he's okay."

At the close of the mission, Clara gave me a picture of Mark. "Now you can put a face to my son," she said. It is a face that reflects life, not death.

In the living worship of God's infinite mercy, we proclaim the paschal mystery of our faith: Christ has died, Christ is risen, Christ will come again. As we make this proclamation, I would like to suggest three possible places we might visit to renew our sacred connection with the communion of saints. The first place is a cemetery. This would be a good time to go for a walk in a cemetery. At the grave of a loved one or a friend we can hear the wind whispering the words, "I am the resurrection and the life. Those who believe in me, even though they die, will live" (John 11: 25). Standing in that cemetery with Clara, I couldn't help but believe it. Listening to Clara's story about her son Mark, Jesus' words to Martha grieving the death of her brother, Lazarus, made sense. Clara is a woman who believes deeply in this promise of life, this sacred connection with her son.

The story of Jesus' visit to Lazarus' grave (John 11: 1-44) echoes the experience of the prophet Ezekiel, who saw a vision of the valley of dry bones and heard God say, "I am going to open your graves and bring you from your graves, O my people" (Ezekiel 37: 12). This was God's eviction notice for the dry bones resting in the shallow graves of the earth. Remember the story: Ezekiel saw a vision of a battlefield cluttered with the dry bones of dead warriors. But what he saw with his eyes was overcome by the vision that was beginning to take shape in his heart. He saw God breathing new life into these dry bones and from the valley of death he saw a return to the glory of the Promised Land.

For the prophet and for the people, these bones represented the period of the Exile. They were symbolic of how the great promises of this people had been left in a heap of bones for the vultures to pick clean. They had been buried in shallow graves without a trace or a name.

But maybe these shallow graves were a blessing in disguise, since deep bones are hard to find with a shovel or pick, or even a story. A shallow grave sets the stage for discovery. The prophet is like a boy pretending to be a scout or an explorer who trips over a clump of dirt with marigolds blooming from its heart. The prophet kicks up the dirt and discovers even more. He explodes with words of hope: "You shall know that I am God when I open your graves and bring you up from your graves, O my people."

God's Spirit will revive these bones, resuscitate these dreams, resurrect these lives. These bones will shout again because the breath of life, God's breath, will cause new flesh to grow on these old bones. Clara knew that it is the Spirit of God that raises mortal bodies to immortal heights; it was that Spirit who raised her son Mark to new life. In the cemetery that day, Clara proclaimed the mystery of faith, the mystery of God's infinite mercy.

REMEMBERING MERCY: SOUL EXCAVATION

A second place we might consider visiting to proclaim our sacred connection with this new creation is another kind of graveyard. We might now go for a walk in that cemetery of the soul where our dreams are buried. It's a place where our severed relationships and broken promises are interred, where our hopes are decaying and turning to dust. As we stand at the tomb of dead dreams, we might ask ourselves, "Dare I roll away the stone?"

A sense of gloom and doom always seems to accompany us as we walk to this tomb where our dreams are turning to dust. Do we have the courage to roll away the stone? Old dreams are decayed by now; old hopes smell of death. As Jesus stands at the tomb of his friend Lazarus, Martha says, "It's been four days now. Surely there will be a stench" (John 11: 39). For some of us, our dreams have been dead for much longer than four days or four months or four years. Yes, it would be much safer to leave the stone in place.

But to proclaim the mystery of faith, to express our belief in the mercy of God that will erupt into a new creation, we might engage in tomb exploration, excavation and reclamation. There are many bones scattered on the floor of this tomb. Dare we believe these bones will live again? Dare we trust that out of this tomb our dreams will come for a walk again? When life itself seems to cave in around us, when the walls of our security crumble and we feel trapped beneath the debris, smothering, suffocating, stifling us with the pungent odor of decay and death, dare we believe in a second chance, a second wind? Dare we believe in this sacred wind, the Spirit of God who will give us the stamina to rise again from the rubble of dusty dreams?

We can if we listen closely to the sound of weeping. Listen closely to the sound of God sobbing over the death of our dreams. That brief verse in John's Gospel, "Jesus wept" (11: 35), perhaps the shortest verse in all of Scripture, gives us the courage to believe again. It says that Jesus is as grief stricken at the death of a friend or the death of a dream as we are. Though he knew that Lazarus would come walking out of that tomb, he imagined for awhile what life would be like without this friend. "Troubled in spirit, moved by the deepest emotions" (11: 33), the story says our dreams, our hopes, our loves, our losses find a home in God's broken heart too.

In the ministry of premeditated mercy, we enter the tomb of our soul to see which of these dreams that have died can walk and which will rest in peace. For, you see, those that should rest in peace are the ones conceived by small hearts, selfish hearts, those dreams that are meant only for our own advancement rather than the advancement of God's love upon the earth.

But God's dreams for us will be revived. They will come shuffling out of those tombs, wrapped up like mummies. "Unbind them and let them go free," is Jesus' invitation to free our dreams, revive our hopes and resuscitate our lives. Then, God pulls the string, and as we spin, God unravels new dreams, new hopes, new life.

This is our prayer when we go to the place in our soul where our dreams are buried to proclaim the mystery of faith: Give us the courage to roll away the stone.

REMEMBERING LIFE: BEING THERE

If it is just too difficult to face the death of a friend or the loss of a dream because the wound is still fresh, the loss too intense, then a third possibility is to go out and meet God halfway. Again, that story of Jesus at the tomb of his friend Lazarus comes into play in the shadows of the mystery of faith.

Why did he delay? He knew his friend was sick. He knew Martha and Mary wanted him close, if not to heal their brother then at least to see

Lazarus before he died and to say good-bye. But Jesus waited. He stayed where he was for two more days. Was he so busy that he couldn't cancel an appointment or two or postpone a preaching engagement to spend time with one who was about to die?

Jesus delayed in coming to Judea to prove a point. He knew that by the time word had reached him that Lazarus was sick, Lazarus was in fact already dead. But he also knew that he would raise his friend from the dead to show that his mission as Messiah was about life, not death. The way this particular episode is situated in John's Gospel suggests that this was the event that caused Jesus the most trouble. The raising of Lazarus led to Jesus' arrest. After all, the dead are supposed to stay dead. Enough said.

Jesus would spend his life visiting the living. I recall the story of a priest who knew that a friend of his, another priest who lived some distance away, was having a very difficult time. He had heard rumors that the priest was on the verge of a nervous breakdown. But he was just too busy to drop what he was doing and drive 100 miles to offer companionship and comfort to his friend. When he received the call that this priest friend had committed suicide, he made plans to attend the funeral. As he was driving to pay his last respects, the truth hit him hard. He would drive the 100 miles to attend the funeral but not to visit his friend when he was alive. As he stood before the casket, he made this promise: "From now on, I will visit the living."

In the ministry of premeditated mercy, we commit ourselves to visit the living. Before we offer our gifts at the altar, we call on a friend we haven't seen for awhile; one who has been distant from us or one that other commitments have kept us from seeing for weeks or months or even years. Mercy invites us to visit the living because the new heavens and new earth shout of life, not death. In following this path of mercy we become a new creation. We celebrate the life of God that is growing within us. Even as we walk on this earth, we celebrate the everlasting life that is God's gift to us when our sojourn in this sacred but sometimes strange land will be complete.

So, in these three ways we proclaim the mystery of faith by embracing the sacred connection that binds us in a personal and eternal bond. We can visit the grave of a loved one who has died and sense the holy ground moving beneath our feet. We can visit that place in the soul where some of our dreams are buried and find the courage to roll the stone away from the tomb. Or we can go spend time with a friend we haven't seen for awhile and catch up on life. All three are spiritual exercises — they exercise the Spirit dwelling within us.

God has placed a divine spirit, a divine image upon our hearts. It is this essence of life dwelling within us that can resuscitate our tired and aching bones. It is this seed-image of God that holds the grace for us to embrace the vision of new heavens and a new earth.

And it is to this sacred space of new heavens and a new earth that our practice of premeditated mercy will ultimately lead us: the place where none shall be missing and all shall be one.

EPILOGUE

Go in Peace:

Finding Room for Reconciliation

Nothing can separate us from the love of Christ.
Not trial or distress or persecution or illness,
neither death nor life, neither the present nor
the future will be able to separate us from
the love of God that comes to us in Christ Jesus.

— Romans 8: 35, 38-39

There is an old saying that "confession is good for the soul." Confession implies an emptying, a releasing, a letting go. "You'll feel better," the advice goes, "if you get it off your chest." This admonition suggests that we store our anger, our fear, our guilt, our greed, our shame, our sin in our chest. Maybe this is why when we gather at the table of the Eucharist, the first thing we do is acknowledge our need for God's mercy. It used to be that at the beginning of every Mass we would beat our breasts while praying the *Mea Culpa* — "through my fault, through my fault, through my most grievous fault." The gentle tapping of the chest was meant to shake the sin loose, to break up the clots of our callousness and carelessness that had clogged the arteries of faith. The Eucharist still begins with a ritual of penance that expresses our desire for God's mercy by acknowledging that we grow closer to God through our most grievous fault. This fault line is the avenue to God's redeeming, forgiving, amazing grace.

But I suspect that most would agree with what novelist Anthony Burgess once observed. "It is never the object of confession," he said, "at least in the Catholic tradition, to present oneself as a likeable character." In my experience as a priest, both as a confessor and penitent, as a presider at Eucharist and a person in the pew, Burgess is absolutely correct. I am waiting for the day when someone comes to celebrate the Sacrament of Penance and says, "Bless me, Father, for I've tried to be good. Made in the image and likeness of God, I know my true identity is to be God's beloved. But at times I forget who I am. At times my mistakes get the best of me. Now, I'd like to tell you about a few things, a few attitudes, a couple of actions, that reflect how I'm not living as a child of God who has been reconciled and redeemed in the blood of Jesus."

Instead, the standard formula for celebrating the sacrament begins: "Bless me, Father, for I have sinned. It's been six months (or a year or several years) since my last confession. Here are my sins." And then the person lists the several items that more often than not reflect a breaking of rules rather than the failure to live as a child of God captured in the covenant of love God made with us and our ancestors in faith. After confessing those sins, receiving a bit of guidance (or comfort or challenge) from the confessor, the penitent receives a penance from the priest, not as a retribution for the sins committed but as a sign of repentance, a symbol of the person's desire to live in the spirit of the reconciliation and reparation that is celebrated. The priest then invites the person to pray an *Act of Contrition*. One of the familiar versions goes something like this:

Loving God, I am heartily sorry for having offended you.
I firmly resolve with the help of thy grace
        to do my penance and to amend my life. Amen.

In the practice of premeditated mercy, both the celebration of Eucharist and the Sacrament of Penance (or Reconciliation) are rituals that encourage individuals to name and claim their truth and amend (or mend) their lives — in short, to find a real ground of reconciliation. Some of my most humbling moments as a priest have come during the Sacrament of Reconciliation when people looked honestly and with hope at the truth of their lives, seen the broken spaces illuminated by the light of God's love, and opened their hands and hearts to God's healing. And yet, some of my most difficult moments have also come in this sacrament when people confess their sins but instead of letting them go have walked out of the room clutching them tightly. I don't believe they were holding on to their faults because they were without hope. They believed that God forgives their sins. But they are unwilling or unable to let their sins escape through the cracks of their broken hearts.

Why do we find it so difficult to forgive ourselves? Perhaps it's because we live out of a belief that we are a fallen race rather than a favored race. We are the human race, made in the divine image. But the emphasis has been placed on our fallen status found in the Genesis story of Adam and Eve's original sin rather than our favored status found in the Genesis story of God's original grace: creating us in the divine image. Our faith communities have emphasized our sinful nature, the original sin, rather than the original grace of God's creative imagination. And so we have experienced large helpings of guilt piled upon our plate rather than embracing the helping hand of God's grace that wipes our plate clean.

But there also could be another dynamic at work in confessing and naming our sin. When we acknowledge the truth about the broken places of our lives by our true confession and accept the mercy of God, we accept the responsibility to amend our lives, to change our lives. Yet, because we are so filled with memories of our guilt and our shame, we don't know how to change. And so we continue to fall into the same patterns of behavior that brought us to the reconciliation room in the first place.

One of my most profound experiences of reconciliation occurred when I was a senior in college. I was struggling with an assortment of issues and was overwhelmed by a sense of guilt. Having been raised a good Catholic, I learned the lessons of shame and blame very well. It was during a retreat that I came in touch with the power of reconciliation. In his conferences to us, the Benedictine monk conducting the retreat spoke honestly about his own struggles with living in the manner of Jesus. His freedom in expressing his doubts and fears unlocked the grip that guilt held on me. Here was a man with the white hair of wisdom and an easy smile of charity telling us, a group of seminarians, that he didn't have all the answers but still trusted that God knew he was trying. His openness gave me the courage to face my own fears and confess the sins that lingered in the shadows of my soul.

As I sat across from him, my hands in his, my voice quivered like an out-of-tune violin. But his eyes shined with an understanding that eclipsed the shadows that hovered over my heart. In his gentle words of counsel and absolution I heard God's voice reminding me, "Joe, I love you. Go in peace."

TRUE CONFESSIONS:
THE GREAT COOKIE DOUGH CAPER

This experience of reconciliation with the wise and humble monk was a turning point for me in my understanding of the Sacrament of

Reconciliation. When I was young, my image of God was of a vengeful judge who took great pleasure in striking me down for breaking the rules. This was the image in place on the day I made my First Communion. My mom made cookies for the party that would follow the Mass. In those days, one had to fast three hours before receiving Communion. But I was not minding the time, not watching the clock. Instead, as I watched Mom put the next-to-last batch of chocolate chip cookies into the oven, I reached into the bowl and slipped a bit of cookie dough onto my finger and into my mouth. Just as I swallowed, I looked up at the clock. Less than two hours before my First Communion. I had broken my fast! I could not receive my First Communion! That cookie dough hit my empty stomach with a resounding thud!

Of course, I didn't tell my mom that I had eaten some dough. I kept it to myself. I couldn't back out now. Relatives were arriving to celebrate the first time I would come to the table of Eucharist. I went to my room to get dressed in my white shirt, blue tie and blue pants. A couple hours later, I joined my second grade classmates at the table. But the guilt of having fasted only two instead of three caused me great anxiety. For a long time, I was certain my First Communion was invalid! Worse yet, I thought that if I died I'd go straight to hell for breaking one of the church's rules.

Though I smile now at my youthful anxiety over the great cookie dough caper, it reflects for me how my image of God has changed. Though the image of a God who is kind and merciful took a long time to develop in me, its evolution leads to the revolution of real presence. Indeed, it's pure grace that allows our image of God to change from a judge who dispenses justice to one who manifests mercy. In Jesus, God has come down from the bench to practice law, except the law God practices is not as a prosecutor but as a defense attorney. God defends us with all God's might. And in the end, even when we are pronounced guilty as charged, God takes our place in the death chamber.

For me as a youth, the confessional was always like a death chamber. I dreaded going in there. Cloaked in darkness behind a heavy curtain, I trembled as I knelt facing the grill that separated me from the dispenser of forgiveness. When the small door covering the grill slid open, I could see the priest sitting in his box but hoped and prayed he couldn't see me. Since I grew up only two blocks from church, I often was called upon to serve at the early Mass or for a funeral. The priests knew me well. So I tried to disguise my voice because I didn't want the priests of the parish to know that one of their favorite altar boys was such a great sinner. And when it was complete, when the laundry list was read, the penance given, the contrition said, there was more relief than reconciliation.

The confessional box hardly provided room for reconciliation. It was more like a closet, dark and dangerous, where demons of blame shamed us instead of angels of mercy consoling us. But since the Second Vatican Council, most churches have replaced the dark closet where we hide our shame with a reconciliation room where we celebrate God's mercy. We've moved from behind the curtains or the screens to more spacious rooms where confessing one's sins is more naming one's truth. This truth of who we are as sometime sinner and sometime saint, as a pilgrim who stumbles now and then on the way of holiness, is named and claimed and given to God. The secrecy of confession remains, of course. The "seal of confession" remains intact. But now there is a sense that this is a seal of God's approval instead of divine disapproval for what we have done and what we have failed to do.

This is not to say that God approves of our misdeeds and missed opportunities to love. But God does approve of our desire to name and claim the truth of who we are and uses the Sacrament of Reconciliation to remind us that often who we think we are is really a mistaken identity. The real mistake is that we forget who we are. Sin seeks to steal our true identity and makes us into something, someone, we are not.

The formula of forgiveness or absolution now used in the Roman Catholic tradition reflects the essence of who we are: children of God for whom the mercy of God is readily available. When sins are confessed, when truth is named, when penance is offered and grace is prayed, the priest-confessor says these or similar words:

> Father of mercy,
> > through the death and resurrection of your Son, Jesus Christ,
> > you have reconciled the world to yourself.
>
> Through your Holy Spirit,
> > you have brought us the forgiveness of our sins.
>
> Through the ministry of the church,
> > may God grant you pardon and peace.
> I absolve you of all your sins, in the name of the Father,
> > and of the Son, and of the Holy Spirit.

And then, the priest says, "Go in peace."

TORN CURTAINS AND COMMUNION RAILS

Peace is Jesus' farewell gift to his disciples. In the Roman Catholic liturgy, these words of Jesus are echoed at every Eucharist when, after the communal recitation of the Our Father, the presider says, "Jesus said to his disciples, 'I leave you peace, my peace I give to you.' Look not on our sins but on the faith of your church, and grant us the peace and unity of your reign where you live forever and ever." Then, before coming to the table to receive the Body and Blood of Christ, the presider invites all those present to offer to each other a sign of peace. Following the prescription of Jesus that we have explored in this book — namely, that before offering our gifts at the altar we should seek reconciliation with each other — this ritual of exchanging a sign of peace would be more appropriate before the Offertory Rite, when we bring the gifts of bread and wine to the altar. And yet, where the ritual is presently practiced, it still speaks of making peace before receiving Holy Communion.

But it seems that for communities of faith today, this peace is an elusive gift. There is much division and separation within and among Christian communities. We have yet to embrace and live the truth of what happened when Jesus offered his life on the cross. When Jesus died, Matthew reports "the veil of the sanctuary was torn in two from top to bottom (Matthew 27: 51). According to the Mosaic Law, there were two curtains in the temple. The first covered the entrance to the temple; the second hung before the Holy of Holies (Exodus 26: 31-36). The law mandated that on the Day of Atonement, only the high priest could enter this inner sanctum of the Holy of Holies (Leviticus 16: 3). Scripture scholars suggest that the implication of the curtain in the sanctuary being torn at the time of Jesus' death is that now all people are admitted into the sanctuary to experience the real presence of God.

When the water and blood flowed from Jesus' side, it created a flood that washed away the barriers that keep peoples apart. In the wake of this rising tide of God's mercy, whatever distance or separateness exists in the human community was eliminated. The death of Jesus destroyed the separation among and between people. According to Paul, "the dividing wall of hostility," symbolized by the curtain in the temple, is gone. Now all people are one. When the flood of blood and water recede, we are left standing on the threshold of a new creation. This new covenant between God and humans is signed in Christ's blood, sealed in the tomb and delivered by Jesus' resurrection from the dead.

However, for centuries, in the design of its churches, Catholics kept this curtain in place. We called it a communion rail. The sanctuary was off-limits to everyone except the ordained and those prospects for "high priesthood," the altar boys. Only the ordained were allowed to distribute communion. The faithful would come to the altar rail, kneel before the presence of the Holy of Holies, stick out their tongues and receive the host. A paten was placed under the chin of the communicant in case there was a slip of the tongue.

With the liturgical renewal mandated by the Second Vatican Council, a new understanding of the priesthood of all the faithful changed the praxis of our celebration of Eucharist. Communion rails began to disappear. Altars were moved forward so that the faithful could get a closer look at the real presence. The language of the service was changed from Latin to the vernacular to encourage the full participation of all those celebrating the Eucharist. The theological and spiritual significance of all these changes seemed to emphasize that before we could recognize the real presence in bread and wine, it was imperative that we recognize the real presence in flesh and blood: the people with whom we gather at the table.

These changes, of course, did not come easily. Much controversy ensued (and in some areas continues to create divisions). In some cases, the distance created by the changes (and more recent modifications in the celebration of Eucharist such as the inclusion of girls as altar servers, women and men as ministers of Communion and as proclaimers of the Word) has been like an "invisible curtain" that separates the so-called right from the left, traditional from progressive, conservative from liberal.

When I worked for a Catholic newspaper in Kansas City in the early 1980s, one of the stories I covered was the lawsuit brought by members of a local parish against their pastor and the bishop of the diocese because the pastor had removed the communion rail from the church. After many months, the lawsuit was finally thrown out of court by a judge. I will never forget the words of the judge when he dismissed the suit because the separation of church and state gave him no jurisdiction over an internal church matter. According to canon law, the bishop had every legal right to appoint the pastor who removed the communion rail. The judge said, "As a Methodist, it saddens me to see such conflict and controversy among my brothers and sisters in the Catholic Church."

I suspect the Methodist judge is not the only one saddened by the separations that exist today among those who bear and claim the name of

Christ; by the divisions that remain among peoples of different faith traditions who all belong to the family of God. As sisters and brothers who seek to practice premeditated mercy — so that all might find a place on the holy ground of our hearts — our theme song might be that old cowboy hymn, "Don't Fence Me In." We cannot limit God's mercy. We cannot fence in God's forgiveness because just when we think someone deserves to be left outside the boundaries of our holy ground, God slips through the fence and brings that one back.

Though we have reflected often on the Gospel of Matthew as our primer for premeditated mercy, chapter fifteen of Luke's Gospel, which is often called the Gospel of the Lost and Found, contains three familiar parables about how we cannot fence in God's forgiveness. These three famous stories about the lost sheep, the lost coin and the lost son make it clear that God is in charge of the world's Lost and Found Department. All three parables are told in a context of a murmuring crowd of religious leaders who criticize and condemn Jesus for welcoming sinners and eating with them. The mercy of God reflected in these three parables is so extravagant that it would boggle the minds of those who heard these stories for the first time. But this was Luke's intention in telling these three stories: to boggle the mind, to stretch the heart, to take down the fences.

How we hear these three parables depends, of course, on whom we identify with. If we have ever felt like a lost sheep wandering aimlessly far from the community, we can sense how remarkable it is for the shepherd to leave the ninety-nine and search out the one who is lost. If we've ever felt like a precious coin that has slipped behind a piece of furniture in a crowded room, we can rejoice in how the woman in the parable — whose image, by the way, Jesus uses to reflect the feminine face of our forgiving God — spends so much time in search of the one coin that is lost. And the third parable presents at least three opportunities for identification: the younger son, who demands his inheritance and spends it foolishly; the forgiving father, who runs out to meet his son when he returns; and the older son, who stands outside on the porch and pouts while the party is going on inside. If we've ever found ourselves in any of these situations, our understanding of these Gospel parables will turn on our personal experience.

One experience in the life of my religious community reflects the parable often referred to as the Prodigal Son. It occurred when one of our members, who left the community in 1981, sought to return to the community in 1991. In the early stages of his coming back to the community, it's fair to say that many of our members were apprehensive about his return. Many of us were like the older brother in the parable. When he left, we had said, "Good riddance." Now, on his return, we were confronted with precisely the same feelings the older brother experiences in the parable. "Hey, we've been here all along, working hard, trying to be good ministers and members of the community. And no one has thrown us a party. No one has even given us a pat on the back or a word of affirmation for all that we've been doing these last ten years."

The thing that is striking to me about the father's response to the older son in the Gospel parable is his acceptance of the son's position. He understands why the older son is feeling the way he is toward his younger brother. But just as he ran out to meet the younger son when he saw him walking down the road, rehearsing his act of contrition, so the father goes out to meet the older son. He meets his children on their own turf, on their own terms.

This parable frames the image of God going out to meet us wherever we might be. Whether we are returning home after being away for awhile; whether we've been lost, wondering and worrying if we will ever be found; or whether we see ourselves in the skin of the older brother, faithful through the years, working hard without much affirmation, and then feeling more than just a little annoyed because all the attention is focused on someone we feel doesn't deserve such recognition — wherever we are in this story — God finds us. That's the sacred truth of God's premeditated mercy: We cannot fence in the forgiveness of God. God will find us. God will seek us out. God will come to stand with us.

As people who seek to practice premeditated works of mercy, we no longer spend our time mending the fences that keep us apart. Rather, now we focus our energy on taking down the fences on this holy ground moist with memory and mercy so that no one — regardless of that person's reputation or sin, righteousness or repentance — will be left out of our heart.

MAKING ROOM FOR THE NEW CREATION

The practice of premeditated mercy encourages us to look honestly at the divisions and separations that exist in our faith communities. We have referred often to the important role memory plays in making peace a real presence in our lives. How one chooses to remember a certain event that caused one to feel isolated, alienated or separated shapes how one will become a new creation. Though we often hear the phrase "forgive and forget," as Father Robert Schreiter points out, this "is singularly bad advice, and is nowhere to be found in the Bible." Rather, Schreiter suggests, "Instead of forgetting, we can learn to remember in a different way."

When we view the past through the lens of God's grace, we begin to put the event that caused our separation in God's perspective rather than our own. Dialogue is crucial in the way we remember because the person with whom I am estranged may view the event in a very different way. He or she may remember the circumstances that led to our estrangement differently than I do. So it is important to listen to the memories of the other to find the common ground that will give us some room to reconcile.

This was brought home to me in a very powerful way as I was finishing these reflections. I had sent the completed manuscript to the publisher on the day I began a retreat with members of my religious community. We met at a retreat center where the expectation was that we would celebrate Eucharist each day with the local community and the people who regularly joined them for daily Mass. The priest and religious sister who were conducting the retreat had prominent roles in the liturgy: The priest presided and the sister offered the reflection after the Gospel. The liturgy was informal but very prayerful.

The next morning, the sisters who operated the retreat center informed the provincial that they were very uncomfortable with the way we celebrated the Eucharist and asked that we hold our own liturgy separate from the regularly scheduled Mass at the Center. The provincial complied with the sisters' wishes, and so two separate celebrations of Eucharist were held at the same time on the same holy ground.

That evening, the retreat directors invited the members on retreat to share a grace or a blessing of that day. But I brought to the table my disgrace that the theme of the retreat was reconciliation and yet because of our differences in the way we celebrate Eucharist two separate Masses were held. Several others spoke of their beliefs, their fears and their difficulties with the way those of us who might be considered more progressive celebrate the Mass. They told the group how often they have felt left out when we gather as a community because they are more traditional in their approach and find themselves in a minority. Many issues we have been wrestling with for years in the community surfaced in the process, but this time the mood was different. People spoke not from the vantage point of defending their positions, taking a stand, making sure they were heard, but rather of simply telling their truth. It was a very honest attempt at dialogue. We put our thoughts, our feelings, our prayers, and ourselves in the center of the table. We reverenced each one's story; we didn't try to convince the other of the correctness of our individual views or the rightness of our causes. We may not have found our common ground about the way we celebrate Eucharist, but what we found and affirmed was our desire for unity, for each one finding a place at the table.

During that dialogue we caught a glimpse of how we can become a new creation. Once we get beneath the labels, the mistaken identities, the ideologies, theologies and ecclesiologies that seek to separate us and begin to see the image of God in each other, the promise of a new creation becomes very real.

The next afternoon we gathered to celebrate Eucharist. The Gospel for the Mass was the one that forms the basis of this book: Before offering your gift at the altar, if you are aware that a companion holds something against you, leave your gift at the altar and be reconciled with your companion. The presider for this liturgy, a priest who serves in Tanzania, invited us at the beginning of Mass to take part in a ritual. He told us that it is a custom in Tanzania to offer one's guests a chance to wash their hands before coming to the table. In an act of hospitality, the host takes a pitcher and a bowl and goes to each guest at the table. It is a ritual of cleansing, of purification, before coming to the altar. So the priest invited each of us to have our hands washed.

He went around and poured clear, clean, refreshing water over each of our hands. When he had moved beyond me, my hands moist from the ritual, I heard someone call my name. From across the aisle, one of the priests who spoke eloquently the evening before, one who stands at the opposite end of the ideological spectrum from myself, extended his hand to me. Though I did not feel particularly estranged from this priest after the dialogue the night before, it was a gesture of grace, a ritual of reconciliation that I will remember for a long time.

Later, when I thanked him for initiating this gesture of premeditated mercy, he shared with me a story from our community's history. Many years ago, two brothers who worked on the farm at our seminary in Ohio argued fiercely over what should be planted in a certain field. Their exchange of words went on throughout one particular day and well into the night. Contrary to the Scriptural prescription, the sun went down on their anger.

But the next morning these two brothers gave one of the best sermons ever delivered in the chapel of that seminary — and neither spoke a single word. As was the custom in those days, the students went to Communion first, followed by the brothers. The two brothers who had had such a fierce fight the day before stayed in the back of the chapel so that they were the last two to approach the communion railing. Before they knelt down side by side, in front of the entire congregation, they turned to each other and shook hands, and then knelt to receive Communion. The priest concluded the story by saying that no one remembers what finally was planted in that field but this story has been passed down through many generations in the community as an example of what this book has named premeditated mercy.

As St. Paul reminds us, in the end "nothing can separate us from the love of God." In God's heart, at God's table, there is room for everyone. As we seek to practice premeditated mercy, we embrace the grace of God that alone can make us merciful toward one another. It is God's gracious mercy that will take us to this new place where we become a new creation. May we go in peace.